Competency-Based Education
Beyond Minimum Competency Testing

AUTHORS:

Arthur Chickering

Charles Claxton

Keith Goldhammer

JoAnne Leigh

Louis Rubin

H. Del Schalock

Scott Thomson

Bruce Weitzel

Competency-Based Education

BEYOND MINIMUM COMPETENCY TESTING

DEVELOPED BY
Northwest Regional Educational Laboratory
Portland, Oregon

Ruth Nickse, *Editor*

Larry McClure, *Associate Editor*

Teachers College, Columbia University
New York & London 1981

Published by Teachers College Press, 1234 Amsterdam Avenue, New York, N.Y. 10027

Library of Congress Cataloging in Publication Data

Main entry under title:

Competency-based education.

    Bibliography: p.
    Includes index.
    1. Competency-based education—United States.
I. Nickse, Ruth.   II. McClure, Larry.   III. Northwest
Regional Educational Laboratory.
LC1032.C67   379.1'54   80-27850

ISBN 0-8077-2606-0 (pbk.)
ISBN 0-8077-2657-5 (cloth)

Manufactured in the United States of America
86 85 84 83 82 81 1 2 3 4 5 6 7

Contents

LIST OF ILLUSTRATIONS

About the Contributors

THE EDITORS

Ruth S. Nickse is an associate professor in the College of Public and Community Service, a competency-based undergraduate college of the University of Massachusetts in Boston. She has had considerable experience in the field of competency-based education, including service as the original project director for the New York State External Diploma Program and its applied performance assessment system for noncredentialed adults. She has written many articles and a recent book about this program. Dr. Nickse has also served as a consultant on competency-based education for the National Institute of Education, for regional educational laboratories, and for state departments of education. She assisted the Massachussetts State Education Department with implementation of competency-based adult diploma programs throughout the state. An educational psychologist, she earned her doctoral degree at Cornell University.

Larry McClure is Director of the Education and Work Program at the Northwest Regional Educational Laboratory in Portland, Oregon, where he has worked since earning his Ph.D. in educational administration from the University of Oregon in 1971. He is author or co-author of three books that have helped policy makers and practitioners lay a foundation for career education K–12, and he has been instrumental in the national development of experiential education programs that place students in the community for learning experiences.

THE AUTHORS

Arthur Chickering is Distinguished Professor of Higher Education and Director of the Center for the Study of Higher Education at Memphis State University. Dr. Chickering has had broad experience in higher education, both in teaching and in administration. He has written extensively in his areas of interest, the psychology of adult learning and nontraditional and experiential education. Formerly Vice President for Academic Affairs of Empire State College in New York State, he has held his present position since 1977. His doctorate was earned at Teachers College, Columbia University, in school psychology.

Charles Claxton is an associate professor of curriculum and instruction at Memphis State University. He has strong interest in the field of experiential education and the assessment of prior learning at the college level. His background includes social work as well as teaching and administration at the college level. Claxton has a doctorate in higher education from Florida State University.

Keith Goldhammer is Dean of the College of Education at Michigan State University. He has extensive background in many aspects of educational research, evaluation, and administration. His credits include classroom teaching and positions as school principal and superintendent. Prior to his present post he held various appointments at the University of Oregon, including Dean of the School of Education. He is well known for his work in the areas of career education and teacher education. Dr. Goldhammer earned his doctoral degree in educational administration and the sociology of education at the University of Oregon.

JoAnne Leigh is a writer/editor for the Competency Based Education Program at Northwest Regional Educational Laboratory in Portland, Oregon. She completed her master's degree at the University of Chicago and has been an instructor in both public and private secondary schools.

Louis J. Rubin is a professor in the College of Education at the University of Illinois. His professional background includes both secondary and postsecondary teaching activities as well as various administrative experiences. He has written extensively in the areas of curriculum development and teacher training. Dr. Rubin completed his doctorate in curriculum at the University of California at Berkeley.

H. Del Schalock is a research professor in the Oregon State System of Higher Education and the Executive Director of the Mid-Willamette Valley Consortium for the Improvement of Education. He received his doctorate in educational psychology and measurement at the University of Nebraska, with research fellowships from the Merrill-Palmer Institute in Detroit and the Tavistock Clinic in London. He has spent considerable time in competency-based teacher education research and development and is now involved in implementing the competency-based education program called for by the new minimum standards for elementary and secondary schools in Oregon.

Scott D. Thomson is Executive Director of the National Association of Secondary School Principals. Dr. Thomson's professional background in education includes a wide variety of activities. He was a classroom teacher, a high school principal, and the Superintendent of Schools in Evanstown, Illinois, prior to joining the staff of NASSP in 1974. He has authored or co-authored several articles related to the subject of this volume, including "Competency Tests and Graduation Requirements" (1978). He received his doctorate in administration from Stanford University.

Bruce Weitzel is currently a doctoral student in educational administration and higher education at Michigan State University. He has had experience in public school teaching and administration. His academic background includes majors in political science and counseling.

Acknowledgments

Thomas Corcoran, Barry Anderson, Rex Hagans, Paul Cawein, and Robert Gourley participated in the initial design and subsequent review of the book. Judy Zaenglein also participated in the review process.

JoAnne Leigh was managing editor. Maggie Rogers and Donna Shaver tracked down innumerable bibliographic citations. Patricia Badnin helped design charts.

René Gentry and Cheryl Prew provided typing support and Adelle McEachern and Sharon Streeter proofread the manuscript.

Introduction

RUTH NICKSE

THOSE WHO have been involved with the writing of this book have had several objectives in mind. Primarily, of course, it is an effort to present information to further understanding of competency-based education. It has been written for a wide audience: those who have responsibilities for the design and implementation of instruction and evaluation, such as school administrators and teachers; those who have a role in directing educational policy, such as local school board members and legislators; and those who are affected by these decisions, namely students and their parents. Its audience is not confined to persons who work in formal institutions, but includes any who seek information about improving the effectiveness of teaching and learning.

It is an attempt to illuminate some of the perspectives that surround the notion of competence itself. Chapter 1 poses the question "What is competence?" Obviously, this is not an easy topic to address, because no one answer will be universally acceptable. And the concept itself is a moving target; what may pass as an adequate answer at any one time in any one arena may be simultaneously premature or obsolete in another. Yet the question must be asked, for how we answer it shapes the programs we design and implement, and they in turn influence our students.

Therefore chapter 1 explores the meaning of competence from the vantages of several disciplines. The authors present four basic principles, underlying the development of competence and its expression, which they derive from several definitions. Then they discuss some of the forces that impinge upon our abilities to become competent and propose some necessary conditions. Issues that pertain to program development are explored, and a model of competence is offered for

our examination, to guide us to a better understanding and appreciation of this provocative and complex topic. Using a familiar visual
metaphor, they liken competence to a generous slice of a Bermuda
onion, persuading us with skill and logic to examine each ring both for
its own integrity and for its relationship to the whole.

In addition, the book seeks to clarify some of the major characteristics that are part of a competency-based approach to education. The
term itself came into use as a phrase to represent an educational
strategy that places primary emphasis on the outcomes of learning, on
learning attainment, rather than on the time spent on the effort or the
process used to achieve it.

This particular focus is another in a series of recurrent attempts by
educators to make what is taught and learned more personally
meaningful, more closely related to individual and societal needs. This
motivation is still a primary force behind the development of new
programs both within and outside formal education. Learner-centered
examples, however, are most commonly found in postsecondary and
nonschool educational offerings, where there are relatively few constraints on the use of time and where custody and control issues are
not central concerns.

At the same time, the urgency of establishing standards for educational performance in elementary and secondary education has taken
precedence over other issues. This has induced public schools to turn
to minimum competency testing, an effort to make education accountable. Although accountability is an aspect of almost all programs, it is
not the most compelling force behind the new and more comprehensive approaches to competency-based education. Because both emphases exist and are affecting our views of purposes and practices,
there is good reason to examine them more closely. Chapters 2 and 5
are directed toward this end.

In chapter 2, the authors review the literature in order to define
"competency-based education" and, naturally, find little support for
any one definition. By examining educational activities in several
arenas, they arrive at a perspective of their own. They propose that
competency-based education is basically an instructional paradigm
that assumes different programmatic forms in different contexts. They
support this chameleonlike condition with a discussion of practice,
and they offer a set of components common to all competency-based
programs.

The role of instruction in achieving the goals of competency-based
education is further examined in chapter 3. "How can competencies be
taught?" The author acknowledges that there is no one best way;

rather, many strategies are appropriate. Guidelines are suggested for planners who seek an organized approach to the design of programs. These have implications for the classroom teacher wishing to develop a competency-based classroom as well as for large-scale systemwide efforts.

Chapter 4 supplements the more general efforts to characterize activities by presenting detailed descriptions of thirteen competency-based programs as they are presently being implemented across the country. These very diverse programs represent many different efforts to design instruction and evaluation according to assumptions about the needs of clients and the best ways of meeting these needs.

Elementary and secondary school programs in Washington, D.C., Wisconsin, California, Kentucky, and Oregon are described. Post-secondary examples include profiles of high school programs for adults, a degree program in a private liberal arts college, and a professional program that validates skills needed by pharmacists in the field.

Moving outside formal educational institutions, the authors describe exemplary practices in service organizations, in the military, and in industry. The Boy Scouts of America, Air University, and American Telephone and Telegraphs's management training institute are featured.

Even a cursory reading of chapter 4 is convincing testimony to the need and the various opportunities for providing new and more sophisticated means for evaluation of educational achievement.

Chapter 5 concentrates specifically on evaluation issues. "How can competencies be assessed?" The author focuses discussion on "role-based assessment." Noting the importance of specifying roles accurately and selecting specific performance indicators, he then describes conditions affecting role assessment. A key concern is that the proper context be chosen and that rater bias be avoided. Further, an adequate sample of evidence must be obtained. These ideas have implications for assessments in states that are concerned with role-based instruction and certification.

Finally, chapter 6 examines some implications of competency-based education for secondary school practice. The author notes that one point is clear: minimum competency testing, considered by many to be only a part of competency-based education, is overwhelmingly what is *going on* in secondary education. Public pressures for accountability in traditional subject matter areas reflects a disenchantment with the schools' ability to document results. Consequently, few schools have realized the potential for change that is inherent in a comprehensive competency-based education effort. According to the author, few have

used the opportunity to rethink their goals, restudy their requirements, reorganize their curricula, or realign their evaluation systems.
However, despite administrative and technical barriers, comprehensive competency-based education programs are not beyond the realm
of possibility for secondary education.

   The idea for this book grew out of an interest in competency-based
education on the part of persons at the National Institute of Education
and the Northwest Regional Educational Laboratory. Individuals in
each of these organizations were involved in research and development efforts in Oregon, as that state took major steps toward initiating
competency-based education.
   At the time the book was conceived, in December 1977, there was
little formal literature on either the theory or the practice of competency-based education; but activities called by its name or having some of
its features were under way all over the country. We felt the need to
pull some information about them together and hoped it would be of
value and interest to others too.
   Of several possible approaches, the present format seemed to offer
the best opportunity for discussion and analysis. In each chapter, the
authors, who are authorities in particular fields, review available materials from many sources for varying perspectives. Quotations from
original sources are used to elaborate and to provide further insight on
major topics associated with the movement.
   Because programs are being implemented much faster than theories
or definitions emerge, it is important to look at them closely in an effort
to understand what they seek to accomplish and how they go about it.
The exemplars described in chapter 4 are representative of a wide
array. Although there were many other possible choices, those included serve the purpose.
   They illustrate the point that programs vary several or many components of the educational process as they search for more effective
teaching and learning strategies. They alter the roles of students and
teachers, the organization of time and instruction, the techniques of
assessing and reporting student progress, and, often, the location of
learning itself, moving outside formal classrooms. Diverse populations are served, including youths and adults in school and out, those
seeking degrees or diplomas and those who are just having fun while
learning. Regardless of differences in approach, these programs have
the same high objective, the development of competence. Their minimum level is excellence.

1

What Is Competence?

ARTHUR CHICKERING
CHARLES CLAXTON

EDITOR'S INTRODUCTION

What is competence? This is a simple question that evokes a complicated response. It is necessary to ask it with full awareness that no universally acceptable answer is forthcoming. It is important to ask it at this time, because persons with both an interest and a stake in education are busily involved in implementing practices (and in some instances legislating rewards and sanctions) as if there were one right answer and as if it were common knowledge.

What is competence? Like many good questions, it is both philosophical and practical. But while there is opportunity to examine the philosophical aspects, there is little time. Because of varying pressures on education, practical aspects take precedence and shape the answers to philosophical ones. However, the issue itself, though difficult and complex, is at the heart of competency-based education. If we can answer this question with courage and intelligence, the most difficult part of our deliberations will be behind us, at least temporarily; but the answer can never be given fully.

The authors of this chapter begin by examining some dimensions of competence, expanding the dictionary definitions relating it to adequacy and sufficiency to include dimensions such as individual differences, and noting the essential motivational aspects first proposed by Robert White. These various opinions lead the authors to propose four basic principles that underlie the expression and development of competence.

These refer to (1) the significance of situations and contexts that shape "competent" responses; (2) the perceptual and biological characteristics that delimit them; (3) the importance of employing diverse learning styles

5

to achieve competence; and (4) the motivational nature of competence itself. By citing research and pertinent writings in several fields, evidence is supplied to support each principle.

The authors remark that our changing society will create situations and contexts more complex than any we have yet confronted. The demonstration of competence is also complicated by new information about the central nervous system and its functions: it may well be that our abilities to respond to changing social, biological, and physical environments are affected by our unconscious needs to preserve unique and essential inner rhythms—in other words, there are organic differences that may limit the attainment of competent behavior.

In addition, individual learning styles and environments affect the degree to which any skill is developed and maintained: the way a person learns is a major factor in personal development and the acquisition of competence. Finally, motivational force, "the desire to have an effect and to become sufficiently competent to do it," is posited as an important variable.

These basic principles are the foundation for program design and development efforts, and they have implications for the success of any curriculum planning.

In their second section the authors identify issues administrators and policy makers must examine as they turn their efforts to the design and implementation of programs. Questions such as those of priority and appropriateness (Which combinations of required outcomes shall we teach and which shall we leave to others?) and the implications and limits of authority in that choice (essential issues of value) collide with issues of local power and politics. And then there are the practical problems of the organization of instruction and its measurement. The authors make the point that it is learning *gains* that should be evaluated in a competency-based system and that both our attitudes and our assessment techniques must become increasingly sophisticated to measure them.

The authors then offer their own model of competence, using the familiar Bermuda onion as a visual metaphor to help us think about competence levels and interactions between them. The surface layers are those aspects of competence that are the most susceptible to change: called survival skills, and closely connected to basic skills, they are essential for daily living, as are those of the next layer, psychomotor skills.

Underlying these in the inner rings, which interact with those on the surface, are vocational skills; and nourishing them are intellectual and interpersonal skills. These in turn draw sustenance from ever deeper layers, the generic abilities of the tendency and self-confidence to learn, which cling closely to the heart and foundation of the onion: ego development and self-determination. This metaphor will be useful to the extent that we understand the interaction of these skills and abilities, for each is dependent upon the others.

In conclusion, the authors point to some significant implications of their model for the design of competency-based programs. There is a need for altering structures of schooling to provide many diverse learning opportunities; and this will call for modification both of curricula and of instructional practices. Student evaluation and its reporting will be altered as well. Schools need to connect with other community agencies for a shared role in teaching and assessing competence. Finally, the authors observe that the notion that school is something that takes twelve years—no more, no less—will have to be set aside. For many, that may be the most difficult idea of all.

R.S.N.

W HAT IS COMPETENCE? The main problem, even with a generous page allotment, is setting boundaries to the answer. We recently asked a Vermont visitor about his steadily expanding acreage. He replied, "I really don't want to have a lot of land—just that which abuts my own." Competency is like that. One parcel seems so naturally connected to the next that we are taken in all directions.

Then there's the story about the Vermonter showing the Texan his farm. "That pine plantation on the far hillside marks the southern boundary. Then you see that tall elm sticking up, that's the northwest corner. And the ridge beyond that pasture marks the easterly line." The Texan, having listened patiently, finally said, "Why, on my farm I can drive all day and never come to my line." To which the Vermonter replied, "Yup, I had a car like that once, but I got rid of it." Well, discussing competence is like that too. You can tune up the Cadillac or the trusty pickup and take off across the landscape, catching the general contours as you go, or you can go by foot, noting the details of all the flora and fauna.

Setting the boundaries for such a fundamental human quality as competence, or deciding how to scout out the terrain, necessarily involves a series of somewhat arbitrary choices. Any synthesis requires selection, questions of order and emphasis, and decisions about what not to say. The outcome inevitably results from interactions between the authors' biases and idiosyncrasies and available research and theory developed by others. This chapter, therefore, does not represent a comprehensive synthesis of all the literature that may be pertinent. It does aim to represent honestly a substantial cross section of recent work. At the same time, like any piece of writing, it is a personal statement.

As administrators (and other persons) define competence, they must grapple with the myriad issues surrounding the topic and must do so in ways that recognize local institutional history, pride and prejudice, strength and weakness, and current concerns. *How* people go about defining competence and selecting areas for program development may be more important than *what* is selected at the outset, because the process will determine the direction of further thought and selection. That is another reason to recognize the important interplay between individual and institutional characteristics on the one hand,

and processes, definition, and selection on the other. Gary Woditsch puts one piece of the issue this way:

> We know that as man's power over nature increases, the future is less and less a function of what actuaries call "Acts of God," and more and more a function of how man wields that power. How man chooses to behave today is the best predictor of tomorrow. Now, if what we want tomorrow is *yesterday*, we can make a good cause for defining competence in terms of what is normative in human behavior today. . . . But if what we want tomorrow is . . . some unprecedented combination of yesterday's successes and today's hopes, the way most men behave cannot be our norm. For a humanity that envisions a future better than its past, those capable only of replicating the past must be judged incompetent.[1]*

With these remarks as background we turn to the question. After sharing some major definitional variations of competence, we address a set of basic principles concerning its nature, development, and expression. Then we recognize some of the problems to be confronted in an attempt to create a competency-based program. We follow with a model of competence, which looks much like a Bermuda onion; its layers describe elements of competence that suit our taste and might add zest and substance to our educational diet. But perhaps it will only make your eyes smart or your mouth pucker. Finally come brief remarks concerning general implications.

DEFINITIONAL VARIATIONS

Appropriately, we go back to Aristotle. Thomas Ewens suggests that competence is what the Greeks called *arete*, "a power which has been trained and developed so that it has become a characteristic of the person who has it."[2] He notes that it is not enough to talk about *arete* in general. It is necessary to specify the *kind* of characteristic or trained ability the person has. Aristotle, Ewens points out, was concerned with high standards as well as constraining circumstances of everyday life. One must possess the ability to function in ways that are most appropriate for a particular situation. "The trick," says Ewens, "is to know how to do it and this is largely a matter of practical wisdom."[3]

After Aristotle came Rome, France, England, America—and dictionaries. Ewens comments that definitions of competence in English and American dictionaries convey "the notion of an adequate supply

---

*Numbered reference notes in standard brief form are gathered at the ends of chapters. All references cited are fully identified in the Bibliography.

or sufficiency; a capacity to deal adequately with a subject; a quality or state of being functionally adequate or of having sufficient knowledge, judgment, skill or strength."[4] Ewens concludes:

> . . . there is a reference to material sufficiency as a kind of necessary base for being competent; on that base are built other competences: in general, that which is fitting, appropriate, sufficient or adequate for doing something or functioning in a given way; there is, finally a reference to the knowledge and experience required to judge certain matters. None of this comes as news. Competence is a very old, eternally contemporary notion.[5]

Then we have a number of added dimensions proposed by contemporary writers. Larrie Gale and Gaston Pol note the inevitability of individual differences:

> Competence, by definition, is tied to a position or role. The ligatures binding the two are abilities, knowledge, skills, judgment, attitudes and values required for successful functioning in the position or role. That is, possession of the critically required abilities, knowledge, judgment, skills, attitudes and values—and proficient use of the same—is what yields competence in an individual.[6]

Competence, then, is a whole that consists of interrelated parts. Gale and Pol suggest that some of the parts may never be identified and actually need not be. Some may be too mundane for an educational program, or too difficult to measure, or too complex to be practical.

These conceptions are consistent with the definition used by the Fund for the Improvement of Postsecondary Education, put by Thomas Corcoran with refreshing brevity:

> The competency-based approach begins with the definition of the knowledge, skills, and attitudes required for successful performance in a particular role. Demonstrated competence under realistic conditions becomes the basis for awarding credentials.[7]

John Raven makes more explicit the motivational element embedded in these formulations, pointing out that

> a key feature of these competencies is that they are motivational dispositions; as a result the methods appropriate to fostering and assessing them are those appropriate to fostering and assessing motivational dispositions.[8]

Alverno College echoes this point:

> A competent student demonstrates certain abilities; she is also committed to using them. Not only can she analyze or communicate effectively, she habitually does so.[9]

Probably Robert White's seminal work has contributed more to this motivational dimension of competence than any other single effort. He views competence in a broad biological sense as "an organism's capacity to interact effectively with its environment."[10] White believes this motivation to learn is not innate. Hence, he sees motivation as a primary characteristic of competence.

White's elaboration of his views and his references to pertinent research and theory take us well beyond the boundaries suggested by the more limited definitions mentioned above. He makes the larger view apparent. We see how important each neighbor's parcel is to the healthy development of our own, and how the stream that waters our garden depends upon the neighbor of our neighbor's neighbor.

White's comprehensive and penetrating perspectives, combined with those from Aristotle through Gale and Pol, give us definitional variations reflecting the multidimensional splendor of competence. Perhaps by shifting our angle of vision we can find another slant that reveals added elements helpful to our understanding.

BASIC PRINCIPLES

One way to think more clearly about competence is to set forth some of the principles that underlie its expression and its development. We shall examine four:

- Competence is internal and external, situational and personal.
- Competence is limited by a person's perceptions, neurological system, and character.
- Achieving competence requires diverse learning styles.
- Competence itself is a motivational force.

1. Competence is internal and external, situational and personal. This is the most critical principle. Competence levels and qualities are dependent upon situations and contexts. Particular contexts and situations interact with particular clusters of predispositions and abilities brought by the person. The outcomes depend upon these complex interactions. Individuals with certain abilities and attitudes may be excellent mechanics, secretaries, nurses, teachers, doctors, lawyers, or administrators in some contexts, but not nearly so good in others.

Norvell Northcutt tells us about these interactions between competence and context for such a "simple" matter as literacy. He notes that the construct of literacy is meaningful only when we consider the specific cultural context and its state of technology. A person who is "literate" in one culture can at the same time be "illiterate" in another. This is particularly significant for complex societies (like the United

States) that are made up of different subcultures. This means that assessing literacy skills calls for continual redefinition of the level and content of literacy:

> Without this provision, we may very well find ourselves claiming that being able to track and kill the sabre-toothed tiger is a requirement for adult literacy when, in fact, there are no sabre-toothed tigers left to kill. The implication, of course, is that literacy must be redefined as technology changes over time.[11]

Further, literacy is directly related to success in adult life. But, Northcutt says, success means different things to different people:

> To some, success means learning to read well enough to understand a want ad in a newspaper—to others, success may mean reading well enough to score high enough on the Law School [Admission] Test to be admitted to the country's most prestigious law school.[12]

The idea of relating literacy to success in life is important in terms of developing ways to measure literacy. Northcutt explains:

> . . . not only must the measure be derived from performances which are taken from the adult milieu (rather than from an elementary or secondary school frame of reference), but that performance on such a measure must be positively correlated to success.[13]

Frederick McDonald believes that in thinking about competence we should use this principle: "Begin with the situation and *within the context of the situation* . . . define the boundaries of the kinds of performances that are relevant in that particular situation."[14] Let us say we are interested in helping people develop cultural appreciation. This implies that they must demonstrate cultural taste by making certain choices (like choosing to attend a performance of the Metropolitan Opera rather than a rock concert?). Given such a context, what kinds of behavior, or performance, would we expect to observe? To make a comparison, we would need to specify what those who have good cultural taste would do in this particular context. McDonald suggests that by defining the context and by comparing a given person's observed behavior as compared with that of persons who demonstrate the desired behavior we have a basis for evaluating the achievement of the competence in question.

Factors that are present in particular situations and contexts operate in fundamental ways that influence how we think. Thus, for example, an individual may be "concrete" in interactions with people and "abstract" in work,[15] or children will analyze and classify persons differently from nations.[16] Cultural experiences exert significant differences in the development and expression of cognitive styles. Gerald

Lesser[17] has demonstrated consistent differences in thinking styles across different American ethnic groups. Herman Witkin[18] has shown differences in kinds of thinking in different cultures, and Jerome Bruner[19] and others have shown cross-cultural differences in the rate and direction of thinking abilities. According to Michael Cole, these differences "reside more in the situations to which particular cognitive processes are applied than in the existence of a process in one cultural group and its absence in another."[20]

The importance of situational factors increases as our lives become more varied and complex. The social changes in the last two hundred years have sharply expanded the range and complexities of the situations in which we work, live, and love.

We are shifting rapidly from goods to services. Having satisfied—though perhaps not satiated—our needs for food, clothing, and shelter, we learn that quantity of things and quality of life do not go hand in hand. The flood tide of material possessions does not steadily lift our ships of happiness, nor does it lift equally all the boats in the bay. When it comes to satisfaction, a sense of worth, and a meaningful existence, many are still stranded on the beach, stuck in the mud, or dragged under by anchors. So there are cries for help. Increasing technological efficiency is freeing human resources to respond. But this shift toward services will take us a giant leap toward increased complexity and escalating expectations in our contexts of working, living, and loving.

The problem is that it turns out to be much easier to create television sets for millions of homes than to create high-quality programs for a few hours each day; and putting a chicken in every pot turns out to be relatively simple compared to seating a stable and well-nourished family around the table.

The social changes that have hurtled us to this point seem destined to continue, unless our resource consumption outstrips our supply and creates a different kind of chaos. *The change toward increased services will create contexts for competence more complex than we humans have yet confronted.* Thus the kinds of factors recognized by Northcutt, McDonald, Witkin, Bruner, Cole, and others will be increasingly significant.

2. *Competence is limited by a person's perceptions, neurological system, and character.* Bob Knott cites five generic cognitive skills:

> (1) ability to receive and discriminate among stimuli, (2) ability to sustain attention to selected stimuli, (3) ability to analytically order stimuli according to problem at hand, (4) ability to reorganize relevant stimuli and apply to problem at hand, and (5) ability to continually censor proposed ordering of stimuli in light of new information.[21]

Now these abilities to deal with stimuli seem straightforward enough. But perceptual and neurological research indicates that it really isn't all that simple. Gardner Murphy gives us a glimpse of how it works.[22] He notes that we each create the world in which we live as we integrate the impressions we receive through our eyes and ears. As we develop our perceptions we also develop sets of expectations that are further colored by our feelings. Our minds become formed in terms of our outlook and expectations. Coupled with this activity are new scientific discoveries about our central nervous system and its patterned and rhythmic response to the environment. All persons, it seems, have an individual internal rhythmic pattern that, in some little-understood way, controls our responses. So it may be that part of our difficulty in adapting to changing social, biological, and physical environments is our need to protect these essential inner rhythms.

Thus each of us carries a unique bundle of deeply seated perceptual and neurological resonances. We may hum sweetly with the external rhythms of certain persons and settings, while others may jangle and clash. "Good vibes" for me may be garbage for you. My Beethoven may be your Bartok, my Gillespie your Presley. Miro for me may be Monet for you. Poe and Frost may speak to me, Eliot and Pound to you. On top of these organic differences we each construct our own stereotypes, dispositions, and theories. We work hard to maintain them, keeping perceptual and conceptual filters in good working order, sustained through absurdity and adversity by logics and faiths of our own creating.

And in the process we shape and sustain our own character, our own personality and identity. That personality in its more general dimensions becomes the foundation upon which the development of particular competencies depends. Knott describes the interacting relationships this way as he discusses curriculum design:

> The requirements for competence in special areas of expertise will vary with the area selected. However, the competence statements should include at least three basic components: (1) specification of minimal levels of knowledge and skills, (2) ability to apply high-order critical and creative thinking skills to the information of the special area of knowledge, and (3) ability to synthesize skills and knowledge of a specialized area and broader knowledge in the construction of informed purposes and means of executing them.[23]

Noting that formal education is only one phase of developing intelligence, Knott goes on to say that a competency-based liberal education curriculum should be designed to fit the developmental level of the student. If this aspect is not considered, students may be unable to relate and use their knowledge effectively, and will not attain the desired level of competence. Knott proceeds to describe a possible approach:

> One such developmental scheme useful for generating a structure for analyzing and promoting student competence has been developed by Arthur Chickering. Chickering identifies seven developmental tasks: (1) developing confidence, (2) managing emotions, (3) developing autonomy, (4) establishing identity, (5) freeing interpersonal relationships, (6) developing purpose, and (7) developing integrity.
>
> Chickering's model provides an excellent framework for ordering the abilities included in the basic competence on personal knowledge. One possible statement of the developmental components of a competency-based liberal education curriculum is made below. . . .
>
> 1. The student demonstrates a sense of confidence in basic intellectual, social-interpersonal, and physical-manual skills.
> 2. The student recognizes and differentiates his basic emotional impulses; assesses the consequences for himself and others, of acting on those emotions; and evaluates his attempts to manage his emotions.
> 3. The student comprehends characteristics of autonomous action and recognizes some internal and external restraints on his personal autonomy.
> 4. The student analyzes the basic dimensions of personal experience he finds most satisfying and assesses some of their potentially creative and destructive consequences for his own identity.
> 5. The student analyzes his relationships with other persons, including peers, parents, and authority figures.
> 6. The student identifies at least one major personal goal which requires the integration of avocational, vocational, and lifestyle considerations and utilizes means of achieving it.
> 7. The student recognizes his basic personal values, assesses them for consistency, and evaluates the consequences of actions influenced by those values.[24]

Rita Weathersby gives us a different slant as she considers the educational implications of Jane Loevinger's conceptions concerning ego development:

> To say this another way, one's ego state is a subjective frame of reference for interpreting and responding to educational experiences, and is the personality framework in which learning of any kind is embedded. What is "learned" is selectively assimilated to one's cur-

ent structures of cognition, interpersonal relations, motivational orientation, and patterns of impulse control and ethical judgment. . . .

People at different stages of ego development react differently to the "same" educational experience. Actually, there is no such thing as the "same" experience because perception of social and institutional environments is always stage-related, at least according to developmental theory.[25]

Developing competence, then, interacts seriously with more fundamental aspects of ego development. We began this discussion of basic principles with Northcutt's observations concerning the situational complexities of functional literacy. Those who have tangled with teaching standard English to minority group persons with strong ethnic identifications also recognize how significantly language learning interacts with such basic personality variables as sense of identity, sense of competence, integrity, purpose, and interpersonal style. That is one reason it works better to teach English as a *second* language than as a substitute for the first. Paulo Freire recognizes this fundamental dynamic when he first asks persons to describe orally their own experiences and makes the written versions conform to their own phonetics and dialects.[26] Only then does he paraphrase their language with the second language to be learned. Unfortunately, we have not yet learned much about how to help persons develop other areas of competence by starting with the skills they have learned on city streets, suburban playgrounds, or rural woods and fields; so it is usually awkward for most of us.

3.   *Achieving competence requires diverse learning styles.*   The going is made more difficult by this, our third principle. Developing a given skill in the first place may require several different learning strategies. Maintaining and enriching skills once learned requires a similar repertoire. David Kolb's experiential learning theory provides a useful model that integrates a wide range of research and is consistent with major approaches to human growth and development. It conceptualizes the learning process in ways that permit identification and matching of differences in individual learning styles and environments. In this model, learning is seen as a four-stage cycle (see figure 1.1). People have immediate, concrete experiences that they observe and reflect upon to form generalizations or abstract concepts. The implications they deduce from these concepts guide them as they become involved in new experiences.

Accordingly, the effective learner needs four kinds of abilities, each with a particular emphasis, as shown in chart 1.1. There are two

Fig. 1.1   Experiential Learning Model

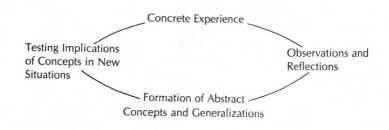

Source: David A. Kolb, "Student Learning Styles and Disciplinary Learning Environments: Diverse Pathways for Growth," in *The Modern American College,* ed. Arthur W. Chickering (San Francisco: Jossey-Bass, Inc., 1980).

dimensions of the learning process: one has concrete experience at one extreme and abstract conceptualization at the other; and the other has active experimentation at one end and reflective observation at the other. People are always choosing which set of learning abilities they will use in a particular situation. Kolb explains: "Thus, in the process of learning, one moves in varying degrees from actor to observer, from specific involvement to general analytic detachment."[27]

Chart 1.1   Kinds of Abilities Learners Need

Ability	Description	Emphasis
Concrete Experience (CE)	The learner becomes fully involved in the new experience.	Feeling
Reflective Observation (RO)	The learner observes and reflects on the experience from different perspectives.	Observing
Abstract Conceptualization (AC)	The learner creates concepts that integrate observations into sound theories.	Conceptualizing
Active Experience (AE)	The learner uses the theories to solve problems and make decisions.	Applying

Many theorists state that as children mature they move from concrete to abstract thinking, and that this is positive. Yet neither kind of thinking is always or exclusively good; rather, each has its advantages. As people go through life they come to deal with situations in characteristic ways, and most develop certain learning styles that emphasize particular learning abilities over others.

One value of the experiential learning model is its recognition that learning is a continuing process of interaction with the experiences in one's life as well as with the tensions caused by them. The way in which a person learns is a major force in personal development and growth. Kolb suggests that people go through three growth processes: *acquisition, specialization, and integration.* First, they acquire basic learning abilities. As they increase their fund of knowledge and experience, a certain learning style and particular kinds of competence are emphasized. The process of specialization leads to increase of competence in particular vocational and personal spheres of life—increase which gradually slows down at midcareer. Finally, they enter the integrative stage and reassert learning styles that have been unused for many years. These are expressed anew as people take up new interests and life goals.

This process of development is marked by increasing complexity and by higher levels of integration among the four modes of learning: concrete experience, reflective observation, abstract conceptualization, and active experimentation.

A major increase in complexity is associated with each of the four modes of personal growth: with concrete experience, affective complexity; with reflective observation, perceptual complexity; with abstract conceptualization, symbolic complexity; with active experimentation, behavioral complexity. In a person's early development, progress in any mode operates somewhat independently of growth in the others. In later years there is a need for a greater integration of the four adaptive modes.

So far, then, we have elaborated three principles involved with the idea of competence. They highlight the significance of (a) situational and contextual variables, (b) perceptual, neurological, and more general personality characteristics, and (c) learning styles and their significance for growth. These principles bring us to the fourth, one that stresses the importance of motivation.

4. *Competence itself is a motivational force.* White uses the term "effectance motivation," the desire to have an effect and to become sufficiently competent to do so.[28] He states that many motives in infants and children have roots in this desire, although he is unwilling

to state it as the primary factor in adult motivation, which he feels is more complex.

Despite White's disclaimer, it may be that effectance motivation is the taproot that stimulates the acquisition of numerous other motives. For motives can be acquired. And they can continue to operate strongly even after the initial need has been satisfied. Gordon Allport emphasized this element of personality development when he talked about the functional autonomy of motives. We may buy our first car because we can't get to work without one. But after that, owning a car (or a car of a certain style or size or status) becomes important in its own right, irrespective of real need. Using a bus or train or taxi, or even leasing a car, may be just as convenient and much more economical, but somehow we find good excuses not to do so. Sporting our very own model is hard to give up. It's true of course that missionaries, the advertising industry, and operant conditioners have recognized the functional autonomy of motives for some time. They have gone ahead creating needs and then meeting them without worrying too much about whether psychologists agree that it can be done.

This fourth principle concerning the motivational power of competence itself and the acquisition of motives is basic. If these dynamics did not hold, competence would seldom amount to much; its particular forms would be limited indeed, as would its application to the affairs of life.

The four basic principles together lay the foundation for a general orientation that should probably undergird any efforts at program development. They make it clear that competence is a macroconcept. It is larger than any collection of discrete psychomotor, intellectual, and affective units. Instead it involves complex interactions among these, powerfully influenced by learning styles and motivational factors.

It follows then that competence and competency-based education are for careers—or, as Ewens puts it, for work, not jobs. He makes this distinction and develops its relevance for education:

> A job is merely an instrument for providing a sufficiency of material means for one's work; one's work, on the other hand, is the task of doing one's life well as a human being. A job is relatively unimportant; one's work is supremely important.[29]

Ewens goes on to suggest that the move to competency-based education has failed to recognize this difference and has been oriented to helping people develop specific competence for particular jobs. What is needed, according to him, is to deal with competences that transcend strict occupational roles. Unfortunately, education in the past has been sold as a means of securing better jobs, which it has been. But Ewens suggests that persons interested in competency-based liberal education need to challenge the belief that education is for jobs. Even though liberal education can improve job performance, its true purpose is to help one "do one's life well."

Ewens and the ancients recognized how blurred the boundaries between work and leisure can become. When the work of one's life is an integrated stream of diverse activities on the job and off, associated with personal, professional, and social relationships, expressing strongly held values, responsive to individual and societal needs, then the cutting points between work and leisure are difficult if not impossible to identify.

So we must also recognize that competence is for leisure and play as well as for work. White shows us that in the close relationship between motivation and play, competence can flow from and serve needs that are essentially playful.[30] He notes that a person is interested in doing something when it creates an effect, but not when the situation is so familiar that actions are routine.

He also points out that it makes sense to speak of the concepts of competence and play together, rather than as unrelated aspects of people's lives. In play, change as an end in itself is not the object. Rather, something is done for the pleasure of the act itself. Effective motivation applies here, in that it "aims for the feeling of efficacy, not for the vitally important learnings that come as its consequence."[31]

We don't have to look far to find friends and colleagues whose primary work is their play, not their jobs. They may be forced to spend more clock hours on the job, but the investment of energy, emotions, ambition, and identity poured into the hours reserved for tennis, bridge, skiing, gardening, woodworking, do-it-yourself projects around the home, or arts and crafts far exceeds that put in at the office or plant. Given the mind-numbing nature of many jobs, those priorities are not surprising. They provide daily documentation of White's point that we all strive for novelty, for variety, for difference-within-sameness. If we can't satisfy those strivings on the job, we search out or create other opportunities to get the continuing sense of increased effectiveness and competence that comes from learning.

There is a message here for educators concerned about "unmotivated" and "lazy" students. Most students so labeled by classroom teachers and school administrators have heavy investments in non-school activities such as recreation with friends, part-time jobs, or projects with the gang. Indeed, many make heavy investments in athletics, clubs, and other school activities not directly related to academics. True, a few are so utterly defeated, deceived, and disillusioned that autonomy has given way to shame and doubt, initiative to guilt, industry to inferiority, and identity to role confusion.[32] For them, little foundation for effective education may remain. But most students display substantial energy, emotion, and identification in some corners of their lives. They may be subdued or beaten in some settings, but remain undefeated and creative or competent in several others. The problem is not laziness or lack of motivation. *It is the disjunction between the students' focal attention and the purposes of the school or between the range of competence developed through nonschool investments and that required for successful school achievement and effective social contribution.*

Surely, much competence is developed through nonschool activities. Indeed, many would say that the more critical problem is the restricted range on which school success depends. Probably it makes most sense to recognize that the pursuit of competence based on individual needs and interests will leave significant gaps in basic skills, general information, and broader social perspectives. What we need to do is diagnose the gaps, then bridge them by recognizing and building on competence developed through nonschool activities. In the process we can tap motives and interests to release latent enthusiasm.

Are there some basic propositions that might guide such an effort? David McClelland has drawn on many research sources to develop several basic propositions that can be helpful in developing a competency-based program.[33]

Experienced professionals will recognize immediately that these propositions describe many basic characteristics of good teaching and good teachers: encourage self-confidence; help the learner see the relevance to real-life needs; conceptualize objectives clearly; combine concrete experiences and abstract conceptualizations; link classroom learning to daily living; connect with significant values; provide opportunities for self-evaluation; establish warm and supportive relationships while maintaining challenging standards; help learners identify and develop relationships with new reference groups. For most of us these propositions may even seem old hat, tired, shopworn. The problems don't seem to lie at this level of abstraction. Instead they seem to involve more difficult questions of institutional and individual resources, energy, and will. As the farmer said to the extension agent promoting the latest developments, "Well, son, I ain't farming half so well now as I know how to." Many of our teaching practices and educational environments are a long way from what we already know to be necessary and effective. It's not new knowledge we need so much as increased ability to apply what we already have.

PROGRAM DEVELOPMENT PROBLEMS

Questions of Priorities and Appropriateness.   Applying what we already know about competence and its development plunges us into a thicket of thorny issues. One of the first concerns priorities. Not enough time, energy, skill, or resources may be available to foster the full range of competencies we judge necessary or desirable. Which combination, therefore, should get top priority and most generous support? Which can be left to informal nonschool socialization? Which can be clearly assigned to other agencies or institutions? And even as we tackle these practical and political decisions we must recognize that the development of some kinds of competence, for certain combinations of persons and contexts, will reduce or interfere with other kinds of competence. Leonard Waks writes:

> To illustrate the concept of competency incompatibility, consider the contemporary work situation. Technological developments erode skill requirements. Instead of acquiring an occupation through skill development in adolescent and early adult years and retaining it throughout life, we may enter an age of constant work re-adjustment. It will be the age of throwaway knowledge . . . knowledge and skills will be obsolete before they are acquired. Within our institutional structure the educational system merely adjusts individuals to evolving workplace conditions. The school could in this situation provide career re-adjustment education, in resume-building, job searching, career re-designing, etc. Work conditions would confront the individual as the man outside the saloon shooting at his feet and shouting "Dance, partner!" Work-role education would be . . . dancing lessons. An alternative response would be to reject the rate of work change as cancerous and to provide effective skills and appropriate attitudes for combatting it. Criteria of workplace performance would include: joining effectively with others and developing collective responses, having a high workplace and occupational commitment, being keen on work operations and retaining pride in work mastery.
>
> These two responses, one individual, the other social, generate different criteria of performance and call for incompatible competencies. The man with a well-developed portfolio of individual work re-adjustment competencies—who has strongly developed skills and habits in resume building, in "networking," in work-search patterns, in market scanning skills, in seeing the direction of work change, in understanding the "needed skills for tomorrow's world" and developing them today . . . such a man simply cannot also have in his competency portfolio such social competencies as strong occupational commitment, pride in work traditions, keenness on specific work operations, high commitment to co-workers.[34]

The Implications and Limits of the State's Authority.   The questions of priority and incompatibility among different types of competence for different persons and contexts raise more fundamental issues concerning underlying values. Who decides what kinds of competence are to be encouraged for whom? And what is the proper balance between determination by the state and self-determination by the individual?

The social and individual consequences of teaching for competence involve many people. They include not only minorities defined by social class, ethnicity, national origin, handicapping condition, or age—to name a few of the most salient categories—but also that "minority group" that is a majority of the population: women. And they also include the other half: men. Today some of our greatest inequities result from the equal treatment of unequals. Who decides the competence and knowledge requirements to be met by all these diverse persons, with their varied strengths and weaknesses, purposes, life styles, values, and aspirations? If our schools and colleges have become the gatekeepers for the full range, where do individual prerogatives for self-definition and self-determination end? Where does the state properly take over? Alex Inkeles observes:

> Everywhere today—by continent, by nation, by region, by class— there is a vast process of social change exerting its force. To manage their lives in a satisfying way, men need new information, skills, motives. New problems and situations everywhere constantly challenge their competence. Tragically, men find that the skills and talents which formerly made them models of competence in their community are of no value or are even demeaned and degraded in the new scheme of things.[35]

Clearly the need is great and will increase. And clearly our schools and colleges have a major role in helping persons who find themselves demeaned, degraded, or obsolete. How should the limits of that role be set?

This, of course, is an old question. But movements toward competency-based education raise it much more sharply now than before. Waks asks, "Does the state have the right to shape life role behavior without limits?"[36] He notes that since the move to competency-based education is meant to have a more direct influence on how people carry out their roles in the society, the question of state power versus individual freedom is raised in a new way. In earlier days, schooling in this country was designed not as a tool of life adjustment but as a way of helping young people see the higher concerns and values in life. With the turn of the century the curriculum became more focused on disciplines. Even with this change, the curriculum was not considered an instrument for developing specific role behaviors. As long as this was the case, the question of state power versus individual freedom, though difficult, was manageable. But the question has become more complex as we have begun talking about role competence education:

> . . . when the compulsory school, an instrument of state power, frames up minimal conceptions of acceptable parenting behavior, and even minimally correct uses of leisure time, and sets in motion compulsory treatments effective in establishing these minimum competencies and tests to ascertain success, the question "by what right?" arises immediately. The state will find no justification for such practices in existing democratic theory.[37]

In classical democratic theory the state was to serve very limited functions, such as protecting life and property against aggressors. Other matters, including education, were left to the individual and other institutions in the society, such as the family and the church. But the incredible changes society has undergone in the last 150 years have altered the ground rules considerably. Environmental and ecological challenges, such as technological development and the increasing scarcity of resources, dictate that we redefine the legitimate boundaries of power and individual freedom. The present runaway resource depletion that characterizes the technologically advanced countries of the world cannot continue. Life role education, says Waks, is one instrumentality for dealing with it. But is the state the entity that defines life role behavior through compulsory treatment and tests in all areas of life, including the appropriate use of leisure time?

Such a move, without philosophical limits, might be akin to totalitarianism. Certainly we would need some consensus on values and on the limits of state intervention. But what we are seeing now, says Waks, is less and less agreement on fundamental values:

> There may be no value consensus in the society sufficient to build a unified LRCE [Life-Role Competence Education] program. Two results are possible. (i) An insubstantial value consensus, insufficient to base genuine LRCE efforts, may be constructed. Taking this way out, the major value questions may be avoided, but no life-role competence satisfying anyone or worth anything will be developed; (ii) the value questions will be faced but not settled, so alternative efforts reflecting alternative value perspectives will need to be developed.[38]

The Dynamics of Power. Of course these value issues, and the alternatives selected, will be decided by those with the power to do so. Some of that power rests with the state. But it is also more general than the state and federal agencies and the legislators who look over their shoulders. It is the power of our deeply embedded social conventions and expectations perpetuated by those who exemplify, reinforce, and profit from them, those whose security, status, identity, and sense of well-being may be threatened by changes. At the same time, this power is more specific—to particular communities, their school boards, and teachers' unions.

McClelland describes these dynamics as they have influenced our definitions and assessments of competence in the past. He points out that by being born in a family with high socioeconomic status a person is provided access to good schooling, college, and entrance into the professions. Part of this process includes good performance on paper-and-pencil tests that reflect middle-class values and orientation.

> When Cronbach (1970) concluded that such a test "is giving realistic information on the presence of a handicap," he is, of course, correct. But psychologists should recognize that it is those in power in a society who often decide what is a handicap. We should be a lot more cautious about accepting as ultimate criteria of ability the standards imposed by whatever group happens to be in power.[39]

These are difficult issues. Yet, wittingly or not, we take a position on them with every educational decision, from the most general (concerning the location of buildings, their facilities, and the qualifications of the teachers and administrators employed) to the most specific (concerning courses, curricular requirements, methods of evaluation, and criteria for success). Any deliberate effort to develop competency-based education will have to confront the questions of value, politics, and local power and resolve them, with greater benefits for some and less for others.

Practical Problems of Reductionism and Fragmentation.   With the uneasy resolution of these basic questions of priority, value, and power, practical problems of implementation remain. Implementation requires that definitions of competence be reduced to manageable terms, broken into recognizable and teachable units, and assessed reliably. Problems of reductionism and fragmentation immediately arise. The complex interactions between persons and contexts, together with the multidimensional nature of competence, make the particulars concerning educational activities, learning resources, and evaluation practices extremely difficult to install and operate. Like the questions of value, priority, and power noted above, these problems are not unique to competency-based education. They are faced by any curriculum committee or teacher undertaking to design a program or a course and by every college professor who lays out a series of lectures and examinations. The difference is that whereas other approaches may let the committee, teacher, or professor ignore the issues, the competency-based approach confronts that sloppiness directly.

Of course, sloppiness is not all bad. Often, tidying up takes more time and energy than it is worth. And the costs in human productivity, satisfaction, and development can be great as well. Casual, shirt-sleeved, feet-up-on-the-furniture folks who have had extended visits in spotless households with precise expectations as to what is done—and when, where, with whom, and for what ends—can understand the frustration and chafing of students constrained by similarly meticulous programming of educational expectations and behaviors.

Paul Pottinger addresses the problem thus:

> Competencies cannot be meaningfully defined by seemingly endless reductions of specific skills, tasks and actions which, in the end, fall short of real world requirements for effective performance. In fact, the more essential characteristics for success will often turn out to be broad or generalized abilities or characteristics which are sometimes more easily operationally defined and measured than an array of specific "subskills" which do not add up to a general competence.[40]

William Spady and Douglas Mitchell put the dilemma this way:

> As instructional opportunities are expanded to support student engagement in achievement of life-role based competency goals, the school's ability to specify the criteria for competency demonstration and certification becomes increasingly difficult. . . .
>
> . . . Reform advocates can secure effective implementation of CBE only if they avoid both narrowness of performance demands and creation of learning opportunities that have no connection to explicit competency goals. Narrow and constraining performance demands destroy vital student motivation, while a diffuse expansion of new learning experiences will leave the students directionless and force them back into role-based modes of behavior.[41]

Assessment Issues.   The problem becomes particularly pressing at the point of assessment. Ewens discusses the close and necessary relationship between initial definitions and ultimate assessment procedures:

> Competence is defined in different ways in different programs. Insofar as an effort is made to define it operationally, the definition is inseparable from the specification of the assessment procedures.

Now it happens that many people tend to understand competency in behaviorist and mechanical terms and they do so because of the kinds of assessment procedures which are in fact used in a number of programs. In many instances, these assessment procedures *are* behavioristically oriented; they *are* extrapolations of an industrial model of performance and efficiency which breaks down given human activities into ever more itsy-bitsy, discrete units. And some people imagine that all CBE programs are wedded to such assessment procedures.

But this is simply not the case. The industrial model of measuring "performance" may be useful for some purposes in some contexts; but it is surely not useful, much less necessary, for measuring competences in the context of liberal education. . . . Competences are holistic, generic qualities, not a trivial series of discrete bits and pieces.[42]

This basic matter of assessment is complicated by the interactions among various types and levels of competence. Developing procedures and criteria for assessment and evaluation in the light of these complications is a challenging task indeed. Pottinger reminds us how much work remains to be done at this level:

It was stressed earlier . . . that competence is not a simple summation of discretely defined skills and abilities. . . . Measures typically used to assess job task performance and performance relating to the mastery of units in a curriculum typically have little bearing on how subunits interact. For any given job, life task, or individual performance, competent skills in one area can compensate for deficiencies in others creating a variety of combinations of individual performance levels which could theoretically "add up to" equivalent overall performance. Thus, minimal levels of performance on individual variables (which compromise overall competence) may have little meaning by themselves. Their interactions with respect to outcomes may have far greater significance. . . .

The implication for CBE is that one cannot *assume* that abilities or skills discretely learned will be integrated in work and life functions and consequently that establishment of minimal levels of performance on isolated skills or "sub-competencies" have much meaning in themselves. Therefore, competency research, new assessment procedures, and test instruments must focus more on the interdependence of skills. Basic research as well as empirical analysis of these interactions in various life functions is desperately needed.[43]

Setting Standards. Then there is the "mean man" problem caused by social-psychological dynamics that flow from establishing general standards to be met by all. Woditsch puts it this way:

> When we search the scene for what is normative in the human saga,
> the arithmetic tells us that most men are not remarkably creative or
> intelligent, tend to be self-serving, and vacillate morally. When we
> look at the bulk of humanity, we witness the placing of safe bets, the
> search for short-term gratifications, and the pursuit of low-risk fu-
> tures. This is the scene the social scientist comes upon, with his
> propensity to classify, count and establish mean scores. "Mean scores
> . . . " The phrase facinates me. It is astonishing that a technical term
> should connote so ironically and perhaps prophetically. When we
> aggregate man, we do in fact arrive at a "mean" description of him. As
> we proliferate such descriptions and use them, as we talk about the
> character traits, opinion profiles, satisfaction curves, migration
> trends, mobility patterns and aptitude scales, our consciousness
> almost irrespressibly boils it all down to an image of "normalcy." And
> normative descriptions of behavior in the aggregate subtly become
> parameters for what is normal and to be anticipated in the individual.
> Finally, what is "normal" becomes society's standard.[44]

Do we set our standards high enough to challenge excellence, recognizing that many may be inspired but few can succeed? Or do we adopt
a "mean man" strategy, aiming at competence levels adequate for
minimally effective coping? There is no sound resolution to this dilemma as long as a general standard is to be applied across the great
diversity of backgrounds, talents, and aspirations among the students
to be educated by our schools and colleges. The recent report of the
Committee on Testing and Basic Skills of the National Academy of
Education recognizes this fact. It forthrightly and unequivocally re-
commends against setting statewide minimum competency standards
for the high school diploma:

> The NAEd Panel believes that any setting of state-wide minimum
> competency standards for awarding the high school diploma—
> however understandable the public clamor which has produced the
> current movement and expectation—is basically unworkable, ex-
> ceeds the present measurement arts of the teaching profession, and
> will create more social problems than it can conceivably solve.
>   It is basically unworkable because in many populous states cutoff
> points for a passing grade that are politically and educatively accept-
> able to parents, pupils, and educators would have to be so low that an
> overwhelming majority of students would be allowed to pass. This
> would make the diploma standard almost meaningless.[45]

The report takes a similarly clear position on the federal role in
relation to testing, whether voluntary or mandated:

The notion that the Federal government should be the Bureau of Standards for educational testing is both professionally unsound and politically dangerous. Since tests reflect the educational goals for many students and teachers, the Federal approval or disapproval of tests is in effect having the Federal government determine what the schools should teach.[46]

The problem of evaluating competence becomes increasingly complex as one moves from elementary and secondary levels to higher education and lifelong learning. Moreover, at these levels it becomes increasingly clear that though norm-referenced and criterion-referenced evaluation are necessary, they are not sufficient for our needs as educators.

Measuring Learning Gains.   The fundamental purpose of schools and colleges is to help students learn. To learn, according to Webster's dictionary, is "to gain knowledge or understanding of or skill in [something] by study, instruction, or experience." Yet, despite millions of hours already invested by thousands of institutions, no standards have been developed for *learning*. There are no standards for *gain*, no standards that suggest how much *gain* in knowledge or skill represents adequate progress, creditable learning, or acceptable performance. There are no standards for *learning* by which a student trying to learn, a teacher responsible for instruction, or an institution supported to create a learning environment might be judged.

We do assess the knowledge, understanding, or skill a student demonstrates at the end of a course, field experience, or program of studies. We do judge teachers and institutions by the status of their students when they finish. But we do not judge by the *gain* which occurs. We assume that learning has occurred among those who perform well. That assumption rests on the view that the beginning student is like a blank slate, having little or none of the required knowledge or skill. For small children or for people first studying highly specialized subjects that assumption may be sound; for others it may be generally valid although its accuracy varies for certain classes of students.

But this assumption becomes almost ludicrous when applied to adult students aged eighteen and beyond, whose knowledge, understanding, and skills may span the full range of human potential. The level of ability and preparation such students bring at entrance will vary greatly in relation to almost every general area of college education. We cannot assume they start out blank, at ground zero. Neither can we assume that simple measures of status, whether they be norm-

or criterion-referenced, reflect learning. If our business is helping students *learn*, and if students and taxpayers are investing dollars, time, and energy for a *gain* in knowledge and skills, then we must develop standards that indicate whether gains have occurred, how much, and of what kinds.

If we are to be serious about accountability and about the performance of our colleges and universities, we must develop the capacity to evaluate *learning*. And it seems likely that we will need a similar approach at the secondary school level if we are to maximize complex areas of competence for all our diverse students. Certainly the methods and instruments are not yet available. But our present sophistication concerning norm-referenced and criterion-referenced evaluation is not exactly gray with age. While we are pushing toward further expertise in these matters we can at the same time develop methods and instruments that will move us toward learning- and learner-referenced evaluation as well.

There are messages here for those who confront the dilemma of cutting points. First, to the extent possible use both norm-referenced and criterion-referenced approaches to assessment and evaluation. Second, emphasize the diagnostic use of the information provided by such approaches. Third, develop multilevel criteria for performance. Fourth, focus on gain rather than on status in evaluating educational effectiveness. And fifth, be clear and tough-minded about the relationships between levels of school achievement and kinds of performance required for real world work, citizenship, and family responsibilities.

COMPETENCE AS A BERMUDA ONION

We have looked at definitional variations concerning competence, posited some basic principles, and noted some fundamental problems in program development. In the light of all these complexities it is utterly presumptuous to attempt a general answer to our basic question, What is competence? But perhaps by doing so we can illustrate a useful way of thinking about competence levels and their interactions.

At the outset we should be explicit about two underlying assumptions: (1) 99 percent of us are normal in most of the characteristics that are important to developing competence; and (2) 99 percent of us have apparent or hidden context- and culture-specific handicaps that need to be recognized.

We take a nice large Bermuda onion as our visual metaphor (see figure 1.2). On the surface of the onion are those aspects of competence that are most susceptible to change and most contextually specific.

They are essential for day-to-day transactions. The deeper layers, which are most generic, are sources of nourishment and support for the surface layers. Each layer interacts most closely with those nearby.

Survival Skills.   The skin of the onion, the outermost layer, is survival skills. Winthrop Adkins calls them "life skills" and sees them this way:

> Life Skills Education is essentially a program area and an innovative method for teaching and learning. The program area is defined by the sets of pre-vocational, motivational and social problems in living

Fig. 1.2   Competence as a Bermuda Onion

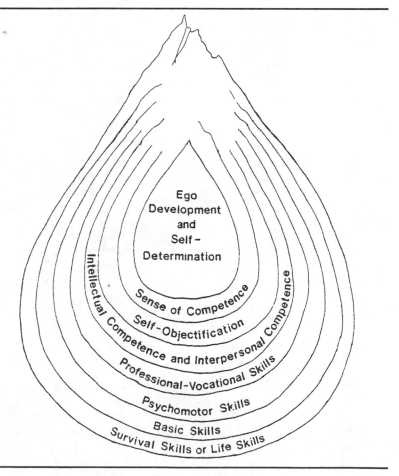

adult learners' experience which interfere with their ability to profit from training and employment opportunities. Such problems are frequently those identified by counselors. They create anxiety and other forms of emotional stress and unless dealt with and resolved can lead to patterns of alienation, anger and withdrawal. Yet they are also cognitive problems. They persist because the learner lacks useful methods for defining them, knowledge, resources and techniques for using them, and basic problem solving strategies and skills which work.[47]

Chart 1.2 indicates some of the major areas to be addressed. Others might posit a somewhat different array, but most formulations would include these major areas in one way or another.

Chart 1.2   Major Curriculum Tracks and Representative Units

Tracks	Representative Units
(1) Managing a Career	Identifying and developing one's interests and abilities, choosing an occupation, locating jobs, conducting interviews.
(2) Developing One's Self and Relating to Others	Caring for health needs, presenting one's self effectively, dealing with conflicts.
(3) Managing Home and Family Responsibilities	Becoming a parent, meeting needs of wives and husbands, budgeting and buying, dealing with the landlord, helping children in school.
(4) Managing Leisure Time	Planning one's time, changing mood and pace through recreation, participative vs. spectator activities.
(5) Exercising Community Rights, Opportunities, and Responsibilities	Dealing with representatives of welfare, health, and employment organizations, handling discrimination, finding one's way around the city.

Source: Winthrop A. Adkins, "Life Skills Education for Adult Learners," *Adult Leadership* 22 (June 1973): 58.

Basic Skills.   Next to the outermost surface of survival skills, and strongly supportive of them, are basic skills. The National Academy of Education Committee on Testing and Basic Skills spoke clearly to this area:

> The term "basic skills" at its periphery is subject to a variety of meanings. Most people would agree, however, that reading, writing and numbers are at the cognitive core. Experts disagree about how developed these skills must be in order to have individuals claim that they are truly competent in them. And many people would argue that certain affective (i.e., socially oriented) skills are essential if children are to become useful citizens and are to be prepared adequately for their various roles in society. . . . The basic skills are the building blocks for the more complex skills of scientific and value analysis; technological and occupational coping; historical, psychological, and philosophical understanding; and political participation. Without the acquisition of the fundamental learning tools of reading, writing, and numbers, no education of value can proceed.[48]

Survival is possible, though increasingly difficult, without these basic skills. Many of our great grandparents got along quite well without one or another of them, or with only rudimentary competence. Some persons manage today. But few go far beyond simple survival without a solid set of these skills.

Psychomotor Skills.   In some contexts psychomotor skills may be more necessary for survival than basic skills. For young persons coping with city streets and playgrounds, good coordination, strength, stamina, and fast reactions are probably more important than reading, writing, and arithmetic. Athletic ability and dancing ability may provide much more ready routes to recognition, self-esteem, and status than good control of standard English. On the farm and in the factory, the ability to handle tools and machinery with sensitivity and precision may give greater guarantees for full employment and increased income than knowing how to write and figure.

Professional-Vocational Skills.   Survival is possible in the absence of a profession or vocation. There are still ways to create food, clothing, and shelter with one's own hands or to earn the means by performing unskilled labor. But those opportunities are increasingly rare. The road to a good life lies in finding a profession or vocation where there is sustained demand and in becoming proficient enough to compete successfully with others running the same track.

Vocational success is possible in some areas without much in the way of basic skills. But most professions and vocations require substantial verbal or computational skills, or both. In many occupations, continued growth in basic skills is both stimulated and required if higher levels of responsibility are to be achieved.

Intellectual Competence and Interpersonal Competence.   Intellectual and interpersonal competence are so functionally interdependent that we treat them as two parts of a single layer. Professional and vocational success, effective citizenship, and healthy marriage and family relationships depend heavily on both. For most persons in most settings, developing competence in one of these areas is highly dependent upon developing competence in the other. Therefore we are better off joining them than by treating them as separate layers.

Intellectual competence is a large umbrella for a very wide array of conceptual frameworks. Perhaps the taxonomy of educational objectives developed by Benjamin Bloom and others is most familiar. The six categories include knowledge, comprehension, application, analysis, synthesis, and evaluation. This taxonomy, with its elaborations concerning test items and educational activities, provides a definitional framework that can be translated into appropriate activities by students and teachers throughout the curriculum.

Conceptions concerning interpersonal competence suggest some of the ingredients necessary to put ideas about intellectual competence into action in an interdependent world where occupational and personal purposes must be achieved with, and through, others. White explains:

> Every interaction with another person can be said to have an aspect of competence. Acts directed toward another are intended consciously, or unconsciously, to have an effect of some kind, and the extent to which they produce this effect can be taken as the measure of competence. When interactions are casual, when we are merely "passing the time of day," the element of competence may be minimal, although even in such cases we are surprised if we produce no effect at all, not even an acknowledging grunt. When matters of importance are at stake, the aspect of competence is bound to be larger. If we are seeking help or offering it, trying to evoke love or giving it, warding off aggression or expressing it, resisting influence by others or trying to exert influence, the effectiveness of our behavior is a point of vital concern.[49]

As with intellectual competence, there have been many attempts to define interpersonal competence and social skills with more precision. J. Michael O'Malley provides one useful perspective.[50] He tentatively defines social competence as the productive and mutually satisfying interactions between one child and peers or adults. Such interactions develop an underlying skill of interpersonal competence, that of understanding the role of another, and of having a variety of strategies available to respond appropriately. However, the ability to use these skills may be inhibited by several factors, such as low self-esteem. O'Malley's approach makes clear the powerful interdependencies between intellectual competence and interpersonal competence, which brings us to the next layer of our onion.

Self-Objectification, Self-Assessment, Tendency to Learn. Continued development of survival skills, basic skills, professional-vocational abilities, intellectual competence, and interpersonal competence depends upon the capacity to objectify and describe one's own purposes and analyze and assess one's strengths and weaknesses and learn in response to these diagnoses.

Raven, in discussing the tendency to learn without instruction, explains that it involves being sensitive to problems, ideas, and data:

> Developing sensitivity to problems and sensitivity to the creative ideas that would help one to do something about them are not things on which schools tend to focus a great deal of attention at the present time. Yet sensitivity to these things is basic to effective action. Sensitivity, whether it is to the physical or human problems that have to be solved, or whether it is to the germs of creative ideas that would enable one to begin to solve them, involves sensitivity to one's own feelings. . . .
>
> Teaching pupils to learn on their own involves making sure that they have ample experience of being able to notice previously unnoticed problems, of being able to make their own observations and seek out existing knowledge that will enable them to build up an understanding of the reasons for those problems or of the reasons for the existence of problems that were accepted as a fact of life. Thereafter it involves making sure that they have ample experience of being able to test the understanding so built up and of collecting vital additional information (and avoiding collecting trivial, useless information), of being able to invent solutions. Pupils need to have experience of being able to come to good judgments, based on incomplete evidence, as to what should be done; of initiating action on the basis of those informed, yet tentative, judgments; of monitoring the effects of such action to make sure that it has the desired effects; of changing the understanding they have built up as the result of observing the consequences of their actions; and of taking effective corrective action when necessary.[51]

Sense of Competence. Self-objectification, self-assessment, and the tendency to learn depend heavily on self-confidence, or on what White calls a sense of competence:

> The competence of a living organism means its fitness or ability to carry on those transactions with the environment which result in its maintaining itself, growing, and flourishing.[52]

Raven summarizes some of the major elements of self-confidence thus:

> . . . confidence that one can work effectively with others; confidence that one's judgment and decision-making ability are good; confidence that one can overcome unanticipated problems and take effective corrective action when necessary; confidence that one can find or invent the information one needs; confidence that one can change the pattern of one's knowledge, skills, and attitudes, should the need arise; and confidence that one can get other people to release their energies in the effective pursuit of important goals, that one can get them to put their best feet forward and pull their weight.[53]

Of course, one's sense of competence depends in part on the realities of one's competencies. A genuine and sound sense of security depends on the ability to solve, or otherwise cope with, life's problems—the ability to maintain equilibrium in the shifting sands of time and social circumstance. This development of skills (psychomotor, basic, and survival) and of competence (intellectual, interpersonal, professional, and vocational) is important. Yet the productivity and effectiveness achieved with a given level will vary greatly with the sense of competence that lies behind them.

Ego Development and Self-Determination.   These layers, ranging from skills close to the surface, through intellectual and interpersonal competence, to self-objectification and sense of competence, bring us to a core that we label ego development and self-determination. This core has to do with purposiveness, managing emotions, and a large sense of values and identity; it is biologically based.

Raven describes some of the ways in which this core must be tuned into our own emotions and reactions if it is to serve rather than subvert our purposes:

> Another pervasive competency would seem to be sensitivity to one's feelings and ability to use the information provided by them. We would include sensitivity to feelings of enjoyment and dislike and the tendency to turn these emotions into goal attainment; sensitivity to feelings indicating that one has a problem or the germ of a solution; sensitivity to indications that one has not fully understood other people's concerns; sensitivity to other considerations that should be included in one's frame of reference when making decisions; sensitivity to summative, impressionistic judgments one may not be able to fully explain; sensitivity to feedback that indicates whether or not one

is achieving one's goals and, if not, why not; sensitivity to resources that can help one achieve one's goals; and sensitivity to conflicts about the desirability of achieving one's goals and the tendency to do something about resolving those conflicts. Once again, it would seem, education could do much more to foster these forms of sensitivity.[54]

But this kind of sensitivity is not easy for all of us to achieve. A primary lesson of childhood and adolescence, rooted in those of us from a Protestant and Puritan heritage, and in many others besides, is: Don't trust your feelings! Resist the feeling of emotion. Stoicism and unremitting self-discipline are sure roads to status and success.

These traditional orientations, drilled into us wherever we have turned, are yielding to greater acceptance of intuition and feeling. As social problems outdistance solutions, despite applications of science and technology, the valid contributions of intuition and emotion are increasingly recognized. As Adam said to Eve on leaving the Garden of Eden, "We are in a period of transition." Like them, we may be leaving a relative Eden for a more difficult existence, and we may need to reach beyond logic and science to make our way. But many of us do not consciously consider emotions and impulses relevant to our present concerns and future purposes; or if we do, we feel guilty or weak-willed. Until we can make such connections, however, our purposive command will be flawed.

It is just this kind of self-determination that Mark Schlesinger puts at the heart of education:

> When we assist students to think critically, to evaluate different sides of a controversy, and to generate a careful position of their own, we may be assisting them in broadening their purposive command over themselves and over the negotiations they as individuals must make with the larger collectivity.[55]

And Richard Giardina suggests that this is the essence of general education:

> . . . it is the development of such a "purposive command" that could earn general education its central role in higher education. If an individual can develop this "purposive command," then he or she has acquired an abiding source of power in this complex and rapidly-changing society of ours.[56]

Well, that's our Bermuda onion. Others would doubtless cultivate a strain with more or fewer layers, or arrange those layers in a different sequence. This formulation does not pretend to be a definitive description encompassing the five-foot shelf of pertinent literature. But whatever the number or types of layers, the fundamental dynamics remain.

The critical point is that we have an onion. Slice it and we can identify the multiple dimensions and the layers that most closely interact. Thus we can start with the layer concerning a particular professional-vocational skill and go toward the surface, identifying the most pertinent psychomotor, basic, and survival skills; then we can go toward the core, identifying which elements of the deeper layers are critically involved. Similar strategies can be used for more complex or more superficial levels of competence.

The most important thing to recognize is that we can't change one layer without influencing other layers closer to the surface or further toward the core. Neither the core nor the skin can survive alone. A flourishing, satisfying, zesty onion requires soils for growth that nourish and strengthen all the layers.

SOME IMPLICATIONS

When we recognize the multileveled and contextually specific nature of competence we face some significant implications for our schools and colleges. Spady and Mitchell note two:

> First, [the reformers] hold that schooling can only become competency based if students have *multiple* opportunities for achieving and demonstrating competency in a given area. If learning opportunities are so structured that students cannot make repeated attempts to develop competency in areas they find difficult, or if they do not get several chances to demonstrate the competencies they have acquired, it is fruitless to expect substantial changes in schooling outcomes. To the reformer this implies that student schedules will require adjustment quite frequently and that the structure of a typical "course" will be altered dramatically.
>
> The second change advocated by the reformers concerns the *diversity* of learning opportunities. If competencies are to be achieved which will enable students to be successful in diverse and complex adult life-roles, meaningful experiences in such roles are necessary; but they are either lacking in needed richness or totally missing in the typical school. To the reformer, this means that CBE programs will require the development of a significant number of learning opportunities which are new in both content and form.[57]

These consequences mean that the school's curriculum design and its instructional delivery will have to be modified significantly. Today these are not built around active life roles, but instead call for largely passive students. Evaluation will look quite different, as will reports of student progress. Schools will have to connect significantly with other agencies and institutions in the community as these become additional loci for learning and for assessing competence. Finally, the idea that school is something that takes twelve years will have to be set aside. For some students it will take less than that, for others more, since the driving force will be pursuit of competence, not serving time in the classroom.

Given these far-reaching and fundamental implications, it is not surprising that defining competence and developing competency-based education is a long, hard task. It presents extremely complex conceptual challenges simply at the level of definition. The program development problems confronted at the point of implementation are formidable. These challenges would be sufficient to overwhelm most hardy innovators, even if they were able to start from scratch building a new institution. But that is not where we are. To be of consequence, competency-based approaches must be established by ongoing systems loaded with tradition and vested interests, staffed by teachers and administrators unprepared for the task.

Even a small beginning with competency-based instruction sends tremors throughout the educational web. Modify one element and the whole system starts to shake. And there are plenty of spiders ready to rush out and seize the unwary or unwitting creature who flies against that beautiful, functional design. It's not surprising that most such brash adventurers are immobilized or sucked dry after a few fitful spasms. And it's entirely to be expected that significant change toward competency-based education will come but slowly, organically, as the web makers themselves gradually learn new designs, more far-reaching and functional for these times and the future.

NOTES

1. Gary A. Woditsch, "Jonathan Livingston Student: Competence for What?", pp. 16–17. All quotations by permission.

2. Thomas Ewens, *Think Piece on CBE and Liberal Education*, p. 14. All quotations by permission.

3. Ibid., p. 16.

4. Ibid., p. 12.

5. Ibid., p. 14.

6. Larrie E. Gale and Gaston Pol, "Competence: A Definition and Conceptual Scheme," p. 20. Used by permission.

7. Thomas B. Corcoran, "Prospects and Problems of Competency-Based Education," pp. 4–5.

8. John Raven, "On the Components of Competence and Their Development in Education," p. 460. All quotations by permission.

9. Alverno College Faculty, *Liberal Learning at Alverno College*, p. 4.

10. Robert W. White, "Motivation Reconsidered," p. 297. Copyright 1959 by the American Psychological Assn. All quotations by permission.

11. Norvell Northcutt, "Functional Literacy for Adults," pp. 2–3. All quotations by permission.

12. Ibid., p. 5.

13. Ibid., p. 6.

14. Frederick J. McDonald, "Assessing Competence and Competency-Based Curricula," p. 25.

15. See C. Stabel, "The Impact of a Conversational Computer System on Human Problem Solving Behavior."

16. See Karen A. Signall, "Cognitive Complexity in Person Perception and Nation Perception," pp. 517–37.

17. See Gerald S. Lesser, "Cultural Differences in Learning and Thinking Styles."

18. See Herman A. Witkin, "A Cognitive Style Approach to Cross-Cultural Research."

19. See Jerome S. Bruner, Rose R. Olver, Patricia M. Greenfield, et al., *Studies in Cognitive Growth*.

20. Michael Cole et al., *The Cultural Context of Learning and Thinking*, p. 233.

21. Bob Knott, "Competency Based Education: State-of-the-Art Position Paper," p. 10. Used by permission.

22. See Gardner Murphy, *Human Potentialities*, pp. 53–55.

23. Bob Knott, "What Is a Competence-Based Curriculum in the Liberal Arts?" p. 35.

24. Ibid., pp. 36–37.

25. Rita Weathersby, "Ego Development and Adult Learning." Used by permission.

26. See Paulo Freire, *Pedagogy of the Oppressed*.

27. David A. Kolb, "Student Learning Styles and Disciplinary Learning Environments."

28. See White, p. 323.

29. Ewens, p. 5.

30. See White, p. 322.

31. Ibid., p. 323.

32. See Erik H. Erikson, *Childhood and Society*.

33. See David C. McClelland, "Toward a Theory of Motive Acquisition," p. 323.

34. Leonard J. Waks, *Education for Life-Role Competence*, pp. 24–26. All quotations by permission.

35. Alex Inkeles, "Social Structure and the Socialization of Competence," p. 283. Copyright © 1966 by President and Fellows of Harvard College. Used by permission.

36. Waks, p. 15.

37. Ibid., p. 17.

38. Ibid., p. 27.

39. David C. McClelland, "Testing for Competence Rather Than for 'Intelligence,' " p. 6. Copyright 1973 by the American Psychological Assn. Reprinted by permission.

40. Paul S. Pottinger, *Comments and Guidelines for Research in Competency Identification, Definition and Measurement*, p. 7. All quotations by permission.

41. William G. Spady and Douglas E. Mitchell, "Competency Based Education: Organizational Issues and Implications," pp. 12–13. Copyright 1977, American Educational Research Assn., Washington, D.C. All quotations by permission.

42. Ewens, pp. 10–11.

43. Pottinger, pp. 20, 22.

44. Woditsch, pp. 15–16.

45. National Academy of Education (NAE) Committee on Testing and Basic Skills, *Improving Educational Achievement*, p. 9.

46. Ibid., p. 12.

47. Winthrop R. Adkins, "Life Skills Education for Adult Learners," p. 57. Used by permission.

48. NAE Committee on Testing and Basic Skills, p. 3.

49. Robert W. White, "Sense of Interpersonal Competence," p. 73.

50. See J. Michael O'Malley, "Perspectives on Competence."

51. Raven, pp. 461–62.

52. White, "Sense of Interpersonal Competence," p. 74.

53. Raven, p. 468.

54. Ibid., pp. 468–69.

55. Mark A. Schlesinger, *Reconstructing General Education*, p. 43. Used by permission.

56. Richard Giardina, Introduction to *Reconstructing General Education*, by Mark Schlesinger, p. vii.

57. Spady and Mitchell, p. 11.

2

What Is Competency-Based Education?

KEITH GOLDHAMMER
BRUCE WEITZEL

EDITOR'S INTRODUCTION

The task of defining competency-based education is not unlike the attempts of the blind men to describe an elephant. One attribute of a complex phenomenon is perceived as primary and taken to define the whole. From one perspective, the main characteristic of competency-based education appears to be its response to issues of standards and accountability. From another, its most important characteristic is its emphasis on instruction based on goals rather than time. From a third, it is primarily an effort to restructure the roles of teachers and students in the interests of shared responsibilities for more effective learning. These are but three examples that illustrate the point; more could be cited.

"Competency-based education" refers to a variety of responses that education is making as it attempts to deal with serious cultural and social pressures. These efforts are said by many to lack cohesion and a dominant theoretical core; and this is in fact the case. However, this is not the first time that education has found itself caught up in a movement it has been unable to define to everyone's satisfaction. Neither is it the first time that varying interpretations have led to quite different educational practices, each based on a real need.

42

The authors of this chapter recognize the difficulty of arriving at a single definition of competency-based education. They share this recognition with several other writers struggling with the same problem, whose cited opinions well illustrate the point that competency-based education is not one thing, but many. Unable to identify a common conceptual or theoretical framework, the authors create their own perspective. They submit that competency-based education is basically an instructional strategy that assumes different programmatic forms in different contexts.

Although they refer to activities in business, industry, and the military, they concentrate on three familiar arenas—public schools, postsecondary institutions, and adult basic education programs. Emphases in these areas are different because they serve different populations and operate through different organizational structures. Nevertheless, the authors identify five issues common to all when competency-based programs are implemented.

These issues represent the choices inherent in the process of combining program elements. They include the identification of suitable objectives, the use of diagnosis, the selection of instructional methods, and the employment of evaluation and certification. Each is discussed, with several implications. As an important aid to identifying the possibilities, the elements are arrayed for discussion in a continuum from traditional to nontraditional practice. The authors note that very traditional subject matter can be taught in a manner that might be viewed as competency based. Some theorists might disagree, holding that whenever time is held constant, the program is not competency-based education.

Next, the authors note some particular patterns that emerge as the three different arenas develop their programs. They observe that public schools emphasize basic skills; postsecondary, generic skills; and adult basic education, life skills. For these authors, distinction centers primarily on the level of instruction, not on the changed organizational structures that interest other observers.

In their concluding remarks, summarizing the distinctions they have made, the authors caution that the real test of the possibilities of competency-based education lies in controlled experimentation of its many forms. Judgments made on the success or failure of a single expression, such as minimum competency testing, are not definitive.

Although Goldhammer and Weitzel differentiate patterns of activities according to educational levels, other schemas are logical and useful as well. Gary Woditsch, in an unpublished letter, points out that many competency-based programs focus exclusively on competencies related to courses; others seek to develop competencies based on roles, and fewer still emphasize generic competencies relevant to many life experiences. He notes that when an elementary school teacher and a university professor are both mainly concerned with competencies related to courses, they share common concerns as they teach. However, a teacher working with competencies tied to roles will have little in common with one who is teaching competencies defined by courses. According to this framework, then, the nature of the competencies being taught and the varying instructional strategies—rather than the levels of education—produce the most significant distinctions between programs.

R.S.N.

Arriving at a theoretical or operational definition of competency-based education is difficult, if not impossible, because of the nature of the movement itself. To a great extent, the definitional confusion can be traced to the variety of concepts that have been incorporated into the expanding movement during the past decade. Performance-based learning, mastery learning, proficiency, accountability, efficiency, equity of outcome, basics, generic skills, criterion-referenced testing, and minimal competency testing have all been subsumed under the guise of competency-based education.

THE PROBLEM OF DEFINITION

Because of this multiplicity, there is no one theoretical or operational definition that encompasses the range of present educational programs called "competency based." In addition, there are numerous and varied programs serving populations at different age and educational levels (K–12, postsecondary, and adult education) that use certain types of instruction or testing that are related to competency-based education. Some of these programs are within the formal education system, and some are outside it—in industry, in the military, in Scouting activities and the like.

What we confront, currently, is not a unified and static movement, but a changing and fragmented one, which evades all attempts at a definitional collar.

There is a further complication to understanding. It is that current practices at different educational levels are based on different philosophies, motivations, and interpretations of the movement. These differences are distinct enough to cause some observers to view the two major sets of activities, minimum competency testing and competency-based education, as entirely separate and unrelated. To others, however, the shared concern with standards is sufficient to link the two practices together. To clarify, minimum competency testing is primarily concerned with setting standards in K–12 education. Competency-based education, however, is a more complex attempt to improve many aspects of the instructional system, and it is most prevalent in postsecondary and adult basic education and in programs that conduct out-of-school training. (See chart 2.1.) Further elaboration of these two practices follows.

Minimum competency testing is an effort to place greater emphasis on the basic skills, so as to "guarantee" that the high school diploma will mean that certain minimal level skills and facts have been mastered. Minimum competency testing is characterized by the use of standardized tests of achievement and reflects the notion that general standards for schools, across all teachers, grades, subjects, and students, should be set. These are comprehensive standards for cumulative learning, to be applied evenly to all students regardless of their courses of study. This differs from the common practice in which individual teachers set standards while considering student ability, effort, and achievement. Naturally, such standards differ not only from teacher to teacher but also with respect to grades, subjects, and schools.

Thirty-six states have legislated, or are in the process of legislating, minimal standards for achievement in basic skills as the goal for the first twelve years of schooling. These large-scale testing programs are often introduced under pressure from constituencies dismayed by

Chart 2.1   Two Contrasting Philosophies of Competence

Minimum Competency Testing	*Competency-Based Education*
The assumption: Minimum competence is the ability to read and compute at a minimum level and a diploma should reflect this.	*The assumption*: Competence is the ability to meet responsibilities and fulfill personal ambitions as an adult.
The problem: Some students who complete their schooling and receive diplomas cannot read well or do basic math.	*The problem*: Schools often concentrate on traditional subject matter and "school skills" (e.g., taking multiple-choice tests) that have limited application in adult daily life.
The solution: Give a multiple-choice test covering basic reading and math skills and award diplomas to students who pass the test and satisfy other requirements.	*The solution*: Revise the curriculum so that students will build the skills in communication, organization, analysis, and other skills they will need to perform as adults (e.g., to go to work, pursue further training, manage a household, participate in the community) and test mastery through applied performance.

Source: Competency Based Education Program, Northwest Regional Educational Laboratory, Portland, Oregon.

evidence of apparent school failure. It is this practice that is often considered to be the whole of competency-based education. However, from other points of view, competency-based education is concerned with several educational components, including standards set far beyond a minimal level.

Six critical components that might characterize a complete *competency-based education* program, extending beyond the demands for minimum skills standards, are suggested by William G. Spady.[1] (1) *Learning outcomes* must be explicit with regard to criteria for performance, and agreed upon and known by all those directly involved with a student's progress. (2) *Time* must be used flexibly in terms of when, how long, and how often opportunities for both instruction and evaluation are provided. (3) *Instruction* must facilitate all students' opportunities for reaching certification standards by providing a variety of instructional activities to help them achieve a required outcome. (4) *Measurement* must entail explicit, criterion-referenced testing of required outcomes, and there must be frequent opportunities for evaluation. (5) *Certification* must depend on demonstration of required outcomes, exclusive of attendance or other bases for determining eligibility, including "credit." (6) *Program adaptability* must be assured through a sensitive management system that provides performance data as a basis for fine-tuning all components to encourage student achievement of required goals.

Not all persons would agree with this construction of competency-based education. There is no lack of opinion on the matter of the most important elements of the concept—i.e., on the problem of its definition. As Walter Hathaway states:

> The fundamental issue is that *there is no common agreement about what competency based education is.*
>
> Given the diverse origins and relative immaturity of the competency based education movement, it is not surprising that there is no single agreed upon definition of it. Nor is it necessary or even possibly desirable that there be such agreement. Career education, the immediate predecessor and first cousin of competency based education, is an example of a movement which has had a substantial impact on education during the last ten years while continuing to evolve its nature and to tolerate diversity of programs. . . . Nevertheless, we would seem to invite communication problems if the coined term competency based education is allowed without distinction to embrace everything from Maryland's proposed program requiring minimal reading levels of standardized tests as a basis for promotion beginning in the second grade, to the joint classroom and clinical competency based law program at Antioch College.[2]

Examining it from a more descriptive approach, Sheila Huff also concludes that the definitional problem stems from the fragmented nature of the movement.

> If one examines all educational institutions or programs that call themselves "competency-based," *there is no uniformity with regard to any of these elements.* There is, for example, no uniformity with regard to educational goals; curriculum, institutional environment and pedagogical techniques; ways in which students are evaluated; or rules and procedures followed.
>
> This fact of nonuniformity is one of the reasons why it is difficult to say what competency-based education is. The activities of CBE institutions do not differ in kind from the activities of traditional institutions. Saying that a program is "competency-based" tells us no more about what the program might look like than saying a program is "traditional."[3]

What, then, can be noted within the competency-based education movement are mixed terms, assumed understanding, and diverse programmatic contexts, all of which add to the definitional confusion. As an example, David Ainsworth submits that

> Competency-based education refers to an instructional system where students are given credit for performing to a prespecified level of competency under prespecified conditions. The system is therefore non-normative with a student's ability determined independently of that of other students in the institution.[4]

Robert Howsam offers this:

> What, then, are people talking about when they refer to performance-based or competency-based instruction? Essentially they are saying that all learning is individual—that the individual, whether teacher or learner, is goal-oriented.
>
> They are saying that the teacher-learning process is facilitated if the teacher knows what he wants the pupil to learn and if the learner is aware of precisely what is expected of him or what he expects of himself. Precise knowledge of results also enhances learning.
>
> Finally, they are saying that the learner or teacher is most likely to do what is expected of him and what he expects of himself if he is accountable for doing what he undertakes.[5]

Michael Palardy and James Eisele:

> CBE is defined in various ways. In its simplest form, however, it means that the recipient (the prospective learner) must be able to demonstrate mastery or attainment of specified criteria. These criteria can be stated so that they include areas in the cognitive, affective, and

psychomotor domains and encompass all phases of education—from the preprimary to the graduate.[6]

In Hathaway's view, a synthesis of *a priori* definitions would state that

> competency based education is a performance oriented process of educating which has a content bias or orientation toward extra-school, high social utility, life functional outcomes.[7]

Perhaps, however, the definition most often cited is that derived from the six critical elements of competency-based education proposed by Spady, who says it is

> a data-based, adaptive, performance-oriented set of integrated processes that facilitate, measure, record, and certify within the context of flexible time parameters the demonstration of known, explicitly stated, and agreed upon learning outcomes that reflect successful functioning in life roles.[8]

Out of these attempts to define competency-based education, two factors emerge.

First, the terms employed to identify competency-based education come from the range of orientations comprising it and have become confusingly intertwined. As the remarks quoted above suggest, many terms, even those considered pivotal by particular authors, are not commonly held and have become obstacles to the construction of a universally accepted and applied definition.

Spady speaks of "life roles" in defining competency-based education; however, the term is not necessarily even a peripheral element in the definitions offered by others. Moreover, it has come to mean different things to various individuals and educational programs. For example, life roles today may encompass citizenship and public responsibility, specific work skills, family and domestic education, interpersonal relations, value and moral education, economic and social survival skills, career education, and other areas, all of which are themselves open to a variety of interpretations.

Second, from the opinions sampled it is apparent that the perspectives from which observers view competency education influence greatly their particular definitions. Those analysts attempting to define competency-based education as it exists within the K–12 public school arena tend to emphasize the elements of outcomes assessment through minimum competency testing certification. Analysts defining competency-based education from the perspective of adult and postsecondary education are more inclined to stress acquisition of generic skills and the individualized nature of competency attainment.

Thus it seems that there are at least three arenas within the formal educational system in which activities called "competency based" are occurring. In addition, there are also out-of-school activities that bear many of the marks of competency-based practice, though they may or may not use this terminology. Examples of these are discussed in chapter 4.

Putting aside the problem of definition, there *are* some common choices that program developers in any educational arena must consider as they begin to design competency-based programs beyond the level of minimum competency testing.

COMPETENCY-BASED EDUCATION IN OPERATION

Because of a common assumption within the competency-based education movement—that learning is a highly individualized process—most applied models have programs organized around a five-step, student-oriented, instructional process. Thus, it is conceivable that competency-based education could be defined according to this basic pattern for instructional design.

The five steps include selection of outcome objectives, diagnosis and pre-testing, implementation of the instructional program, evaluation and post-testing, and the certification of competence. (See figure 2.1.)

First, the specific objectives to be achieved by the student are explicitly defined in advance of instruction or assessment so that all members of the learning process are made aware of the specific objectives and learning requirements at the outset of instruction. Spady's definition implies that

> the outcome goals of a CBE process [must] be stated in terms that are clear and explicit with regard to the criteria of performance that are expected and that they be known and agreed upon by all those with a direct interest in the student's educational progress. In other words, CBE takes the surprises out of the instructional-certification process by encouraging collaborative decision making regarding goals, by placing these goals "up front" as guides for both teachers and learners, and by attaching those goals to explicit and reasonably concrete behavioral referents.[9]

Palardy and Eisele put it this way:

> The first stage is establishing for any given school activity, such as a course or a unit of work, a listing of behavioral outcomes.[10]

Second, a form of diagnostic pre-test is conducted to determine how well individuals are prepared, what specific learning needs they have,

Fig. 2.1   Competency-Based Education Instructional Process

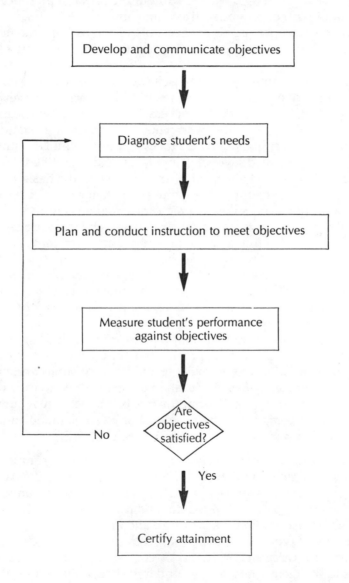

and what instructional methods are best suited to meet those needs.

Third, learners receive planned instruction in order to meet the pre-established outcome goals. Instruction may thus take place inside or outside school settings, with or without the physical presence of a teacher, and with or without a fixed time limit.

Fourth, competency assessment or post-testing is implemented to measure the learner's competence against the initial outcome objectives.

Finally, if the outcome goals are reached or surpassed, some form of acknowledgment or certification is presented the learner. However, if the objective is not attained, the process reverts to step two: learning problems are diagnosed and instructional methods are evaluated, redesigned, and reemployed. This process continues until the student achieves the designated level of competency and is certified.

These five steps can be viewed as an approach to the design of the instructional process supporting many competency-based education programs. If, however, so many practicing programs are based upon this structure, why is there so much debate between various competency-based education proponents and programs in the field? The answer is that even though these steps don't encompass all of the choices within competency-based education, each contains a range of possibilities. Therefore, at each stage of the process individuals devising a competency-based education program have many options in selecting an instructional focus.

The range of choices among components offers each designer of a competency-based education program an opportunity to create a unique identity. It is thus possible to have a very subject-oriented, traditional competency-based education program, or a radically different one. Whatever the final form, the five components just outlined are the basis for competency-based education's fragmentation and for the variety of foci established within it. (See chart 2.2.)

The Choice of Competencies.   The initial question for most competency programs is, Which competencies should be identified as the basis of our program? The answer is extremely important in determining the personality of the particular program, and it will heavily influence all remaining decisions about its structure and emphasis.

The choice of types of competencies to emphasize is the chief issue separating the three major arenas of competency-based programs: basic skills for elementary and secondary schools; life role skills for adult education; and generic skills for postsecondary programs. Although all types of skills may be addressed in each arena, one type usually dominates.

Chart 2.2 Choices Within the Competency-Based Education Process

---

DEVELOP OBJECTIVES

Skills

1 Basic skills in communication and computation

2 Specific subject area skills

3 Skills needed for adult roles

4 Generic process skills

Participants

Teachers/staff

Department of Education

Students

Community

PLAN AND CONDUCT INSTRUCTION

Differentiation

Uniform instruction for most students according to age

Special classes for some groups

Independent study classes

Variable instruction for individuals or groups

Time

Fixed time allotted for completion

Make up one competency while working on the next

Complete one competency, then proceed to the next

Places

Classrooms

Field trips

Home

Community placement sites

Instructors

Certified staff

Community experts coming to classrooms

On-site community experts

MEASURE LEARNER'S PERFORMANCE

Means

Paper-and-pencil tests   School products   Simulations   Performance

---

CERTIFY ATTAINMENT

Scope

Learning in school

Experiences outside the classroom

Mode

Evaluation by teacher

Certification by community expert

Possible selections range from the specific knowledge objectives of a particular unit, class, or program to the generic skills of higher-order thought processes such as critical thinking and problem analysis. Between these extremes is everything from the process skills of reading, writing, and numerical computation to the life role competencies that can range from specific knowledge and processes to value clarification and interpersonal relations. (See chart 2.3.)

Most K–12 public school competency-based education programs select only a portion of this spectrum, limiting their choices to basic academic skills (such as the traditional three Rs), to postschool life role skills or a combination of these two, or to competencies concerned only with specific skills, knowledge, and performance within a particular unit of study.

Consequently, the range of alternatives has perhaps been better exemplified in some postsecondary programs. College and university programs with competency-based education approaches have tended to emphasize generic skills much more than their public school counterparts have. As a primary example of this, Alverno College in Wisconsin has eight outcomes that are demanded of each student; and of these, three (analytical capability, problem-solving ability, and facility in forming value judgments within the decision-making process)[11] are generic skills.

Aside from selecting competencies, the three arenas also must determine whether skills are to be assessed as applied in school or in real-world situations outside the institution. Most K–12 programs require students to demonstrate academic skills in the school, assuming that these basics will carry over into the world outside.

Adult education, which perhaps is more aware of the realities of our changing society, has generated new competency-based programs to teach students to *apply* basic communication and computational skills in situations common to the real world. Edith Roth observes that as adult education's new programs are presently developing, they tend to rely heavily upon real-world experience and application of general and individualized skills.[12]

Postsecondary programs, especially those for undergraduate general education, posit general process skills as a means of bridging the gap between competency applications inside and outside the institution. These generic skills, which "underlie all productive intellectual functioning"[13] and are closely aligned to problem solving, can be applied to a range of disciplines and problems.

It should be noted that decisions concerning the selection of required competencies are highly susceptible to political realities and prevailing

Chart 2.3   Examples of Four Kinds of Skills

1 Basic School Skills

> read with comprehension
> communicate clearly in writing
> compute correctly
> listen with comprehension
> communicate orally
> attend class regularly and punctually
> listen quietly when a teacher is talking
> follow oral directions accurately
> spell correctly

2 Skills for Specific Subject Areas

> dissect a frog
> name foods in the four basic food groups
> recite the dates of major Civil War battles
> change a spark plug
> name works of major contemporary and classical composers
> type 30 words per minute
> run 100 yards in less than 20 seconds
> identify congruent geometric figures
> diagram a sentence
> classify literary works by genre

3 Skills Related to Adult Roles

> *citizen*: utilize voter information to make informed choices about candidates and issues
> *producer*: make informed job or recreation choices based on personal abilities and interests
> *consumer*: collect information on a potential purchase and select the best buy in terms of cost, convenience, effectiveness, and efficiency
> *family/group member*: relate to others in a way that indicates tolerance of differences and acceptance of the dignity and worth of other individuals
> *learner*: locate learning resources for an adult task

4 Generic Learning/Thinking Skills

> solve problems
> apply the scientific method
> use community learning resources
> locate information on a given topic
> construct questions to elicit desired information
> make judgments based on stated criteria
> synthesize information from two or more sources
> plan and conduct personal learning experiences

public expectations, including mandates issued or legislated by state governments and the pressure to avoid instructional innovations in the face of declining enrollments at K–12 levels. These factors play a more important role at the elementary-secondary level than at levels of education that are normally less visible to the public eye.

The Choice of Instructional Coordinates: Time and Place. A second question for those constructing a competency-based education program is: Where will the instruction take place? Within the range of possible programs, instruction may occur totally inside or outside the school. The decision rests heavily upon the choices preceding it. As Spady states:

> Essentially the more closely outcome goals reflect competencies that require problem solving, personal initiative, and social skills in connection with life-roles that are broader than those of student, worker, or consumer, the greater is the need to expand the instructional program beyond the walls of the school and to tap as instructors resource specialists outside the formal school staff.[14]

This point is central to the adult programs that have employed competencies as a means of providing credit for learning acquired outside formal educational systems.[15]

Also, decisions must be made concerning time. How much time will be allowed for a competency to be successfully demonstrated by the student? Will the learning process be limited to standard quarter or semester units of academic scheduling, or will it take place according to the individual's own rate and ability to learn? The answers to these questions conceivably have radical implications for our present educational system of chronologically grouping students into levels K–Ph.D. and confining instruction mainly to the classroom.

The Choice of Test Types. A third decision confronting those designing a competency-based education program is: What type of measuring device should be used to assess a student's level of competence? Should paper-and-pencil tests before and after instruction be the sole means of measuring competence? Or should actual performance in real-life situations be the basis for assessment? Four choices among possible measurement systems geared toward a standard of minimum competency are these as outlined by Brickell:

> 1.   *Paper and pencil tests* in the classroom—what we usually think of as "tests." Most of these measure a narrow band of knowledge or skill and are far removed from performance required in real life. . . .

2. *School products and performances.* These are essays, paintings, experiments, clarinet solos, brake jobs, speeches, touchdowns—things students make or do while studying in school. . . .

3. *Simulated performance* situations set up in the schoolhouse to resemble those in later school or on the job. . . . The student demonstrates minimum competency in artificial situations like the real ones to come. . . .

4. *Actual performance* situations in later school or on the job. . . . The student demonstrates minimum competency by entering and graduating from the next level of schooling or getting a job and keeping it.[16]

The Choice of Standards. A fourth decision centers on the question of standards. Will learners be assessed and compared according to standard norms, or should they be assessed according to their ability to meet a pre-established minimum achievement level?

The Choice of Certification. A final choice must be made as to how the certification of competence will be recorded and to whom it will be reported. In some systems, certification of competency achievement is stated publicly and is the basis for grade promotion or graduation. In others, there is no special recognition, diploma, certificate, or stamp. Rather, the learner's attainment of competency levels, known and assessed solely by the student and the teacher, is used to diagnose weaknesses, gains, and strengths, and to indicate the next goal. Falling between these two extremes are various combinations of practices for reporting instructional outcomes to individual students and to the public.

The preceding discussion does not represent the entire range of choices each program must make; it merely sketches the choices that underlie the basic orientation of any competency-based education program. It is possible to describe the instructional profiles of most current programs according to the positions of their various elements along any of the continuums shown earlier in chart 2.2.

PROGRAM PATTERNS

Particular patterns emerge as various programs are developed from the array of available choices. College and adult education programs generally seem to emphasize innovative and nontraditional aspects of competency-based education, while K–12 public school programs usually select the more traditional options. Gary Woditsch points to the fact that competency-based education does have a variety of forms,

and that the existence of two dramatically different thrusts leaves us
with both traditional and radical possibilities:

> In its many forms, competency-based education proposes to matricu-
> late competent graduates. When it makes this proposal with an eye
> toward behaviors and roles currently sanctioned by society, CBE
> doesn't differ overly much from our better traditional examples of
> vocational education. The task is one of shaping students in accord
> with some societal blueprint. But when CBE proposes graduates who
> are capable of leading productive lives in a radically changing world,
> whatever the blueprint, it sets its foot where there is no path.[17]

Descriptions of both public and postsecondary competency-based
education programs show this general pattern of bifurcation, which
results from the public schools' desire to return to the basics and the
collegiate attempt to offer attractive and meaningful general education
programs.

Collegiate and adult programs such as those at Alverno, Mars Hill,
Bowling Green, and the New York State External High School Diploma
Program align themselves more or less in accordance with the generic
and life skill competencies. There is, of course, some overlap, but the
key tendency seems to be greater emphasis upon basic skills in the
public school programs. As Spady states:

> According to information compiled by Clark and Thompson (1976),
> no states outside of Oregon appear to use language consistent with
> the life-role conception of competency in either their current or pend-
> ing regulations pertaining to mandated student proficiencies. The
> possible exceptions refer to the need for occupational and consumer
> mathematics skills.[18]

Between these two poles lie the adult programs that emphasize basic
academic and life role skills along with real-world career exploration.
As Ruth Nickse says about the New York State External High School
Diploma Program:

> The new diploma recognizes performance in basic skills areas (math,
> reading) as well as in life skills (consumer, scientific, citizenship and
> health awareness, and occupational preparedness); it rewards ad-
> vanced occupational/vocational, academic, and specialized skills.[19]

A second basic trend also appears when programs are analyzed
according to these three educational arenas. Postsecondary and adult
education programs not only tend to select the more nontraditional
choices, but also tend to select a broader area of the continuums.
Meanwhile, the K–12 public school sector is narrowing its focus to

those options closely allied with traditional curricular approaches. Chris Pipho reports these specifics:

> Among the 31 states that have taken official action in this area, most seem to agree on the identification of basic skill areas. Virtually all mention reading or communications and mathematics. Florida mentions life skills; Rhode Island, survival skills. Colorado leaves all identification of basic skills to the local districts, while California and Florida allow local districts to add subject areas at their discretion.
>
> Only Florida and California have enacted legislation that permits early exit from high school. Early-exit laws allow school districts to award the equivalent of a high school diploma to students who pass a designated test, even if the students have not earned the minimum number of credits traditionally required for graduation.
>
> Twenty of the 31 states have minimal competency testing standards that will affect regular high school graduation. These states are Alabama, Arizona, California, Colorado (local option), Delaware, Florida, Idaho (local option), Kentucky, Maine, Maryland, Nevada, New Mexico, New York, North Carolina, Oregon, Tennessee, Utah, Vermont, Virginia, and Wyoming.[20]

Not only are there varying emphases in the three main arenas practicing versions of competency-based education, but also there is an increasingly large gap developing between public school programs on the one hand and adult, postsecondary, out-of-school programs on the other. These differences appear to be growing, not diminishing.

SUMMARY

Competency-based education is a multidimensional movement that encompasses at least three major educational arenas as well as out-of-school programs. These arenas and their programs vary greatly from one another. The most publicly identifiable form is at the elementary-secondary level, where minimum competency testing is viewed as a rational and systematic response to a general public desire for programs that are economically efficient, socially uniform, accountable, and traditional. The emphasis on basic skills in these programs has been determined mainly at administrative or legislative levels—something less than a grass-roots response to locally defined needs.

Within our complex society, moving back to basic skills and processes which are to be employed chiefly within academic fields and settings is an interesting denial of the role of expanding technologies in our lives.

At the same time, the postsecondary, adult, and nonschool arenas have developed in different directions from the K–12 form of competency-based education, and have generally remained outside the public's view and assessment. Postsecondary programs have tended to define more abstract and higher order skills than the three Rs. Their search for improvement in the teaching of learning and thinking skills has led them to the goal of graduating a broadly informed student who can apply process skills to standard disciplines.

While K–12 and postsecondary competency programs have been reexamining what skill needs their student populations have, adult education has been moving more toward an appraisal of what actually constitutes a learning experience and what situations—both in and out of the classroom—foster particular skills. Both of these arenas are experimenting with new forms of assessment, including applied performance testing and simulations.

However, if the public continues to view the competency movement as a single approach, the real dimensions of the movement may not be perceived. If this is the case, the fate of competency-based education will rest entirely upon the success or failure of only one of its forms—minimum competency testing. Such nearsightedness would, of course, result in the loss of untried variations, many of which could offer provocative alternatives to more traditional programs.

Competency-based education has been able to develop within different educational arenas, primarily because it revolves around no true theoretical core. What competency-based education has offered is a general instructional approach within all educational arenas.

Although its ultimate potential remains unknown, it is clear that competency-based education can affect traditional schooling only if many of its forms are developed experimentally and applied selectively to learning situations. It is essential that people recognize that the value of competency-based education lies far beyond minimum competency testing. Such efforts will depend on general public awareness and support.

NOTES

1. See William G. Spady, "Competency Based Education: A Bandwagon in Search of a Definition," pp. 9–14. Copyright 1977, American Educational Research Assn., Washington, D.C. All quotations by permission.

2. Walter Hathaway, "Competency Based Education: Definitional Issues and Implications. . . . ," p. 1. All quotations by permission.

3. Sheila Huff, *Problems in Implementing Competency-Based Programs*, pp. 3–4. Used by permission.

4. David Ainsworth, "Examining the Basis for Competency-based Education," p. 322. Used by permission.

5. Robert B. Howsam, "Performance Based Instruction," p. 35. Used by permission.

6. J. Michael Palardy and James E. Eisele, "Competency Based Education," p. 545. All quotations by permission.

7. Hathaway, p. 2.

8. Spady, p. 10.

9. Ibid.

10. Palardy and Eisele, p. 546.

11. See Alverno College Faculty, *Liberal Learning at Alverno College*, p. 6.

12. See Edith Roth, "APL: A Ferment in Education," pp. 6–9.

13. Bob Knott, "Competency Based Education: State-of-the-Art Position Paper," p. 9. Used by permission.

14. Spady, p. 11.

15. See Ruth S. Nickse, "The Central New York External High School Diploma Program," p. 123. Copyright 1975 by Phi Delta Kappa, Inc. All quotations by permission.

16. Henry M. Brickell, *Let's Talk About Minimum Competency Testing,* pp. 6–7. Copyright © 1978. Used by permission.

17. Gary A. Woditsch, "Jonathan Livingston Student: Competence for What?" p. 19. Used by permission.

18. Spady, p. 13.

19. Nickse, p. 123.

20. Chris Pipho, "Minimal Competency Standards," pp. 34–35. Used by permission.

3

How Can Competencies Be Taught?

Some Observations and Suggestions

LOUIS RUBIN

EDITOR'S INTRODUCTION

A primary educational goal shared by all is to improve learning effectiveness and opportunity. To this end, programs designed to be competency based have altered some critical elements of the teaching-learning paradigm, emphasizing one or another, or some combination, for their own purposes and according to their own needs. These elements include specifications of desired educational outcomes related to some agreed-upon criteria of performance, and variations in uses of time, types of instruction, and types of measurement, as well as requirements for certification. Each system, prompted by varieties of pressures and desires, makes decisions and implements changes that seem both desirable and feasible. Most efforts in schools, operating under both real and perceived constraints, proceed with one change at a time. New programs organized according to some version of a competency-based philosophy orchestrate several variations as part of the process of program design.

For those programs that posit "competency-based education" as an opportunity for providing multiple learning experiences to help learners achieve some required goal, there are many possibilities. Instructional approaches may include mastery learning techniques, discovery learning, Keller's PSI method, and the many available versions of individualized instruction. For purposes of instruction, media presentations, small group learning teams, learning packets, handbooks, workbooks, and learning projects are all employed.

In theory, individual differences in learning speed and style are acccommodated by the use of many strategies, for there is no one best way to teach competence. The availability of a wide variety of instructional resources and strategies is both necessary and healthy. Opportunities to use community resources such as libraries and museums expand as such sites for learning gain increasing legitimacy. Learning at home, a viable strategy for a large number of people who will not or cannot avail themselves of institutional learning, gains importance as well.

In addition to using various appropriate instructional strategies and learning sites, some competency-based programs employ craftspersons from business and industry, as well as their own alumni, to augment the professional staffs' talents and skills. Community members may be specially trained by educators and used to evaluate competence in programs where instructors feel less well prepared to make judgments.

It is clear that competency-based education offers ample opportunity for a wide range of instructional approaches. What seems needed is some systematic approach to observation, data gathering, and analysis of effective strategies, so that those that seem successful are nourished and can serve as models for study and adaption. We need to know, too, what doesn't work and why, so that scarce resources are not squandered.

The author of this chapter about the task of teaching for competence points out first that there are essential differences in instruction when it is intended to meet the objectives of minimum competency testing and when it is designed for competency-based education of a more complex nature. From his perspective, teaching for competence is related to the successful management of programs that (1) feature instruction based on goals rather than time, (2) encourage a high degree of individualization and the development of competence in real-life settings, and (3) depend importantly on the commitment of both teachers and learners.

He cautions that teaching for competence must proceed with a clear emphasis on the coordinated development of abstract book knowledge and concrete experience. By outlining a set of eight important steps, he provides useful guidelines for planners who seek an organized approach to the design of competency-based instructional programs. In concluding, he suggests some strategies that have the potential to link knowledge and skills, an important instructional objective.

Although they are intended to direct large-scale instructional programs, the guidelines suggested by Rubin can be modified for use by any individual with teaching responsibilities. Educators can follow these steps to identify desired outcomes and their subcomponents, plan effective and diverse methods of instruction to assist students' learning, identify appropriate learning strategies, provide continuity across courses to support the learning of the desired objective, provide for individual differences in learning styles, make provisions for learning outside the school, and carefully evaluate progress.

Classroom teachers who develop competency-based programs in a systematic manner need support for these ventures. Successful implementation on a small scale can do much to refine these concepts and can lead to greater understanding both of the problems of competency-based approaches and of their potential.

R.S.N.

IT BECOMES apparent even from a cursory reading of the literature that competence can be and is defined and assessed in a variety of ways. Whatever interpretations are made or accepted, they will necessarily have great influence upon any subsequent recommendations for teaching. Moreover, it is of great importance to distinguish between competency-based education and minimum competency testing. Although both concepts have attracted considerable attention, they are quite different in both character and intent. They therefore require dissimilar instructional operations and pose contrasting obligations for students and teachers.

The focus on minimum competency testing (in K–12 public education) is clearly designed to measure achievement in specific areas of study. The primary purpose is to verify cognitive development. Essentially, it is an effort to make the existing systems of instruction and certification accountable, with no drastic change in either. Consequently, the teaching strategies must concentrate on delivering substantive information, conceptual understanding, and reasoning. This is a laudable effort, even if narrowly conceived.

Competency-based education, however, differs markedly from minimum testing programs. The substance of the instructional content derives from the functions of adult life; affect is integrated with cognition and manual capability, and the assessment devices used to verify competence are oriented more toward performance than knowledge. In addition, there is a focus on the achievement of desired outcomes and goals, not just on time spent or attendance. There is a focus on the application of skills as well as on information recall. Historically, these emphases represent a different teaching-learning paradigm for education and must be accommodated in any competency-based curriculum. They demand a new concept of the use of time in instruction, of multiple learning opportunities inside and outside formal schooling structures, and of new goal-oriented roles for both learners and teachers. (See chart 3.1.)

The changeover from old instructional systems to new ones will need to proceed gradually, step by step, in order to provide a shelter against apprehension and alienation among learners and their instructors. With all due deference to the architects of competency programs and to the spirit of the revolution, the contemplated shifts are based upon notions and convictions that do not yet add up to a tested rationale. Systematic trial and error in the implementation of competency-based education programs would therefore seem to be crucial.

Until more is known, contradictions about the effects of different organizational structures and roles within a competency-based educa-

Chart 3.1   Potential Changes in Schools Adopting Competency-Based Education

Competency-Based Education May Require Schools to Move	
Away From	*Toward*
instructional content derived from subject discipline knowledge bases	instructional content derived from functions of adult life
separation of affective from cognitive and psychomotor domains in determining instructional content	integration of affective, cognitive, and psychomotor domains
assessment oriented towards knowledge	assessment oriented towards performance
focus on attendance and course credit requirements	focus on student attainment of desired outcomes
information recall	application of skills
single learning and assessment opportunity	multiple learning and assessment opportunities
curriculum planning primarily within grade levels and courses	comprehensive curriculum articulation, K–12
independent planning of teaching activities	teacher communication and coordination between grade levels and subject areas
teacher-directed learning	student self-directed learning
instruction entirely in classrooms	instruction in both school and community settings
communication flowing one way, from school to clients	communication flowing two ways, between school and clients
instructional content based upon a determination of "what's good for" a group of students	instructional content based upon identified individual student needs
teaching ideas in the abstract	teaching ideas within personal contexts and experiences

tion system probably are unavoidable. Nevertheless, they should be watched closely; some of the experimental endeavors may be barren or counterproductive, just as some may prove manageable and fruitful. Since so much is unclear, it would be a great advantage to accumulate as much empirical evidence as possible and to bring dispassionate judgment to bear upon its subsequent analysis. False assumptions that are not brought to light and corrected always lead eventually to massive distortions and pernicious side effects.

The measure of our illiteracy with respect to teaching for competence is perhaps best conveyed by David McClelland's prescription for needed research:

> In summary, research on ways of acquiring competencies should be supported which focuses on the following areas:
> 1. Natural variations in competencies;
> 2. Educational environments (or institutions) that produce wide variations in competencies;
> 3. Subject matters that are especially appropriate for producing various competencies;
> 4. Experimental studies of educational treatments that produce various competencies provided they focus on the elements that produce learning and take into account the requirements of social delivery systems [among the treatment variables of particular interest are classroom management techniques, the media, and various types of organizational arrangements for delivery];
> 5. The relationship of educational "treatments" to characteristics that the person possesses at the outset. Of particular importance is the investigation of what educational treatments work best for those who start very low on the competency in question.
> Research support should be for a series of interrelated studies of how to increase a particular competency. Single-shot experiments have little cumulative pay off in the educational field.[1]

McClelland's last paragraph is particularly significant. It forewarns, first, that a considerable amount of exploration will be necessary and, second, that any given competency can probably be developed through alternative teaching procedures. Because the achievement of competence is a cumulative process that must be reinforced in a variety of contexts, teachers must have access to a comprehensive program of student monitoring, so that individuals are taught—year by year and subject by subject—through methods that best nurture the desired competence. Effective pedagogy will need to be based on the learner's characteristics, the nature of the particular objectives, the characteristics of the instructional environment, and the teacher's work style.

Prefabricated, universally applicable prescriptions are not likely to be of much real help. (See chart 3.2.)

Within these constraints, then, what observations can be made on teaching for competence?

A major departure from convention in competency-based education is that demonstrated competence replaces the customary system of grades and semester hours. If educational institutions follow this pro-

Chart 3.2   Characteristics of Personalized Instruction

Personalized Instruction Is	
Not Necessarily	*But Usually Involves*
one student working with one instructor	some one-on-one time, especially for planning activities and evaluating achievement
conducted in small groups	grouping strategies and activities, including peer tutoring
self-paced	time flexibility, so that the student masters one competency before proceeding to the next
self-directed	student choice, with teacher guidance, of learning materials and activities
	student participation in planning and evaluating learning
	some independent work
outside the classroom	some activities outside the classroom, linking school experiences with the rest of the student's life
ungraded	some flexibility in grading procedures, to grant credit for previously mastered skills and to permit all students to master criterion skills or competencies
	more extensive feedback about performance than letter grades provide
an individual education program for each student	flexibility in assignments and materials and strategies to meet the needs of students individually

Source: Competency Based Education Program, Northwest Regional Educational Laboratory, Portland, Oregon.

cedure, the competencies selected as primary educational targets will need to be attacked systematically in all subject areas and at various age levels. A comprehensive thrust must therefore be made part of the entire curriculum. Teachers must know what students have encountered *before* a particular learning unit and what they will experience *after* it.

Moreover, since individualization is critical in effective competency development, every teacher must also have some sense of *each* student's strengths and weaknesses. Thus, the need for routine teacher communication and collaborative interaction both with students and with other teachers is substantially greater than in traditional formats. In the absence of a carefully orchestrated plan, faculties could easily work at cross-purposes with one another.

Students, too, must be more heavily involved in self-directed growth. As in any other endeavor involving the cumulative enhancement of performance, they will progress more rapidly when there is a clear understanding of the goal, a sustained sense of progress, and a recognition of specific weaknesses that require strengthening.

All of this suggests that practitioner commitment to the underlying aims of competency-based education is indispensable. For if some teachers subscribe to its intent and spirit and others do not, students will inevitably flounder amid conflicting pressures. Consequently, an extensive program of teacher orientation is essential. The inherent advantages of competency-based education must be made obvious; a belief in its underlying principles must be kindled; and considerable in-service training must be devoted to assisting both teachers and administrators in the accomplishment of their mission.

Without question, the precondition of greatest moment is practitioner commitment. Revisionist theorists sometimes assume that any reasonable change can be introduced on the basis of its logical advantages. Life, alas, is not so made; principals and teachers who prize traditional brands of instruction may not find it easy to accept the competency-based education philosophy. Furthermore, since the ambitions of the competency programs are exceedingly high, much depends upon the teacher's willingness to take on a far larger responsibility. Some will be sufficiently impelled by the potential to do so; others will conclude that the liabilities outweigh the assets. It goes without saying that a healthy self-concept and a complex array of life skills together constitute a greater teaching challenge than the Roman wars. Hence, if teachers cannot be convinced of competency-based education's virtues, it will be a lost cause.

Another problem concerns the difficulties of developing real-world competencies within the confines of the school environment. While it is conceivable that public education can be taken beyond the walls of the school into the community proper, effective provisions for this will be difficult to orchestrate. Nevertheless, authentic life skills must be conditioned and refined in actual settings. Even more important, their mastery can be tested only in actual situations.

The ability to handle some, but not all, aspects of an operation does not reflect true competence, just as understanding is not the same as proficiency. Appreciating the skills of a great tennis player is of a different order than being able to play adeptly. Similarly, the odds are good that if the verification of a competence is best done in a direct performance situation, its development probably will also be expedited in a naturalistic setting. Many writers, in fact, have argued that these "real" learning experiences offer maximum effectiveness and efficiency. There are, as a result, further compelling reasons for relating in-school learning to outside experiences.

A good deal of ingenuity, one suspects, must go into the invention of competency-building activities that can serve as a bridge between formal and informal education. As more and more attention focuses upon a stronger collaboration between home and school, and as further investigations into the potential of community-based learning continue, one may expect to see practices like those outlined in chart 3.3. Even so, it seems likely that teachers will need to reconceptualize the traditional nature of homework and search out authentic competency-building exercises in the student's environment.

There is a secondary consideration, which must also be resolved. Competence, by definition, implies sufficiency; a competent person is one who has *enough* skill and knowledge to behave effectively. The amount of knowledge and skill required for successful performance, however, differs from situation to situation. Most of us occasionally find ourselves in circumstances in which we feel incompetent. We then seek to delegate, circumvent, or escape responsibility in some way. Such maneuvers are sometimes the most sensible course of action. The question, therefore, is how the schools should pursue the cultivation of those life skills that must be tailored to a specific set of events. The primary dilemma is that competence is not defined by mastery of arbitrarily determined skills, but rather by the ability to survive in whatever circumstances one happens to be in. Because these cannot be readily anticipated, a number of writers have cautioned against teaching to predetermined learning objectives. Leonard Waks, for instance, argues that the best solution lies in direct experiential learning:

. . . the principle of least treatment, states that direct pedagogical treatments intended to promote specific pre-determined learning objectives should be used only where other instrumentalities for life-role learning are demonstrably inadequate. Stated prescriptively, the principle says: make maximum room for the growth and utilization of non-pedagogical instrumentalities and self-determined learning in life-role education. . . . Similarly, instead of combatting the youth culture while at the same time attempting to convey social skills through artificial school interventions, the schools should learn to

Chart 3.3   Opportunities for Community Participation in the Educational Process

School/Community Links	
SELECT OBJECTIVES	Community members help define the competencies
DIAGNOSE STUDENT'S NEEDS	Community instructors notify teachers when a student needs special help to complete a project
PLAN AND CONDUCT INSTRUCTION	Community members act as instructors at their own work sites
	Students see what competencies are needed in jobs
	Students apply what they've learned in school to community experiences
	Students analyze learning opportunities in community experiences
	Parents and teachers collaborate on home projects for students
MEASURE STUDENT'S PERFORMANCE	Community instructors evaluate performance of students whose projects they supervise
	Community members may join teachers on assessment committees at the school
CERTIFY ATTAINMENT	Community instructors certify that students have met project requirements

Source: Competency Based Educational Program, Northwest Regional Educational Laboratory, Portland, Oregon.

respect youth culture for its positive values of association and mutual support, and learn to encourage the development of other positive youth-related instrumentalities, supplementing or contending against these only when necessary . . .

. . . If a person is not competent, this means that he does not satisfy the competency requirements of a given role. The situation may be changed if the person acquires new knowledge and skill. But it also may change if the role requirements change so as no longer to demand the missing knowledge and skill. Competence is not merely a function of the possession of "competencies," it is an interaction between competencies and requirements.[2]

A pedagogy shaped for competency development must also contend with values. It can scarcely be denied that there often are contradictions between the values espoused in the curriculum and those reflected in the societal mainstream. As a primary socializing agency, the schools are expected to imbue the young with a sense of what could be, rather than merely with what is. Socialization and the kindling of idealism, it is generally believed, should go hand in hand. As a result, when exploring a suitable teaching strategy for competence it is necessary to ask whether students should be taught to deal only with the existing world or with some more perfect society as well. If, for example, competence is regarded as the capacity and willingness to deal with things as they are, it could be argued that the schools will serve mainly to perpetuate the status quo and to prolong weaknesses in the social system. Chickering and Claxton touch upon a similar point in chapter 1 when they observe that in any thorough competency-based education program, difficult questions of value, politics, and local power will arise and will have to be resolved with varying kinds and degrees of benefit for those involved.

There are also liabilities on the reverse side of the coin. It is falsely assumed in many quarters that once explicit standards have been imposed, learner achievement will rise dramatically. This, unfortunately, will not always be true. Effective human behavior cannot be guaranteed—through chemicals, compulsion, or even good teaching! The achievement of competence is heavily influenced by the learner's incentive, mind set, and previous learning experience. A student, for instance, who attributes earlier academic failure to lack of effort will encounter less difficulty than one who attributes it to lack of ability. Similarly, while a good deal of superior teaching goes on, it cannot reasonably be presumed that no student will ever encounter ineffectual instruction. The bond between student competence and teacher competence is strong.

There are three further concerns to be considered with regard to teaching for competence, apart from the technical procedures that must be employed.

First, we cannot doubt that total disregard of the standard disciplines would be unduly threatening to both the profession and the client. The young must have some exposure to the accumulated cultural heritage. Yet formal study of the traditional disciplines pursued in traditional learning modes cannot by itself be counted upon to engender functional competence. Accordingly, particular concepts that are especially useful in developing specific social competencies must be located in and developed through the disciplines. This, in effect, constitutes the significant distinction between education based on disciplines and education based on competency. From a study of history, for example, students can come to understand that a participatory democracy does not work if the citizenry fails to participate in decision-making activities.

Second, teaching must identify and emphasize the cognitive processes through which acquired intellectual concepts can be used to increase social proficiency. In and of themselves, even the most powerful ideas are inert. It is only when they are applied directly to a problem that their potency takes effect. As a result, teaching for an objective such as social competence must enable the student to analyze a given life situation, determine the critical factors at play, apply relevant concepts from organized human knowledge, and then deduce and carry out appropriate action. In discussing a problem-solving approach for instruction in a competency-based general education program, Gary Woditsch makes these suggestions:

> They should be problems that collectively, and in some cases individually, exhibit the following traits: 1) problems that compel scientific and systematic modes of thought about self, environment and society, 2) problems that require setting value priorities regarding self/environment/society, 3) problems that involve the translation of theories and idealized values into practice, 4) problems that try modes of conflict resolution, and 5) problems in determining a basis for cooperation in the face of divergence. They should also be problems that disciplinary exemplars have, to some degree of satisfaction, brought to resolution or solved. We need exemplary processes of solution not so they may be copied, but so that students may use them in contrasting and assessing their own problem solving efforts and capabilities, the better to set new skill aspirations.[3]

Still, for most social competencies, conceptual knowledge and exemplars from the disciplines will not be enough. The greatest part of human behavior is prompted by attitudes and beliefs that derive from life's happenings. Curriculum and instruction, consequently, must also deal with mechanisms through which learning embedded in personal incidents is preserved, utilized, and adapted to new circumstances. Experience, if not the best teacher, is at least an influential one. Yet the lessons learned from social encounters are not always constructive. It is only when we learn to analyze and interpret their meaning, to avoid distortions, and to internalize the resulting wisdom that life's occurrences can be used to make us stronger and more adequate. Teaching for competence, accordingly, must continually seek to correlate abstract book knowledge with concrete personal experience.

Third, there is a body of skills and knowledge that is essential to functional competency and that may not have developed through the student's experiential background. Teachers must use some kind of inventory to identify these missing elements and devise a pattern of activities, inside and outside the school, that will help to fill the void. It will sometimes be more convenient for students to acquire the necessary knowledge base through active experience; sometimes the study of a formal discipline will be needed. In short, effective teaching must provide for a *comprehensive* attack upon a diagnosed competency need, combining old and new experience, formal and informal subject matter, and direct as well as indirect learning into a well-orchestrated composite. Only in this way can the school hope to fulfill the requirements of a complete competency-based curriculum and meet more traditional expectations at the same time.

It seems clear that the architects of competency-based education regard it both as process and as terminus. Put another way, the end goal of competency-based education is to nurture individuals who can thrive in their social milieu as fully functioning persons. Social adeptness of this sort, as many writers have noted, must derive from a variety of capabilities that differ both in nature and in complexity. It follows that the teaching techniques directed toward these capabilities must vary accordingly.

Hence, a series of coordinated procedures must be set in operation. These eight obligations will be mandatory, irrespective of how competency-based education is implemented.

First, a particular competency—social awareness, for example— must be identified.

Second, the anatomy of the competence must be dissected, so that the particular skills, understandings, and attitudes it embodies are identifiable.

Third, instructional devices for each of these competency components must be selected, so that a systematic developmental program can be organized. In the case of social awareness, the instructional content and learning activities must be arranged in some kind of logical order so that there is a rational beginning, middle, and end.

Fourth, a repertory of teaching strategies must be devised so that teachers can attack given objectives in the most appropriate ways.

Fifth, provisions for interdisciplinary applications must be arranged so that the knowledge, attitudes, and skills acquired in one context can be reinforced in another.

Sixth, controls that ensure continuity as students progress through the schools must be established. Individuals differ in the manner and rate at which competence develops, so the learning program must allow for variations.

Seventh, since many of the designated competencies are likely to be influenced by experiences outside the school, these must be taken into consideration as instructional options are planned.

Eighth (cf. Schalock in chapter 5), an assemblage of evaluation mechanisms must be acquired, administered, interpreted, and incorporated in the continuous effort toward self-correcting improvement. Since competencies cannot all be evaluated in the same way or by the same personnel, regular assessment will be necessary as a basis for readjustments.

Speculating about a target roster of competencies for general education, Woditsch lists five kinds of behavioral capability:

1) Selective attention: ability to control the class of stimuli which receive conscious focus.
2) Sustained analysis: a capacity to probe a complex situation until all its components are identified.
3) Analogizing: a capacity to test known relationships for similarity with those potential to a new situation.
4) Suspension of closure: prioritizing (synthesizing) factors before shaping solution.
5) Autocensorship: testing a solution covertly, before affirmation.[4]

Then, in discussing generic skills (general abilities not readily discernible by inspection), he warns us that authentic skill development involves both internalization and a capacity to recognize when and where the skill is applicable:

> Generic skill development is a two-phase process. First, one must make sure that the skill literally emerges, and that the learner is not merely simulating emergence by employing some complex of lower-

order capabilities. But to do this much is not enough. Next, one needs to see that the skill is in fact *genotypic* of the learner's behavior, which means phenotypes are exhibited across the full range of the skill's utility. To do this, the learner must exercise the skill in a sufficiently broad range of experiential settings to explicitly recognize the skill as fruitfully transferable, or "generalizable." When the learner exhibits a proactive, or habitual, tendency to exhibit the skill in new situations, we can speak of a *genotypic* competency.[5]

Finally, he poses the critical question: How do we develop genotypic competencies in the five kinds of behavior? His answer:

> By confronting the student with exemplars of those real problems that circumscribe the human condition and that are amenable to some resolution only through the exercise of conceptual thought and its tools. For instance, problems embedded in the muddy, imprecise, or deliberately devious use of language, which on the one hand alarm and impede clear thinking, and on the other set a snarl only clear thought can unravel. Problems such as these can develop not only conceptual acumen, but a reasoned appetite for precision in the use of language. Or again, problems that stem from conflicts in value systems, or in seeking immediate as opposed to deferred gratifications, where the difference between well-reasoned and unreasoned resolutions can be disastrous. Problems of this sort can also nurture a healthy respect for history as a diagnostic of varying standards in human action. Problems that pose the need for human cooperation can at one and the same time demonstrate the genotypic worth of conceptual abilities and establish the "relevance" of skill in communication, and underscore the importance or probity of politics.
>
> There exist a number of pedagogies and programs that hold promise for developing the kind of genotypic conceptual competencies we have outlined. Unfortunately, many of these curricular efforts are not sufficiently aware of the centrality and priority of their role in general education. Their employment is perfunctory, or they address "cognitive skill development" as a component of some broader introductory mission.[6]

From the perspective of Woditsch, then, it is apparent that:

- Concepts from the disciplines can be applied to events in the real world.
- Involvement in the real world is useful in developing particular objectives, such as social competence.
- A major aspect of competence lies in recognizing when and how acquired skills should be deployed.
- Self-actuating engagement in which the student practices new skills in the social environment is indispensable.

From another perspective, James Block acknowledges the natural congruence between mastery learning and competency-based education:

> This conception of the competent student re-emphasizes the linkage between learning for mastery and learning for competence. It suggests that students must learn for mastery if they are to become competent. The conception also encourages that mastery learning ideas and strategies are used broadly and humanely. It admonishes mastery learning advocates that their ideas and strategies cannot be limited to the acquisition of only simple intellectual and motor skills nor can they be implemented in a mechanistic fashion that would sacrifice student feelings about what they were learning.[7]

Given all of our observations thus far, the outlines of an approach to teaching for competence begin to take shape. No single method or procedure will suffice. Students vary in their personal history, warehouse of skills, and fund of knowledge. Their learning styles, moreover, are equally diverse. Some thrive in simulated situations while others must have direct involvement; some develop insight step by step while others make intuitive leaps; some flourish in group situations and others do better alone. Competency-based education must be pluralistic in method, content, and aim.

One of competency-based education's major advantages is that acquired knowledge is put to practical use. Theorists have long agreed that the learning of subject matter is not the ultimate goal of education: rather, the objective is to use accumulated knowledge in dealing intelligently with life's situations. Hence, in teaching for competence it is important that learners progress systematically through increasingly difficult assignments so that their skills mature. In short, teachers must organize instruction in such a way that a learner's competence is enhanced, generalized, and made permanent.

The heart of competency-based education, as many writers have observed, lies in provisions that help to guarantee student achievement. These provisions must integrate cognition and affect, incorporate instructional mechanisms that allow for individualization, permit sustained growth and development, afford internal reinforcement, and facilitate the regular evaluation and feedback crucial to efficient learning. Inherent in such an approach is the belief that respectable performance standards can be met if there is a sufficient amount of learning time and adequate variation in teaching procedures. In the quest for competence, a learner must master one level of knowledge and skill before moving to another. An orderly arrangement for identifying and correcting difficulties, as well as for directing students to more difficult tasks, must therefore be built into the system. In short, instead of holding teaching methods and learning time constant, allowing students to learn whatever they can, the time and method are varied to ensure that each student attains the desired performance level.

An emphasis upon planned variations in teaching methods, designed to accommodate individual learning idiosyncrasies, greatly increases the likelihood of identifying and enhancing special talents. Patricia Cross has pointed cogently to this concern:

> . . . some students will take to traditional academic learning like a duck to water, while others will struggle to remain afloat. Never mind that our sinking duck can run like a gazelle or fly like a swallow. What we are not yet ready to concede is that running and flying are as good as swimming and that our world is better for the existence of all three talents, appropriately used.[8]

The benefits of competency-based education are obviously dependent upon the usefulness of the goals and role models that are selected. These must be clearly understood and highly valued by the student. When these conditions are not met, the necessary incentive is lacking and only limited benefits occur. Whether we are interested in learning to play golf, use a new power tool, bake bread, or master a second language, our achievement rate is directly related to the extent of our interest and desire. An effective competency-based education program must first win the learner's commitment to its goals, then encourage continual practice, and finally facilitate self-directed growth after the instructional unit has been concluded.

Motivation, so crucial to building competence, is perpetuated by four kinds of classroom activities: role playing, simulation, problem solving, and assignments outside the school. These, to be sure, are neither the only devices that should be used nor sufficient unto themselves. They nevertheless make irrefutably good sense because they connect knowledge and skill. All four procedures have attributes that are of considerable value. They are operational, realistic, multidimensional, attitude-shaping, and oriented toward behavior.

Role playing, for example, is beneficial in that it allows the learner to practice behavior that will be invoked repeatedly during adulthood. Likewise, simulation provides a means of incorporating life situations in a curriculum that otherwise would lack practical application. Problem solving, when the right problems are selected, provides a vehicle for joining useful insights gleaned from the disciplines. Consider, for instance, the diverse kinds of knowledge that must go into the sensible purchase of a home. Homework assignments tied directly to the learners' environment increase relevance, encourage individuals to apply concepts, and, above all, help them gain a personal *sense* of competence. How many of us are defeated, not by a lack of ability, but by self-doubt?

One further advantage of these kinds of learning exercises is also worth mentioning. Whenever human behavior is reduced to discrete, observable phenomena, the dangers of oversimplification become very great. People engage in a complex constellation of activities as they go about their business. It is this, consequently, that is most germane. Until better evaluation methods are devised, student competence in *life skills* will undoubtedly be determined through human judgment. Such judgment is fallible, however, and the evaluators must take care to avoid confusing contributory skills with competence. A student, for example, may be able to identify the hazards of nicotine and tar and describe their effect on the body. These, however, are only intermediate skills; the true test is whether the student chooses to smoke. Competent action, we would do well to remember, depends not only upon knowledge and skill but also upon one's values, beliefs, and inner strength. As a result, classroom teaching and its evaluation must deal with the total framework of human adequacy.

For the skeptical, such an attempt to embrace the overall range of capabilities required for competence may seem impossible. Models, however, are beginning to emerge, and the next chapter will describe variations within schools and colleges and also some nonschool settings. Alverno College, for example, has implemented a competency-based curriculum. While this private college has somewhat fewer constraints than an elementary or secondary school, its program nevertheless could be replicated or adapted. The curriculum centers around eight core competencies, and instruction provides multiple learning opportunities.

Another model is to be found in the Scouting movement. Again, it does not operate within the same environment as a public school, but the merit badge program illustrates how competency goals can be joined with individual self-direction in developing functional attainment of life skills. The merit badge program not only demonstrates ways in which different categories of knowledge can be fused into a competency, but it also serves as an example of potential links between the school and the community. It is easy to envision a social studies unit for, say, seventh-graders, that would dovetail nicely with the merit badge personal management activity.

Finally, if competency-based education is to be viable rather than moribund, if it is to summon students to a higher order of values, and if it is to discharge education's responsibility for raising consciousness, some attention must be given to the competencies of greatest moment. High competence used mindlessly or deployed toward tawdry ends takes a great toll. History, after all, is replete with instances in which people have pursued bad things with extraordinary skill and cunning. We must not forget, therefore, that competence has its own moral overtones, as well as its hierarchy of the trivial and the significant.

NOTES

1. David C. McClelland, *Pedagogy and Competency-Based Education*, p. 14. Used by permission.

2. Leonard J. Waks, *Education for Life-Role Competence*, pp. 31–32. Used by permission.

3. Gary A Woditsch, *Developing Generic Skills: A Model for Competency-Based General Education*, p. 48. All quotations by permission.

4. Ibid., p. 22.

5. Ibid., pp. 23–24.

6. Ibid., p. 25.

7. James H. Block, "The 'C' in CBE," pp. 14–15. Copyright 1978, American Educational Research Assn., Washington, D.C. Used by permission.

8. Patricia K. Cross, *Accent on Learning*, p. 17.

4

A Sampler of Competency-Based Education at Its Best

LARRY McCLURE
JOANNE LEIGH

EDITOR'S INTRODUCTION

Competency-based education is a goal, not a program. Terms like competencies, learning objectives, criterion-referenced tests, and individualized learning occur together often enough to give the sense of a national movement; but the fact is that competency-based education practices as much diversity as it promotes. In the quest for competence, educators devise programs according to their assumptions about the educational needs of their students and the best ways of meeting these needs.

Consequently, in pursuing competence as an educational outcome for youth or adults, a program may concentrate upon classroom organization, curriculum development, teacher responsibility, community experience, learning packages, integrated tasks, or some other approach deemed capable of producing results. This sampler of 13 existing programs surveys a broad range of practices with elements of competency-based education as discussed elsewhere in this book, even though they may be called by other names. Materials representing or describing the programs, assembled and edited by the chapter authors, were provided by the persons named at heads of sections.

Elementary and Secondary Education.   Three quite different approaches to K–12 competency-based education have transformed public school systems in Janesville, Wisconsin, Washington, D.C., and Milpitas, California. Janesville concentrates upon individualized learning, suspending traditional grade levels. Washington, in its primary concern for curriculum development and delivery, distributes three-part learning packages of objectives, instructional activities, and assessment tasks so that teachers have what they need to conduct classes. Milpitas, too, prepares detailed curriculum standards—in four subjects—then entrusts teachers with introducing, reinforcing, or assuring mastery of skills assigned to given classes. Teachers develop their own competence through practices such as the Bay Area Writing Project so that they in turn can guide students.

The Hood River School District in Oregon introduces competency-based education at the high school level. Students simultaneously pursue state-mandated minimum competency standards and individualized career preparation competencies through a system of individualized learning and open scheduling.

Other districts adopt elements of competency-based education to satisfy specialized needs. The Harrison County Vocational Center in Kentucky finds it feasible to prepare students for several entry-level jobs by providing learning modules for them to master on their own. Jefferson County Public Schools in Colorado encourage junior high and high school students to carry out self-styled projects in the community and have selected competencies certified by adult experts outside the school.

Postsecondary Education.   Postsecondary applications of competency-based education include high school diploma programs, a private liberal arts college, and a state-operated professional school. New York State assesses—but does not teach—generalized basic skills and individualized career competencies as the basis for awarding high school diplomas to adults. Chemeketa Community College in Oregon offers an adult diploma through a program that teaches and assesses life role competencies along with required subjects. Alverno College continues to refine its thoroughly reformed curriculum to produce the outcomes of a successful liberal arts education, and the University of Minnesota's College of Pharmacy orients its professional program toward validated skills needed by pharmacists in the field.

Outside formal education institutions, service organizations, the military, and industry adopt competency-based procedures to perform some of their educational functions. The national office of the Boy Scouts of America sets specific merit badge requirements in many skill and occupation areas for boys to demonstrate to the satisfaction of community experts. Air University and AT&T's Large Team Management Training Institute both identify mastery performance and set objectives to help their personnel reach it.

These programs differ in populations served, geographical location, and instructional practices, but they share a commitment to high standards. The staff people involved seldom talk about minimum competencies because their sights are set far beyond them. When they say someone is competent, they mean it as a compliment.

J.A.L.

The Janesville Public Schools and IGE

The Janesville Public Schools in Wisconsin were among the
first to become involved in Individually Guided Education
(IGE), created by the Wisconsin Research and Development
Center, housed at the University of Wisconsin in Madison.
During 1978–79 the district had a total K–12 enrollment of
12,800. Until his retirement at the close of the 1977–78
school year, Fred Holt was Superintendent of the Janesville
Public Schools.

WHAT IT IS

The Janesville Public Schools equate competency-based education
with individualized learning. They have been reforming their program
since 1960, when a Ford Foundation grant to the University of Wisconsin School of Education caused Janesville to be selected for an experi-
ment in team teaching. Working together, teachers found they could
combine their strengths and spend more time with individual children. The success of the method convinced the district that students,
especially at the elementary level, respond more enthusiastically to
personal attention. They committed themselves to identifying the
individual needs, abilities, and interests of each child and designing a
nongraded program for continuous-progress learning.

During the second semester of the 1965–66 school year, Janesville
became one of the first districts to replace classes grouped by age with
nongraded Instruction and Research Units, the initial form of Individually Guided Education.[1] The curriculum was reorganized and
staffing patterns were changed to produce a multi-unit school. In
succeeding years, the remaining 13 elementary schools converted to
similar programs, so that now all 14 can be called Individually Guided
Education schools. Their programs include these seven components:

- multi-unit organization, in which a unit leader and three or four
  other teachers are responsible for 100 to 150 children with a
  three-year age span
- instructional programming for individual students
- evaluation before, during, and after instruction to facilitate decision making
- compatible curriculum materials that students can learn and
  teachers can teach without massive in-service training
- home-school-community relations to help educators build support and remain sensitive to public opinion

- facilitative environments, meaning the organization of units and the physical design of buildings as well as the contributions of outside groups—state education agency, intermediate education agencies, teacher-training institutions, and teacher and parent organizations
- continuing research and development

Decision making in a multi-unit system is shared. An Instructional Improvement Committee, consisting of all unit leaders and the principal, meets weekly to plan building activities. Occasionally teachers of music, art, physical education, and programs for the handicapped are invited to assist them. A Systemwide Program Committee chaired by the district superintendent brings together central office staff, multi-unit school principals, unit leaders, and teachers to help plan at the district level.

By 1972 all Janesville elementary schools were organized into units. Approximately 6,000 to 7,500 children in K–6 have participated annually in Individually Guided Education since then. Elements of the program have also been introduced in three junior highs and two senior highs.

HOW IT WORKS

Small groups within elementary teaching units and secondary departments meet to organize strategies, instructional materials, and resource persons for the school year. They agree upon objectives and administer pre-tests, which they compare with post-tests at the end of the year. The Janesville schools agree upon a set of common objectives for *all* students—like basic skills in math and reading—and also offer others to engage individual interests—like art and music. In either case, the objectives may be introduced sequentially or independently and may require a uniform level of mastery or varying levels teachers accept for individuals.

During the 1977–78 school year, Wilson School outlined priority objectives in language arts, math, and media skills for K–6 students. Media skills for the kindergarten children included:

- entering the Media Center with a purpose, working quietly, and leaving in good order
- listening attentively to fairy tales, nursery rhymes, sound filmstrips, and television
- locating the easy book section
- signing a book card with first name and last initial, placing the card in the correct pocket, and returning the book to the cart

- holding books properly, keeping them clean and free from damage

At the sixth-grade level students were expected to demonstrate their competence in using media skills by performing these tasks:

- read eight books from these different categories: fairy tales, science, mystery, biography, animals, sports, tall tales, adventure tales, poetry, history, humor, plays, myths, science fiction, war, and classical literature
- compile a bibliography of one book, one magazine article, and one encyclopedia
- write a report with a cover, table of contents, and bibliography
- identify reference book most useful for a particular question
- properly use sound filmstrip equipment and opaque, overhead, and 8-mm projectors

Unit teachers assess each student's current performance level, rate of progress, learning style, and motivation in order to plan courses of instruction. They decide whether at any given time it is best for students to study alone, one-to-one with a teacher or instructional aide or another student, in small groups, in large groups, or with the entire unit. Whatever the teaching strategy, staff evaluate students regularly to measure progress toward objectives.

In a unit, teachers proficient in the basic skills and concepts of subject areas organize content into units of instruction. Regular interaction with teachers of different specialties encourages some interdisciplinary approaches. Teachers assign each student materials and activities from several curricular areas and expect them to master the objectives in approximately three to six weeks. These programs of materials and activities prepared for each child are quite different from commercially distributed programmed learning packages of identical books, films, and tests for groups of students.

Students are often grouped and regrouped as they work toward objectives. Since they progress at their own pace, they complete their assignments at varying rates. When some finish ahead of the others, they may be regrouped with other early learners for the next unit, undertake more objectives, or tutor classmates who need extra help. Students who do not satisfy the requirements in a given time may continue with their groups to the next unit and try to meet both sets of objectives, repeat the same objectives with other nonattainers or with a group just getting started, or work toward simpler objectives in a new group.

Maintaining Flexibility.   Schools practicing Individually Guided Education are committed to flexibility. It is built into their organization and operation. Staff at district and building levels share decision making and solicit parent and community opinions to keep their programs accountable. In the units, teachers adjust individual programs for continuous-progress learning. If one set of materials and activities does not help a student reach an objective, another set is produced. Students exercise some control by choosing among elective objectives and deciding when to pursue nonsequenced ones.

To reduce physical space and time constraints, Edison Junior High, completed in 1971, has open areas—for English, languages, math, social science, and natural science—surrounding a large instructional media center; and Parker Senior High since 1974 has had a mod-flex program of twenty-three 20-minute mods, allowing class sessions to range from 20 to 120 minutes. Among other benefits, this schedule facilitates a school-within-a-school alternative program for potential dropouts.

Management Considerations.   After originally allowing children more free time than they could manage, staff introduced more structured activities. Teachers now stress student responsibility for carrying through assignments on time, exposure to materials at grade level, less movement within units, and more class-grouped instruction.

Individualized learning has required some additional personnel as well. Supervised instructional aides assist students so that teachers have time to work with small groups and individuals. Teachers, aides, and administrators cooperatively plan students' schedules, help them master mechanical functions associated with their materials and learning devices, and keep accurate records. Children's work is stored in individual folders, which staff may consult when it wishes to evaluate student progress or consult with parents, counselors, or school psychologists.

Staff Development.   During the early days of the program, staff learned from on-the-job teaching plus seminars and summer courses conducted in Janesville by faculty from the University of Wisconsin at Madison and Eau Claire. Instructors from the nearby Whitewater campus have since taught Janesville teachers.

Those involved in individualized learning in Janesville recognize that staff needs carefully planned in-service training, which accomplishes most when staff and well-accepted resource persons willingly share ideas and experiences. But the system is too comprehensive to be presented exclusively through in-service sessions. Teacher-training institutions need to acquaint their students with the theory and practice of competency-based education. In Janesville, student teachers from the University of Wisconsin at Whitewater and Madison work for a full semester in the Janesville schools to become familiar with Individually Guided Education concepts and methods.

ONGOING CONCERNS AND FUTURE DIRECTIONS

Whenever a school system introduces innovations, it meets some resistance from misinformed or skeptical parents, community members, and media people. The public has generally supported the district's educational reform program but still wants evidence that the new system is better.

Applying a new approach to old educational problems challenges current school staff as well, and it is still in the process of adapting to different roles and expectations. New teachers and school board members will need to understand and accept district goals.

Janesville's former superintendent believes that local teaching staffs and administrators will investigate and adopt principles of competency-based education without state or federal mandates. They can build upon what is working well locally and elsewhere. Educators at the secondary level can adapt competency-based procedures to subject areas and make their curricula increasingly student-centered. Janesville's progress is apparent in the open-design building of a new junior high school and in a mod-flex program with team teaching in a senior high.

Janesville's administrators believe that competency-based education, at least Individually Guided Education, is here to stay. For one thing, individualized learning produces results. A study of the mean percentile scores on the Metropolitan Achievement Tests for second- and sixth-graders in multi-unit and traditional schools between 1971–72 and 1976–77 documented the superior progress of students participating in Individually Guided Education. They surpassed their peers in all areas except sixth-grade spelling.[2] That is the kind of evidence "back to the basics" critics appreciate.

The Public Schools
of the District of Columbia

The Public Schools of the District of Columbia favor
community involvement in formulating educational goals.
In response to community needs, the district began to
implement its Competency-Based Curriculum at the
beginning of the 1978–79 school year. Nearly 6,500 teachers
and 600 administrators and supervisors serve
approximately 121,000 students, K–12. Joan W. Brown is a
special assistant directing development of the
Competency-Based Curriculum.

WHAT IT IS

The Competency-Based Curriculum installed during the 1978–79
school year by the District of Columbia public schools centers attention
where local educators and the community believe it should be—on the
curriculum as the foundation of the learning process. Curricula for
pre-K–12 (before kindergarten through twelfth grade) in the priority
areas of reading, mathematics, science, and language arts have been
thoroughly revised and validated to develop consumer/producer,
analytical, communication, social/political, and self-actualization
skills. Under consideration is a plan to modify graduation requirements to include exit competencies reflecting these general skills,
which the district believes students must possess to meet the goals
chosen by school personnel and ranked by the community. (See chart
4.1.)

The newly written curriculum has six essential attributes:

• It is *individualized*. Instructional plans are adjusted to accommodate varying rates of student growth and learning styles.

• It is *progressive*. From before kindergarten to twelfth grade, students work at their personal development levels (rather than grade
levels) and move upward to more complex levels.

• It is *sequential*. Students enter a learning hierarchy at their own
preassessed competency levels, then work through a series of hierarchical objectives to reach a terminal objective, or mastery level.

• *Behavioral objectives* are emphasized in classrooms. Teachers use
learning packages prepared at the district level. These contain one
objective, two instructional activities, and three assessment tasks.
Students who master one objective continue to the next; others work
on modified activities until they achieve mastery.

• *Criterion levels* are specified. For each assessment task there is a cutoff point for mastery.

• It supports the district goal of facilitating students' active *participation* in society and their development of a *positive self-concept*.[3]

The content of the new curriculum is essentially the same as that of a traditional one. The differences are that it has been organized into progressive *learning hierarchies* with specific behavioral objectives packaged for delivery and that it has been *extensively validated* in 29 pilot schools. Before fully implementing the program, the district tested it fully to be sure:

• Each behavioral objective states *who* is to perform; *what* is to be performed; the *conditions* under which performance is to occur; and *criteria* for success.

Chart 4.1   List of Educational Goals for the Public Schools of the District of Columbia

---

Educational Goals

• command of fundamental communication skills
• command of the skills that constitute mathematical, scientific, and technological literacy
• ability to think critically, constructively, and creatively
• attitudes and self-discipline necessary to meet everyday situations realistically
• command of the skills that promote sound physical, mental, and emotional health
• understanding and appreciation of intergroup relationships and acceptance of responsibility within various groups
• skills and attitudes necessary to plan one's future
• ability to relate knowledge and capabilities to individual needs and aspirations
• ability to demonstrate marketable skills that may lead to economic independence
• command of the analytical skills that lead to sound consumer choices and practices
• ability to use leisure time wisely and constructively
• understanding of the cultural, economic, and political backgrounds of the peoples and nations of the world and their interrelationships
• knowledge of governmental processes and the implications of changing political times
• knowledge, interpretation, and appreciation of literature and the performing arts

---

- For each behavioral objective there are at least two instructional activities to provide alternative approaches to learning.
- For each behavioral objective there are at least three assessment tasks actually testing the behavior expected.
- The criteria for successful performance are clearly stated and are consistent with the objectives.
- The reading level of materials is appropriate for the indicated grade level.
- Each learning hierarchy has entry level, enabling, and terminal objectives.
- Objectives are arranged in the correct sequence.
- The difficulty of a task is appropriate for the students involved.[4]

HOW IT WORKS

Typically, at the beginning of each class session where these materials are used, the teacher lists performance objectives or skills on the chalkboard and introduces two or more individual or group activities so as to help students master them. Since classes, by law, are heterogeneous, teachers individualize lessons to meet each student's needs. Several testing modes help teachers assess mastery according to performance standards set by groups of teachers under the direction of supervisors.

For example, one objective of laboratory science in biology at the senior high school level is for students to be able to demonstrate the proper method of preparing a temporary wet mount slide. The learning package for this objective includes (a) an introduction explaining that many microorganisms must be slowed down or stained to become visible; (b) two activities to familiarize students with the process (preparation of slides of onion cells and protozoa according to detailed instructions and participation in a class discussion about the appearance and movement of the specimens); and (c) assessment tasks (students demonstrate that they have met the objective by preparing three wet mount slides).[5]

Competencies range from simple to complex along the pre-K–12 continuum. In the present system, students who work quickly are assigned extra tasks but remain at the same grade level.

The D.C. schools' Competency-Based Curriculum has not emphasized teams of teachers from varied areas working together, so instruction still tends to be focused on standard subject matter disciplines. However, coordinators playing support roles offer an interdisciplinary perspective on curriculum content, skills mastery, assessment, performance objectives, and instructional techniques. Since similar issues are faced in various subjects and levels, teachers are learning more about the common problems that bind them together.

Maintaining Flexibility.   Since mastery is the goal, students progress at their own rates toward achievement of a performance objective, then move on to the next objective along the instructional continuum. Those who demonstrate self-discipline are given considerable latitude in allocating their time, but others may require more structure and supervision.

The Competency-Based Curriculum program is still very much in the process of development and refinement. Prototype schools[6] are working out system "bugs," and pilot schools[7] are collecting data on curriculum effectiveness. As community priorities change, the curriculum can be altered to accommodate them, inasmuch as such changes are generally slow and amenable to the process of revision. When teachers prove that a learning sequence needs to be modified, it can be. If an adequate sampling indicates a performance standard is too high or is low, the standard can be rewritten. As the program continues, staff anticipate revisions in the curriculum based on student performance data and characteristics.

Staff Development.   Because the district adopted an innovative idea—a competency-based curriculum—staff received training in three year-long phases.[8] After a design for a pre-K–12 curriculum was proposed and approved in 1976, three teams were created to set the program in motion. The coordinating team provided overall leadership for the school system; the instructional support team concentrated on team approaches to improving teaching and learning processes; and the implementation team helped to introduce instructional activities and to mobilize school system resources.

During the conversion period, approved staff received training in three year-long phases. The "Year of Awareness," 1976–77, was a time for workshops and seminars to orient staff and community people to the concept of a competency-based curriculum—what it is, what it purports to do, and what implications it has for behavioral changes in learners and teachers. During the summer two courses were conducted. Teachers experienced in curriculum writing attended classes to improve their skills—and some were selected to help specialists write materials. Team members met to explore ways of planning and implementing the program at each level from classrooms to the total system.

During 1977–78, the "Year of Understanding and Professional Commitment," staff participated in workshops, televised courses, and forums to explore more fully the Competency-Based Curriculum support roles and responsibilities of various offices and departmental units of the school system and to become adept at applying competency concepts in actual classroom instruction. For 29 schools it was a period of pilot testing and validating the curriculum, with involved teachers requiring specialized and more sophisticated training in the use of competency-based curriculum instructional procedures and in the process of validation.

Additional training and review of both theoretical and practical aspects of the Competency-Based Curriculum helped prepare staff in 1978–79, as they entered the "Year of Implementation."

Management Considerations.   Staff are organized into teams to carry out program goals. Writing teams from each subject area contribute to the curriculum. The coordinating and instructional support teams supervise the development and review of curricula and produce learning packages for teachers to use. The management team plans the logistical support necessary for staff training activities.

In classrooms, teachers or students chart individual progress toward meeting instructional objectives. Because students have different learning styles and rates, teachers continually introduce and manage diverse activities and assessment procedures. They also group and regroup students according to momentary needs and assign personalized tasks to each individual.

ONGOING CONCERNS AND FUTURE DIRECTIONS

The Public Schools of Washington, D.C., recognize they must overcome the usual difficulties of implementing a new program. Teachers and administrators must be receptive to new instructional ideas and roles if they are to adopt new ways of doing things. Personnel and material resources needed for the program have to be identified and secured. Individuals, offices, and departments must be reoriented or reorganized to achieve program goals. Thorough groundwork has prepared the way for effective implementation of the Competency-Based Curriculum, and extensive experimentation and validation in pilot schools should lead to controlled program modification and expansion. In time, the program will involve the entire high school population, and the curriculum will include more abstract and humanistically valuable behaviors.

Issues related to nongraded placement, continuous-progress instruction, courtesy promotion, and graduation requirements based on competence rather than on time still need to be defined and officially endorsed by both the school system and the community. These are the subject of ongoing dialogue and, in some instances, experimental research.

Involvement with the Competency-Based Curriculum thus far has taught District of Columbia staff that it is wise to:

- involve administrators, teachers, parents, community groups, and professional organizations in the earliest stages of planning
- select personnel who have the expertise and skills to carry out the program and free them from routine tasks
- design and conduct a full-scale orientation program for school personnel, parents, and community representatives
- secure maximum support from all concerned parties
- maintain a program of education and reeducation in the competency-based approach for both school personnel and community people—and don't alienate them with educational jargon
- conduct intensive training sessions for supervisors, teachers, administrators, and typists before starting to write the curriculum
- keep up with developments in the competency movement through ongoing research
- establish an evaluation system for a thorough and objective assessment of the program
- validate the curriculum

Although hard data are still pending, participants in the public schools of the District of Columbia are optimistic about their Competency-Based Curriculum. To date, the time, materials, and human resources invested have produced a reasonably cost-efficient program. More importantly, staff enthusiasm has created an educational ambiance of "great expectations."

The Milpitas Unified School District

Milpitas Unified School District in the San Francisco Bay area of northern California has responded to a mandate to introduce proficiency standards for its graduates by implementing standards in basic disciplines for K–12 students in all of its 16 schools. Dr. Richard E. Schmieder is Director of Curriculum.

WHAT IS IT

After July 1980, graduation requirements for California students will include passing tests in reading, writing, and mathematics to demonstrate mastery of minimum competencies determined by individual districts. Milpitas Unified School District has chosen to add social science as a priority area and to develop three levels of standards to help students reach increasing levels of proficiency.

A competency, in Milpitas terms, is an activity that can be performed—such as balancing a checkbook or writing a business letter. Proficiency is the level of expertise attained in a competency—such as balancing a checkbook within half an hour or writing a business letter without errors. To demonstrate competencies at given levels of proficiency, students need skills or operative knowledge of facts—such as addition, subtraction, punctuation, and vocabulary.

The program is still being refined for the district's school population of 4,815 elementary students and 4,100 secondary students. Parameters are:

- To graduate from high school, students must satisfy clear and specific criterion-referenced outcome statements.
- The instruction and evaluation of students must embody these outcomes directly.
- Students know the expected outcomes before they begin course work.
- Alternate forms of instruction and evaluation must be available for students who do not progress under existing methods.

The Milpitas competency-based approach is not limited to developing minimum survival skills. Rather, it helps students meet increasingly demanding standards. In order to graduate, all students must demonstrate their mastery of functional standards by passing the district's uniform test. They are encouraged to meet desirable or advanced standards to prepare them for job entry at higher levels or for further education. Although these three levels are identified, students are not tracked. Rather, they work through one level to the next, and all are urged to proceed as far as possible.

Initially, open meetings at two junior high schools allowed all interested persons to suggest competencies students need to function as responsible members of society. These basic life skills were reviewed by an advisory committee and revised by teachers until a satisfactory list was produced. Teachers from each of the four priority subject areas involved worked with curriculum and evaluation experts to identify prerequisite skills undergirding the basic life skills. Committees distinguished between functional, desirable, and advanced standards and designated which courses are responsible for introducing or producing mastery of each objective.

HOW IT WORKS

Each of the four subject areas has major objectives that it seeks to realize through setting functional, desirable, and advanced standards. For instance, the language arts program lists five major objectives:

- Each student will develop effective writing skills.
- Each student will develop the ability to speak effectively in both formal and informal situations.
- Each student will develop critical listening skills.
- Each student will develop skills to read, analyze, and interpret a wide variety of literature.
- Each student will receive ongoing counseling by instructors with respect to the student's skills in language arts.[9]

Teachers for each class know exactly what they must introduce, reinforce, and bring to mastery to help students meet these objectives at each level. For instance, to help students develop effective writing skills, eighth-grade language arts teachers do not have to introduce any new skills, but they must help basic students at the functional level reinforce their ability to:

- write legibly
- spell accurately
- capitalize and punctuate correctly
- write dictated material
- write instructions for something they can do or make
- draft an informal outline

- develop clear, logical, grammatically correct paragraphs with acceptable topic, developing and concluding sentences[10]

They must help these same students master writing skills necessary to:

- express a complete thought in a sentence
- unscramble a disordered sentence
- correct usage errors
- describe an incident, scene, or observation
- employ personal point of view
- develop a sequence of events
- express cause and effect relationships
- record a verbal message
- state a problem in written form[11]

These are typical language arts skills, and the district lays no claim to novelty of purpose. However, listing skills is only one step toward developing them; and the district is turning to the highly successful Bay Area Writing Project approach to actually produce the results English teachers have long sought. The Bay Area project, which was initiated at the University of California, Berkeley, in 1971 and first implemented there in 1974, has now spread nationwide.[12] Teachers are brought together with one basic assumption: that people learn to write by writing—often without the threat of red marks. After building their own writing fluency and confidence, these teachers return to their schools to help their students become enthusiastic writers.

Words do not flow unless there are ideas behind them, however; so students learn first (if necessary) to generate and organize thoughts. Teachers share oral and written stories with young children to develop a strong oral language base; and students talk over their ideas before they write, so they do not draw blanks when pencil and paper meet. These experiences during the elementary years build students' confidence, and they feel prepared to write analytically as they grow older.

Teachers have previously hesitated to make writing assignments because they take longer to review and grade than do multiple-choice or true-false tests. To offset this disadvantage, the Bay Area Writing Project encourages holistic grading based on reaction to a work as a whole rather than reaction to details.

Similar procedures are followed for other subject areas. Teachers know what objectives students must meet to satisfy different standards, and they seek the best methods to achieve them. Social studies teachers, for example, also share responsibility for study techniques, vocabulary development, writing competence, and other broadly used communication skills. All teachers have copies of language arts standards so they can reinforce students' linguistic facility.

Students are evaluated in each class, but they also take comprehensive districtwide proficiency tests during the eighth and tenth grades. The first is primarily diagnostic, identifying areas in which students need alternate instruction. The second must be passed before students graduate.

Maintaining Flexibility.   The district has established a K–12 curriculum with instructional responsibility for each skill clearly designated. Because the objectives are oriented toward basic skills, they are not likely to change much. However, if additions are necessary, responsibility can be assigned to appropriate classes.

Although the system posits fixed objectives, it allows considerable latitude in achieving them. Teachers use whatever methods and materials they find effective. If particular instructional plans do not work with individual students, teachers introduce alternatives. The program is adjusted as necessary to help all students master the skills required to pass the district exam.

Management Considerations.   To accommodate the goal of having each student satisfy each objective at the functional level, the district is devising a monitoring system to track each student's progress on each objective. Teachers will receive printouts three or four times a year so that they will know which students need other learning tasks to master objectives.

Staff Development.   In the early stages of development, the district provided workshops to develop curriculum materials, a monitoring system, a graduation examination, and alternative means of instruction. Because the success of the program depends upon effective classroom behavior, teachers have been exposed to new methods. They have responded well to in-service training in writing and other areas. As the monitoring system identifies teacher strengths, the district will compile a "cookbook" of successful practices to help teachers meet particular objectives.

ONGOING CONCERNS AND FUTURE DIRECTIONS

Teachers in the four subject areas involved at Milpitas are expected to orient their classes to meet specific goals. In-service training has been necessary, often at the expense of hiring substitutes. Local tests are being created. Persons directly participating in effecting the changeover are enthusiastic, but other staff need more information and assurance of the program's permanence. In reviewing the implementation procedures to date, administrators realize that the more teachers are engaged in shaping the program the better, since active contributors are likely to be supportive.

Those responsible for long-range planning assume the trend is toward competency-based education. Some states require students to demonstrate their competence before graduation, and others—like California—allow students after the age of sixteen to earn a high school diploma by passing proficiency tests. The most active advocates of competency-based education at Milpitas would like to specify hierarchical objectives for the entire curriculum and assign course responsibility for them. As yet they have no statistical data to cite in favor of their plan, but they can point to well-defined programs, in four major scholastic areas, that have gone far beyond minimum competency testing.

Hood River Valley High School

Hood River Valley High School, located in an Oregon agricultural and lumbering community along the Columbia River, developed a competency-based approach to education long before the state adopted minimum competency graduation standards in 1976. The school is recognized as a pioneer and has surpassed many with its individualized instruction and flexible scheduling. Charles Bowe is principal.

WHAT IT IS

Hood River Valley High School developed a competency-based program of secondary education with continuous-progress learning in 1968 and implemented it in 1970. Each year an average of 750 students in grades 10, 11, and 12 take advantage of schoolwide individualized instruction to master basic learning, living, and career preparation skills.

Education at Hood River High is goal-oriented. Students attend classes to master basic competencies and to prepare for their preferred next step after high school—job entry, vocational-technical training, or college. All students must demonstrate 26 competencies to satisfy the state's minimum competency law. (See chart 4.2.)

The 26 required competency areas are built into a group of course offerings called basics, which all students are required to take or demonstrate competency in. These include speech, writing, reading, social science, driver education, health, physical education, personal finance, and career exploration. Satisfactory completion of the objectives for these required courses indicates that the competencies have been met. In most cases there are several courses that satisfy the competency.

During the eleventh grade, tests developed by the district are given in reading and mathematics to assess retention. A standardized reading test is also administered. Students who fail to perform at the competency level are required to take additional work in the basic skills.

Students at the school go beyond these minimum survival skills to develop their individualized career preparation competencies. On the basis of personal interest, extensive testing, and counseling, all students tentatively select a career area and meet its requirements.

HOW IT WORKS

All incoming sophomores and transfer students take the Stanford TASK test of basic skills, the Ohio Vocational Interest Survey, and the General Aptitude Test Battery. Counselors use such information when they meet with students and parents to choose for each student a tentative career cluster and a "guide": one teacher who helps the student make week-by-week course selections and provides counseling support throughout the student's three years at Hood River High.

Students enroll in 15-hour learning units that satisfy cluster and competency requirements. These units contain course goals, general course content, learning activities, anticipated learner outcomes, and procedures for evaluation. For instance, all students must take a course in speaking to understand communication as a process and to practice organization, delivery, and listening skills. There are no prerequisites. Learning activities include oral presentation, discussion, library visitation, demonstration, use of texts or teacher-prepared materials, reading, and writing. To complete the unit, students must:

- identify and analyze speech communication as a process through individual reading and small group discussions, to the satisfaction of the instructor

Chart 4.2   List of Basic Competencies Developed by Hood River Valley
High School

What Students Need to Learn to Do

- orally communicate ideas effectively before an audience
- learn basic skills and processes of reading, to be able to function competently at the entry level of an intended job goal and in other community, business, and social activities
- make use of appropriate written formats often used or encountered in personal life
- understand that society has developed political and social institutions to preserve and enhance human dignity
- participate in school and community affairs
- learn methods of social control, used by society and by various organizations, that do not require "strong arm" tactics
- understand that a citizen should support the constitutional rights of all individuals
- know the main structure and functions of local, state, and federal government
- understand problems of international relations
- acquire the knowledge, skill, and understanding necessary for improved performance as a motor vehicle operator or occupant, or bicyclist, or pedestrian
- acquire knowledge and understanding necessary for improved performance as a citizen in interaction with the environment
- know the role of good nutrition in establishing and maintaining a high level of health, and develop an individual food program designed to serve the needs of the individual
- know about the major communicable diseases: their causes, methods of transmission, prevention, cure, and where assistance and guidance can be obtained for prevention or control
- know about the contributing factors, danger signals, and means of prevention and control of the major degenerative diseases
- know about the structures and functions of the male and female reproductive systems, the processes of reproduction, pregnancy, childbirth, and related problems
- acquire appreciation of and respect for the theory and practice of physical fitness: functional posture, sense of well-being, and skills of movement
- learn to move skillfully and effectively through exercises, games, sports, dance, recreational activities, and/or aquatics
- demonstrate a sensitive awareness of others and a positive self-concept
- learn wise shopping and buying procedures
- know how to shop for credit and make appropriate choices
- learn that accurately kept records facilitate income tax reporting and help families maintain financial stability

(Continued)

Chart 4.2   *(continued)*

- know that sound financial planning is the key to successful personal money management
- know how to purchase and maintain property such as a home or automobile
- recognize several satisfying career choices from a wide range of possibilities
- understand that groups of employees can organize to influence conditions of employment, and know how state and federal laws governing employment practices protect workers
- learn that the character, attitudes, and responsibilities of both employer and employee are as important for job success as skills and abilities

---

- practice the use of gestures, facial expressions, and eye contact through participation in three informal speaking presentations to be evaluated in an oral critique on a pass-fail basis
- listen to a taped speech and complete with 80 percent accuracy a written analysis of the speaker's development of content and use of delivery skills
- complete with 100 percent accuracy a written outline of a speech which meets the requirements of the speech department
- deliver a three-to-five-minute speech from an approved outline and participate in an evaluation feedback session with the instructor

Upon completing these performance objectives, students receive both course credit and competency credit for orally communicating ideas effectively before an audience.

Students choose learning units and work at their own pace. Depending on the unit, the teacher has learners work alone, or in subgroups pegged to the rate of the slowest member, or in groups with freedom to go to greater depth.

Teachers use many teaching methods—including small groups, lecture, demonstration, laboratory work, and individual research. Some team-teach interdisciplinary units (a science teacher and a social studies teacher jointly offer environmental education), and some from different departments share responsibility for units (teachers in home economics, social studies, math, and business prepare discrete components of a unit in personal finance).

Students work on units at their own pace until they meet performance objectives. No one fails. However, continuous progress is expected; so if a student is in a class more than 20 days or fails to enroll in another learning unit after completing one, the student's teacher guide investigates the problem.

Teachers evaluate performance within two days after units are completed and give a "C" for meeting the objectives. Students can earn an "A" or "B" by showing special responsibility or producing work of exceptional quality, and since they know what is required for the higher grades, many now work for them.

After students complete one unit, they enroll in another. About 65 percent of the units are sequenced, so students continue the same subject with the same teacher. As far as scheduling is concerned, this is essentially the same as a traditional system. The difference comes in the nonsequenced courses that students may work into their programs. Incoming sophomores are restricted to sequenced units, but as they show personal responsibility, they are allowed to add variety to their schedules by taking nonsequenced units too. To earn this right, students must have:

- completed at least 12–15 learning units
- had not more than two whole day absences
- been referred for discipline no more than once
- had the approval of their parents and guide for release from the structured program

At the same time that students are completing learning units, they are acquiring the basic competencies. When they are ready to demonstrate mastery, they meet required performance objectives. Those who demonstrate the basic competencies and meet all career cluster requirements in less than three years may graduate early, take more high school courses, or work part-time and study part-time. Students who need more than the usual three years return the following year to finish.

Maintaining Flexibility.   When students finish a learning unit in a sequenced course they continue to the next one. When they complete learning units they enter a new class unit the next day. Each day some are changing classes. If their career goals have shifted, they are also able to change to another career cluster with the approval of guide and parents.

Ongoing evaluation makes staff sensitive to changing conditions. As needs are perceived, they are referred to a cabinet, which makes recommendations to administrators. Recently staff responded to concerns expressed in a community survey by improving communications with parents and allowing sophomores to take nonsequenced courses only after they showed self-discipline.

Management Considerations.   Continuous change is a way of life at Hood River High. It becomes manageable through the diligence of the teacher guides and the daily data-processing updates. All certified staff serve as guides for 15 to 20 learners, whom they advise and encourage.[13] Guides meet daily with their multi-age groups to take roll, make announcements, and schedule appointments with individual students.

Each morning the guides receive printouts from the data-processing center that tell them who has finished a unit, what grades have been given, who has dropped a course, who has entered a new class, and who has been absent or tardy. Guides are responsible for recording this information for each student in their respective groups. The system operates smoothly as long as teachers submit information on time. When the records show students are having trouble, guides make necessary referrals.

The success of the school's program depends upon community support, so staff cultivate good public relations. Guides contact parents regularly to let them know how students are performing, and the principal issues monthly newsletters. For wider circulation, the school releases news to the local radio station and the weekly newspaper. To keep information flowing both ways, school officials seek the recommendations of an elected advisory committee.

Staff Development.   When the school converted to continuous-progress individualized learning, existing staff retained their positions, but they had to perform new functions. Teachers became managers of time, people, space, and resources. They learned to utilize aides, volunteer adults, and student helpers. Administrators wanted teachers to feel comfortable with their new roles, so they provided time and money for training. Now staff leaders are able to replace outside consultants as trainers. Occasional rotation of assignments helps the school maintain a constant pool of trained personnel for various positions.

ONGOING CHALLENGES AND FUTURE DIRECTIONS

In its eight years of operation, the competency program has had problems and made improvements. Present concerns include these:

• Staff accustomed to dispensing information need to become better advisers. In-service training and assistance by certified counselors are helpful.

• Community members who don't understand the program reject it because it is different. Better communication has lessened resistance, but some still remains.

• Staff needs more time to develop new materials. Fortunately the district provides extra time one afternoon a week and allocates money for curriculum development during the summer.

• Teachers feel the new system is better, but they have only a few follow-up studies and opinionnaires to support them. A cooperative research program with the University of Wisconsin Research and Development Center promises to provide adequate assessment.

Hood River Valley High School staff believe they have found a good system. They have avoided a traditional administrative orientation toward college preparatory training and have concentrated instead on the needs of all students. Their experience is that competency-based education works well with individualized learning. If it is tagged to a strictly college preparatory model, they fear it's in trouble. But alternatives like their competency-based program are available to those who are willing and able to make the adjustment.

Harrison County Vocational Center

The Business and Office Education Department of the Harrison County Vocational Center in central Kentucky participates in the V-TECS program, a consortium of 17 states established in 1972 to produce educational performance objectives based on job analysis. Catalogs of objectives, once available only to members, can now be purchased by others on a cost recovery basis from the V-TECS office in Atlanta, Georgia.[14] Ms. Pat Burkett teaches at the Harrison County Vocational Center, an area occupational skills center that serves four high schools and has an average yearly enrollment of 300 students.

WHAT IT IS

The Business and Office Education Department of the Harrison County Vocational Center in Cynthiana, Kentucky, supplements its traditional course offerings with competency-based entry-level training for future secretaries, bank tellers, and legal secretaries. The department's three full-time teachers conduct classes for 100 junior- and senior-level students from three surrounding counties.

For each of the competency-based programs, specific skills objectives were identified by V-TECS. Workers were asked exactly what their jobs entailed and their responses were compiled in a catalog of performance objectives. Each state then assumed responsibility for disseminating the catalog of objectives and preparing instructional materials.

In Kentucky, the State Board of Education and the Curriculum Development Center at the University of Kentucky collaborated to produce individual learning modules incorporating the objectives. For instance, the program for secretaries includes 66 modules covering clerical skills—typing business letters, typing business forms, filing alphabetically, preparing bulk mail, sending telegrams, preparing stencils, preparing payroll reports, preparing monthly statements, and determining office layout, to name a few. Teachers at the local level add their own special materials as they choose.

HOW IT WORKS

Each module, or learning package, contains objectives, directions, learning activities, self-check exercises, and checkout activities. If students already know how to perform the tasks, they arrange to complete the checkout activities; if they need to learn more, they work on instructional sheets and self-check exercises until they are ready to be tested.

For example, the objective of "Module 7, Typing Tabulations," is to teach students to set up a balance sheet and an itinerary in tabular form. Those who think they are ready ask the instructor for a checkout. Those who need more preparation read Instruction Sheet I, "Producing Typewritten Financial Statements," Instruction Sheet II, "Producing Typewritten Itinerary," or other material the instructor suggests, then practice setting up tabulations by completing Student Self-Check I, "Typing a Balance Sheet," and Student Self-Check II, "Typing an Itinerary."

Students are evaluated only on criteria mentioned in the Instructor's Final Checklist form included in the module, so the instructor and students know exactly what must be done. Usually all students take the same test on a given competency, although supplementary tests are available. Grades are given for work on each module and are averaged at the end of the reporting period.

Students know in advance what is expected and set their own pace to meet goals—which requires considerable self-discipline. They are highly motivated, partly because this kind of education is new to them. Breaks in routine learning patterns—like slide-tape presentations in many of the modules—add variety and make lessons more appealing.

Traditional instructional patterns of group demonstration, group testing, and unit organization do not work very well in this system, since students work at various levels on different modules. The instructor acts as a manager, rather than as a teacher-lecturer, and provides individual attention to slower students while faster students move on. However, if there is need, students are grouped for lectures and discussions.

The subject matter is not intentionally interdisciplinary, but if students are struggling with their modules because of weaknesses in other subjects, a teacher offers whatever additional help is needed.

Maintaining Flexibility.   Teachers meet assigned classes one day a week to give out assignments, lecture to the group, or introduce guests. On the other four days the students have three-hour blocks of time that they budget to complete assigned tasks. For example, a student can choose to spend three hours on accounting or one hour on accounting and two hours on office practice and machines. Since the program is at the secondary level, open entry and open exit are not possible. However, after students complete one instructional unit they can move on to another.

The program's flexibility makes field trips and guest speakers assets to learning rather than interruptions. Other enrichment activities and supporting materials such as reference books and slide-tape presentations are also encouraged.

The modules themselves are adaptable. In Harrison County's Business and Office Education Department one instructor is primarily involved with the V-TECS competencies, but other teachers find the modules useful in their classes too.

Management Considerations.   To facilitate steady progress, the instructor maintains an adequate supply of materials, monitors individual accomplishments, allows time for student checkouts, and records grades for each module completed. Every student has a personal skills record; when a competency is mastered it is marked on the form, along with comments about work habits, attitudes, and level of performance. For example, all 66 modules included in the secretarial program are listed on the record and are marked as they are completed. A student who demonstrates all competencies is considered ready for employment.

Staff Development.   Instructors are able to benefit from state and local resources as they prepare for their new roles. The competency-based education unit at the Kentucky State Department of Education and the Curriculum Development Center at the University of Kentucky willingly give whatever assistance is needed. In-service training and workshops orient teachers to competency-based education and give them opportunities to ask questions. Ongoing communication with employers and clerical workers in the community helps the school maintain relevance and quality.

ONGOING CONCERNS AND FUTURE DIRECTIONS

Except for difficulties in finding adequate filing space for the large collection of resource materials, the competency-based vocational education program has run smoothly—partly because of staff comfort with individualized learning. A recognized need at present is for instruction in employment skills. Job skills are well taught, but job-seeking and application procedures are not. Plans are under way to remedy this by preparing units on finding and applying for jobs.

A competency-based approach to vocational education has proved its worth, and with adequate funding the state objective of developing new programs should be met. Harrison County Vocational Center plans to introduce new units as soon as they are available. The method generates enthusiasm because instructors know they are teaching up-to-date techniques verified by actual field conditions. Students who perform the required tasks accurately can feel confident they will do well in their chosen jobs.

Because of the competency program, school personnel and community workers have more contacts. As a result, the school receives donations, guest speakers, and requests for prospective employees. A recent survey showed that 82 percent of business and office students found entry-level jobs in 1977–78.

Jefferson County Public Schools: Career Education

Jefferson County Public Schools in Lakewood, Colorado, serve a rapidly growing urban population supported by a diversified economy. As part of their career education program, the schools have adopted a limited version of the Experience-Based Career Education model[15] created by Northwest Regional Educational Laboratory (NWREL) in Portland, Oregon. Dr. Robert E. Blum is the Career Education Coordinator.

WHAT IT IS

The Jefferson County Public School District weaves competencies throughout its part-day career education program called Exploring Careers in the Community. Students in grades 8 through 12 apply basic skills, practice life skills, and come to understand career development both on campus and at a variety of community sites. During the 1977–78 school year, approximately 450 students in seven schools participated in the regular program, and approximately 120 students identified as gifted and talented in six schools were enrolled. Since the program began in 1977, 720 have been involved.

Students spend a major part of their time on individual learning projects that require involvement and "sign-off" by volunteer community resource persons. This core activity translates back into traditional school credit for each student.

Another component of the program requires mastery of selected competencies. During the first year of program operation, the professional staff in three pilot high schools, assisted by advisory committee members, chose to retain these five competencies from NWREL's original model developed in Tigard, Oregon:

- filing federal income tax returns
- maintenance of a checking account
- fire and crime prevention
- operating and maintaining an automobile
- physical health and nutrition

Eventually competencies for the high schools are expected to be established countywide. Before the second year, a special task force, representing three field-test junior high schools, parents, students, and the community, selected four competencies for the junior high version of the program:

- RTD (rapid transit)
- job application
- first aid
- choosing to change

Staff members of the Exploring Careers in the Community Program believe students are competent when they are able to demonstrate certain skills, knowledge, or behavior. They assume that:

- Students need certain skills, knowledge, or behaviors to adequately fulfill lifelong adult roles.
- These competencies can be identified, defined, and measured.
- Students move through the program by demonstrating competence rather than by spending a certain amount of time in classes.
- Individuals meet competency requirements at different rates.
- Competency-based education should not completely replace other approaches that provide important enrichment.

HOW IT WORKS

Students enroll in Exploring Careers in the Community to supplement their traditional education, not to bypass it. They are encouraged to spend one term in the program. During this term they may negotiate projects with employers in the community. In addition to performance required in these individual projects, all students must demonstrate core competencies and be certified by community experts.

For junior high students, one of these competencies is using public transportation. After an RTD representative shows a film about the RTD system and explains how to use maps and schedules, groups of five to ten students plan and take two bus trips. Students individually complete observation forms—listing landmarks, streets crossed, the bus driver's responsibilities, transfer details, and so forth—and evaluate what they learned. To demonstrate competency, each student must pass with 80 percent accuracy a written test administered by teachers. Upon completion, each receives a certificate, presented by the RTD representative if possible.

This example shows how students integrate various subject matter skills to satisfy competencies. They use *mapping skills* to plan trips; *communication skills* to get route and schedule information, ask bus drivers for directions, and call for assistance if lost; *math skills* to pay for rides and count change; and *writing* and *analytical skills* to complete their observation and evaluation forms.

At the high school level, transportation skills extend to operating and maintaining an automobile. The competency is organized into eight activities, each with suggested resources and criteria, which a community certifier evaluates. In these activities the student must:

- define listed parts of an automobile
- locate specified parts of an automobile on a drawing
- check designated parts (shock absorbers, radiator, spark plug wires, and so forth)
- sketch the instrument panel
- outline an automobile's service schedule and describe a tune-up
- show understanding of tire care
- explain octane rating, discuss gasoline types, and specify the best fuel for his or her car
- list pollution control devices and write a paragraph articulating his or her position on automobile exhaust regulation

Junior high students are usually taught in groups and are certified in groups or individually, but high school students are more likely to take their own initiative to complete each requirement. Ordinarily students demonstrate their competence individually to resource people at their workplaces, but occasionally community instructors certify competence at school. For instance, banking representatives come periodically, because *all* students must show they are able to maintain a checking account, and local bank officials believe it is most efficient to come to the school to certify students.

Standards or criteria are set by Exploring Careers in the Community staff members in cooperation with community volunteers and are published in a student manual. Criteria are not differentiated by age or level, although different competencies are expected of junior and senior high school students.

Maintaining Flexibility.   Program flexibility allows staff to respond to changes in the community or in learners. Required competencies are reviewed each year and adjusted as appropriate. If modifications are necessary either during the year or between school years, competency guides are updated.

Time lines are less fluid. Junior high students must have certain competencies to progress through the program, so they receive group instruction and are certified according to program needs. For example, most acquire the regional transit competency within the first three weeks of the program because they have to understand the transportation system before they begin their three-to-five-day career explorations in the community.

High school students work much more independently, but they must meet completion deadlines, and when group instruction is offered they must schedule themselves into sessions set by program staff.

Management Considerations.   Jefferson County has devised a system to:

- recruit competency certifiers
- make available materials and scheduling information necessary for student preparation
- keep records for each individual for each competency during a term
- work through competencies with groups of students
- check the progress of each student toward developing competencies
- obtain feedback from certifiers

Records are kept for the program each term, but as yet they are not part of the permanent system, so the school is not able to supply competency certification information for students who transfer to other schools.

Staff Development.   Staff must be prepared for a new way of teaching students in this program. It must decide which competencies to offer, how to recruit certifiers and work cooperatively with them to design competency procedures, how to deliver the competencies to students and work comfortably with individuals in a group, and how to manage the logistics and paper work necessary to an organized approach.

ONGOING CHALLENGES AND FUTURE DIRECTIONS

Jefferson County has not encountered any major problems in implementing this particular competency-based program, but staff recognize they still need to:

- identify a broad array of competencies that satisfy both general and individual needs
- offer competency-based credit through the program in preference to incorporating class sessions into it
- interface the competency approach with the class approach practiced in the rest of the school program so that students who demonstrate language arts competencies, for instance, in the

Exploring Careers in the Community Program will not have to repeat similar instruction in their regular classes
• integrate Exploring Careers in the Community with districtwide competency-based education strategies

Jefferson County believes competency-based education's potential lies in its double capacity to foster necessary skills and knowledge and to free students to pursue individual educational goals once they have mastered basic competencies.

Because the approach can offer so much, staff believe it is important to work out existing problems such as finding appropriate and economically feasible measurement techniques. They recognize that the competencies they have established in the Exploring Careers in the Community Program are easy to identify, define, and measure; but they fear a competency-based approach to abstract concepts may be simplistic or irrelevant.

Program staff see these as their accomplishments:

• developing a format to individualize competency development and certification
• providing training and instructional procedures that enable teachers to work with students individually and in small groups
• devising processes to determine necessary competencies and criteria for success
• developing procedures by which community instructors or school personnel certify competencies

A significant strength of the program is that the procedures and materials established through it could be transferred easily to other subjects and used by any appropriately trained teacher.

The New York State
External High School Diploma Program

The New York State External High School Diploma
Program, initiated in 1973 with a three-month Ford
Foundation grant and funded by the New York State
Education Department's Division of Continuing Education,
is now available in six locations throughout the state. Judy
Alamprese-Johnson is Director of the Research and
Training Center at the Syracuse University Research
Corporation, which works with all six sites as they offer an
option to adult learners.

WHAT IT IS

The New York State External High School Diploma Program is a
competency-based, applied performance assessment system offering
adults another way to earn a high school diploma.[16] Adults who have
become skilled without formal education are now able to receive high
school credentials by demonstrating their competence through simulated adult life experiences.

The system was created to assess—not teach—competencies. Community learning resources are ample, and adults should be sufficiently
motivated to seek them out. If some learners do have trouble, program
staff refer them to appropriate resources.

The program is now available in six geographically heterogeneous
locations. Between March 1975 and June 1979, 2,100 adults received
their high school credentials through the program. As of June 1979,
over 1,300 persons were enrolled.

This program was validated as an exemplary model by the Joint
Dissemination Review Panel of the U.S. Office of Education in the
spring of 1979. Both the assessment process and instruments used
have met rigid standards of reliability and validity, according to this
panel. It is one of the two adult education models ever selected.

The program regards competency as a specific skill or knowledge
that a candidate can demonstrate at the request of an assessor. Those
who wish to earn their diplomas must master 64 basic skills in communication, computation, self-awareness, social awareness, consumer awareness, scientific awareness, and occupational preparedness.
They must also demonstrate an individualized occupational or vocational skill, advanced academic skill, or specialized skill in an area such
as art, music, or community organization.

The competencies were established during 1973–74 by a group of 14 educators in the Syracuse area working with the external diploma assessment staff at the Regional Learning Service, an educational and career counseling agency for adults. They were reviewed by representatives from small businesses, industry, unions, school personnel, and social agencies, and then refined by Regional Learning Service staff. A Regional Committee, selected from a cross section of education, business, labor, and community leaders, approved the competencies in its capacity as school board for the program. The assessment plan and competency requirements were then sanctioned by the State Education Department in 1974.

The external diploma program incorporates the following conditions in its working definition of competency-based education:

- The skill or knowledge to be assessed is explicitly stated and known to the candidate and the evaluator.
- The candidate may help determine the timing of a test.
- The candidate knows the conditions under which testing will occur.
- The testing process puts candidates at ease by allowing them to perform adult tasks.
- The candidate knows the process and content of the evaluation.
- Testing is criterion-referenced, not norm-referenced.
- Immediate feedback is given to the candidate after the evaluation.
- The verified demonstration of competencies is the sole criterion for the candidate's success and certification.

To be considered competent, candidates must demonstrate the 64 generalized basic competencies with 100 percent accuracy and have an expert in the field acknowledge their possession of individualized competence on the basis of one or more of the following: successful employment, a performance assessment of occupational skill, certain New York State occupational licenses with evidence of work, an acceptable portfolio of documents (such as standardized test scores) indicating ability to do college work, or a special skills assessment.

HOW IT WORKS

Candidates are able to demonstrate their competence through a two-phased program of diagnosis and final assessment. Interested persons attend an information session at the assessment site to learn about alternative high school diploma programs available to adults in the state. Those who prefer the external diploma program register and become applicants. Program advisors administer diagnostic pre-tests in math, writing, and reading comprehension and help identify occupational interests, aptitudes, and skills needed for the individualized competency assessment. In the process, applicants become more familiar with competency requirements and advisors are able to estimate their capabilities in the required areas. If the diagnosis shows weaknesses, advisors specify the exact competencies needed and available community resources. After learning occurs, the diagnostic process is repeated.

After applicants successfully complete the diagnostic phase, they become candidates, and their mastery of the 64 generalized competencies is evaluated through a series of "tasks" involving assessment interviews and take-home projects. Since candidates may use outside resources for take-home projects, assessors tell them at the beginning that specific competencies will be spot-checked in a closed setting. The tasks are:

Task I: Community awareness: Through a simulated search for community resources, candidates demonstrate computation, measurement, reading, and map skills.

Task II: Personal and family health: Candidates convey their understanding of first aid and health through structured interviews with an assessment specialist.

Task III: Occupational preparedness: Candidates reinforce job-seeking skills by comparing and classifying jobs advertised in newspapers, writing a resume and a letter of application for a job, and identifying payroll deductions.

Task IV: Personal and social awareness: In interviews with an assessment specialist, candidates show awareness of music and art, identify contributions of different cultures, indicate an understanding of how groups affect one another, show evidence of regular reading of various materials and demonstrate the ability to listen.

Task V: Consumer awareness: Candidates complete a take-home project to demonstrate reading, reasoning, and writing skills relevant to consumer practices.

Task VI: Consumer decision making: In a take-home simulation exercise candidates demonstrate competencies needed to make decisions about major household purchases and to gain consumer information (reading, computation, map reading, distinguishing between fact and opinion).

A given task may involve various activities, depending on the candidate's individualized skill emphasis. For example, in the interviews for

Task IV, personal and social awareness, candidates may be asked to perform activities like these:

• Write a paragraph that contains at least four sentences about yourself, your job, or your education. Your paragraph must have: (*a*) a sentence introducing the subject; (*b*) one or more sentences giving the reader more information about the subject; (*c*) a sentence summing up what you have to say. Make sure you indent the first word of the paragraph and use correct grammar, spelling, capitalization, and punctuation.

• Please show me an example that you have found in a newspaper or magazine that describes a specific instance involving civil rights. What civil right is involved? In what document is it written?

As these activities suggest, the tasks prompt candidates to integrate multiple competencies bridging subject areas. For instance, Task IV may require proficiency in reading, listening, viewing, writing, speaking, self-awareness, social awareness, scientific awareness, and aesthetic awareness. Varied assessment methods also draw upon multiple capacities. For instance, candidates must be able to participate in an interview, provide documentation, and pass a paper-and-pencil test to satisfy the requirements of Task IV.

Candidates complete Tasks I–V or Tasks II, III, IV, and VI, depending upon whether they prefer an urban or a rural orientation. In the process they have the opportunity to demonstrate the required 64 generalized competencies. The assessment specialist gives candidates evaluation forms after each task, so that they know exactly how much progress they have made.

After candidates have successfully demonstrated the generalized and individualized competencies, their names are presented to a local school board and they are granted high school diplomas. The external diploma staff holds graduations each year to recognize candidates' achievements.

Maintaining Flexibility. Learning is self-paced, and participants may "drop in" or "out" of the program as they choose. During the diagnostic phase, applicants usually meet with advisors weekly; but if breaks are necessary they resume where they stopped. In the assessment phase, candidates have one week to complete each task. During post-task assessment, candidates have as much time as they need. As long as candidates are actively pursuing their diplomas, they have unlimited time; but if they interrupt their progress they must resume work within a year or begin the entire program again.

The external diploma program has been designed with a certain amount of flexibility, but the assessment sites offering the program must conform to implementation and evaluation standards as set forth in a series of manuals. Sensitivity to changing needs has led to modifications such as these:

- revised program materials
- creation of a less urban task, Task VI, consumer decision making, which rural candidates may use in lieu of Tasks I and V
- regularly updated lists of learning resources and newly printed learning materials
- consideration of ways to adapt the program for special populations—the handicapped, speakers of English as a second language, and youth under eighteen years of age

Management Considerations.   The State Education Department must choose sponsoring agencies to administer assessment sites. The pilot site was a not-for-profit agency administered by the Regional Learning Service. In replicating the program, the department field-tested three school districts and two intermediate service agencies. In evaluating the sites, the department must consider cost-effectiveness, the needs of adults, and the impact that location has on their willingness to participate in a program.

Program implementation requires the enlistment of a local school board to grant diplomas and the selection of appropriate personnel. It is important that program staff be able to work with adult learners and understand their needs, express themselves articulately, conduct interviews, and evaluate program competencies. Those who advise and assess should be available to keep the site *open*—days and evenings. One staff member must act as coordinator to conduct staff meetings, manage staff activities, and report to the sponsoring agency.

The large flux of candidates and activities becomes manageable through a detailed record-keeping system. Program staff can identify a candidate's progress at any time by consulting portfolios that contain complete, accurate documentation of diagnostic tests, generalized assessment tasks, and individualized assessment. Candidates themselves can review their achievement by examining the progress forms they received when they completed tasks. After candidates have fulfilled all program requirements, a transcript listing competencies and documenting successful completion is filed at the district office.

Staff Development.   The State Education Department has required all staff to be trained by the Technical Assistance and Training Center administered through the Regional Learning Service. Some two-week sessions are conducted at the Syracuse site. Training includes:

- orientation to competency-based education
- overview of the history and operation of the external diploma program
- a simulated assessment process
- detailed instructions about individual jobs
- advice on coordinating an assessment program, selecting program personnel, conducting public relations, and choosing an assessment office
- in-service training

ONGOING CHALLENGES AND FUTURE DIRECTIONS

Although developers are pleased with their extensively tested model, they have encountered problems in replicating it. Staff members, including many who formerly worked in district schools and the intermediate service agency, have had to adjust to a very different system. Misunderstanding of the program's rationale has made some want to change processes and materials without an adequate field test. As the program is implemented across the state, the model must be adopted as designed, and program standards must be met to maintain the integrity of the credentials.

Other concerns center on finances. The external diploma program and training package must be as cost-effective as possible, and a permanent base of funding must be secured.

Those engaged in the New York State External High School Diploma Program are convinced of its merit but wonder whether the competency movement as a whole is too diffused. They believe educators could help adults by developing the notions of generic competence and transferable skills and by increasing the reliability and validity of instruments to test minimum competencies. Their present contribution is a replicable and appealing assessment model that has possibilities for use with secondary students as well as adults. As they refine their occupational skills assessment, they expect to make significant contributions in that area too.

Chemeketa Community College Adult Diploma

Chemeketa Community College, located in Salem, Oregon, is one of 13 regional community colleges serving the state. Over 23,300 students are enrolled in lower division, vocational, and other courses. Colleen Owings is the High School Completion Coordinator.

WHAT IT IS

Chemeketa Community College now offers students an opportunity to gain high school credentials through its Competency Based Adult Diploma Program. This new program was created in 1970 to provide adult students with (a) the skills they need to succeed in further vocational or academic training, (b) a meaningful diploma, (c) an option to the GED, and (d) credit earned through demonstrated competency rather than "seat time." In any one year approximately 300 students participate in the program, and betwen 70 and 100 receive diplomas.

Chemeketa regards competency as the possession of skills, knowledge, and understanding that can be demonstrated. Its core competencies are tailored to meet the life roles specified in the Oregon Board of Education guidelines: individual, learner, producer, citizen, consumer, and family member.

Representatives from several Oregon community college diploma programs met and reviewed lists of competencies established by local school districts and adult educators. A common core of competencies was identified and organized under the categories of read, write, speak, and listen; analyze; compute; use basic scientific and technological processes; develop and maintain a healthy mind and body; be an informed citizen in the community, state, and nation; be an informed citizen in interaction with the environment; be an informed citizen on streets and highways; be an informed consumer of goods and services; and function within a career or continue education leading to a career.[17] Performance indicators were written and a management manual was produced. Each participating college agreed to implement the common core and add to it if necessary.

The core competencies are written in terms of life applications. For instance, these represent the ability to *analyze*:

- analyze and apply a decision-making process to problems related to life experiences

- select and analyze a conflict situation and apply a decision-making process
- analyze how the consumer's decision to buy may be affected by direct and indirect forces (propaganda)

In credit courses at Chemeketa, the common core competencies are supplemented by additional competencies, which are usually identified by the instructor with input from students. The instructor organizes the competencies in a course outline and submits it for review by a curriculum committee made up of the program director, the coordinator, and teachers. After the outline is approved it is sent to the Community Services Division for final sanction and adoption.

Program staff let students know exactly what they have to know, tell them if they know it, suggest how to learn the part they don't know, and assess mastery. Students proceed at their own learning rates and acquire practical skills. They often demonstrate competencies by performing tasks. For example, students don't recite the steps of a decision-making model; they use the model to solve a life-related problem. In performing these tasks, students draw on knowledge and skills associated with many subjects, making the process truly interdisciplinary.

HOW IT WORKS

Persons sixteen or older may enter the program; those under eighteen must have a high school release. To receive diplomas, students must earn 21 credits—11 in required subjects and 10 in elective subjects—and demonstrate the ten core competencies. Students earn many of their credits by taking courses at Chemeketa Community College. Most classes meeting 30 hours or more a term give half a high school credit—and some classes offer high school and college credit concurrently. Elective credits are often accumulated in college or vocational programs. Students may also receive credit for work done elsewhere, including:

- courses completed through accredited secondary schools, technical schools, military service, correspondence schools, or adult education programs
- work experience (at the rate of one high school credit for each year of full-time work experience, including military service, up to a maximum of three credits)
- life experience fostering special skills and accomplishments, such as home management and community participation
- abilities demonstrated through standardized tests[18]

Although adults are able to earn credit through these many outside sources, those wishing to receive their diplomas through Chemeketa must enroll for a minimum of two terms or earn a minimum of two high school units of credit at the college.

To develop competencies students attend classes, go to the Competency Lab, use relevant packets, worksheets, or workbooks, ask family members or friends for help, or meet with a tutor at the Study Skills Center. When students feel they are prepared to demonstrate a competency, they schedule an appointment to have it assessed by the teacher of a class in which the competency is taught or by an assessor in the Competency Lab. If they meet the criteria, they are considered competent. If they need more work, a new instructional plan is devised. Students are not assigned to levels or rated by degree of competence: they are judged either competent or not.

Maintaining Flexibility. Students can build flexibility into their programs by planning carefully and by selecting learning environments that range from totally individualized open-entry open-exit arrangements to highly structured and regimented classes. Their programs can be adjusted as needed, and they are free to leave and resume work at any time.

Management Considerations. In order to keep track of where students are in their programs, staff updates their files at least once a term. These files contain an evaluation of the transcript and competencies, a permanent record, competency and credit completion slips, and, if appropriate, documentation of life and work experience credit. Accuracy is essential; if records are lost or incorrectly evaluated, both staff and students lose confidence in competency-based education.

Staff Development. Staff adapting to the concept of competency-based education needs precise job descriptions and work plans, as well as ongoing staff development opportunities. Ideally, staff training is itself a model of competency-based education. It is geared to the needs of staff members and increasingly involves them in the process. At first they become aware of program needs, then they help implement a program, and finally they identify problems in the system and help solve them.

ONGOING CONCERNS AND FUTURE DIRECTIONS

To overcome the complications produced by instituting competency-based education, Chemeketa recognizes the need to:

- develop staff commitment toward implementation
- help students understand the system
- encourage students and staff to offer suggestions
- develop relevant, uncomplicated record-keeping forms
- devise a method of charting student progress and of updating records as students complete credits and competencies
- clarify job descriptions and reorganize staff so thàt advisors are not also assessors
- locate additional funding
- win the support of those who resist the program
- develop an objective criterion-referenced assessment model based on life roles
- identify or develop appropriate instructional materials
- secure additional staff for record-keeping and competency assessment
- increase program flexibility so that more people can earn their diplomas

Staff at Chemeketa envision more widespread use of competency-based education in community colleges, especially in vocational programs, college transfer programs, and staff management and training. The outcome can be greater unity of purpose. At Chemeketa, staff in different departments have begun to work more closely together because of their common interest in competencies. Those involved in the adult diploma program look forward to a time when more refined assessment will make it possible for all who demonstrate their competence to get their credentials without spending a specified number of hours in class. For their part, staff believe their contribution now lies in the areas of record-keeping, curriculum development, and assessment.

Alverno College Comprehensive Instruction Program

Alverno College was founded in 1936 in Milwaukee, Wisconsin, as a four-year liberal arts school for women. In 1970, in the midst of declining enrollments, Alverno reexamined its position and began to reorganize its curriculum around the specific outcomes of liberal arts education. The result was a comprehensive competency-based instruction program. Mark Hein is a member of the Academic Dean's staff.

WHAT IT IS

Demonstrated competence has replaced grades and semester hours as the basis for graduation at Alverno College. Faculty members have defined the desirable outcomes of a liberal arts education and have reoriented their courses to develop and assess them. Students continue to study traditional humanistic subject matter, but go beyond that to demonstrate sensitive and practical skill in using it. In the process they become more confident in self-management and self-assessment.

When staff at Alverno refer to competence, they mean a general ability that underlies performance of many particular tasks in varied situations. For example, a student who is competent in communication can deliver a speech, write a report, read or design a chart, or prepare a slide or film presentation. By the time she graduates, she is certified *in toto*, after repeatedly validating each particular component of the general ability in different settings.

Faculty at Alverno have concluded that their students must develop *eight liberal arts skills*, which they call "competences."[19] Graduates must learn to communicate, analyze, solve problems, make value judgments, interact socially, consider their relation to the environment, understand the contemporary world, and respond to the arts and humanities.

These skills can be developed to varying levels of sophistication and can be improved throughout a lifetime. For the purposes of the college, each *competence* is organized into six *levels* of ability or facility. For each level students demonstrate within each competence, they earn one *unit* toward graduation. To graduate, they must reach Level 4 in every competence, for a total of 32 units, and accumulate 8 additional units at higher levels, with at least one competence mastered at Level 6. A student demonstrates these advanced skills in a major area of concentration and in a support area, these areas corresponding roughly to an academic major and minor.

For example, Competence 5, "developing facility for social interaction," is organized into levels thus:

Level 1   Recognize and assess one's own behavior in a group.
Level 2   Systematically analyze social behavior of self and others.
Level 3   Evaluate effectiveness of one's own and others' behavior in a group.
Level 4   Act appropriately in varied settings.
Level 5   Interact satisfactorily in tasks involving differing cultures and subcultures.
Level 6   Exhibit organizational leadership.[20]

At the sixth level, a student with a major area of concentration in management may study theories of organizational change in order to build competence in managing the change process. To demonstrate this ability, students may be asked to take the role of a divisional management team and design a strategic plan for their division's implementation of a companywide move to "management by objectives."

Faculty volunteers serving on interdisciplinary competence divisions for each of the eight competences review the teaching and assessment techniques and materials being used for the competence and operate a clearinghouse and consultation service for the rest of the faculty.

Alverno currently enrolls approximately 550 full-time and 250 part-time students in the weekday college. The Weekend College, opened in 1977, presents the same curriculum in a four-year (80-weekend) baccalaureate program serving about 225 full-time and 175 part-time students. An additional 250 women participate in courses and counseling services offered through outreach programs.

HOW IT WORKS

Students develop competences in the content and context of particular courses and off-campus learning experiences. They may work in several courses simultaneously toward a given level of analysis—for example, in English, biology, sociology, and history. All students are expected to complete assigned exercises and assessments for a course whether or not they plan to have this work count toward competence validations. Those who do seek validations have several assessment opportunities in each course and may choose when to try.

Most assessments are conducted by course instructors. They may require individual work, like writing an analytical summary of an assigned text or a description of social interaction; or team work such as that involved in preparing a biology lab report; or group interaction as in simulated problem solving.

General assessment criteria for each competence level have been gathered and reviewed by the competence divisions; specific course criteria are set by individual instructors or supervisors of learning experiences. Since the same competences are taught in different courses, the school tries to keep criteria as equal as possible by requiring multiple validations in varied settings, having each competence division review all assessment techniques for a given level, and occasionally adopting generic instruments for a given level.

About 20 to 25 percent of assessments are too complex for individual classes, so they are conducted at the Assessment Center. Well-trained volunteer assessors—from an available pool of more than 100 business people, professionals, retired professionals, and alumnae—join faculty in evaluating student performance and providing feedback. For instance, for the first level of the communication competence all students must go to the Assessment Center to complete tasks in reading, writing, speaking, listening, and creating and using graphs.

Later on, when students have acquired individual competences, they participate in simulation exercises at the Assessment Center to demonstrate the degree to which they have integrated the competences. For example, students might simulate being members of a decision-making board of citizens asked to choose one of three city budget proposals. They give persuasive speeches, write business memos and letters, and meet with others to pick a workable spending plan.

As students advance, they become independent enough to help design their own on-and-off-campus learning experiences—the latter with the help of 55 volunteer mentors at community work sites—and also contribute to their own assessment criteria and procedures.

Maintaining Flexibility.   Because Alverno is a private college, it is not subject to the kinds of community pressures imposed upon public institutions. And because its competences are not tailored to specific job roles, the college needs only to adjust instruction in its areas of concentration to accommodate and encourage gradual professional shifts. The changes Alverno makes are essentially responses to its own recognized needs and goals, as its revised program attests.

The new program offers students flexibility within a fairly fixed system. Students may choose when to attempt validations, but they cannot skip levels or develop too wide a spread between competences (being at level 5 in three competences, at level 3 in two, and at level 1 in the rest, for example). Most students complete graduation requirements in four years, partly because the program was designed on the four-year model, but some students finish a semester early.

However, because the system is based upon competence rather than time, the faculty has been able to adapt it for career women unable to attend school full-time. The college has accommodated these students' time constraints by offering a four-year weekend program.

Management Considerations.   Alverno keeps a file for each student which includes audio or video tapes and writing samples from the Assessment Center (both successful and unsuccessful validation attempts). Semester units for completed courses do not apply toward graduation, but they are noted for the benefit of other institutions. No grades are given. Uncompleted courses are recorded but not reported outside the college. Transcripts include the student's course record and competence certifications, as well as summary profiles by the student's major faculty supervisors.

The Assessment Center stores and indexes assessment records. Students may review their own records and use them in preparing portfolios. Complete files are retained for five years after a student graduates or leaves; after that, summaries are kept.

For an institution of its size, Alverno has engaged in unusually extensive and many-faceted evaluations—of its assessment techniques, of the competences themselves, of the relationship between its competences and those shown by successful professionals—and unusually intensive longitudinal and postgraduation follow-up studies. Despite the demands of creating, operating, and refining its program, Alverno sponsors visitation days, seminars, and workshops for colleagues and others interested in its work.

Staff Development.   In the years preceding implementation of its new learning approach, Alverno faculty debated and shaped their ideas in special seminars, student-faculty convocations, committee work, and faculty institutes. In 1972, four faculty members were released half-time to write the curriculum in detail.

To maintain momentum after program implementation began, the school increasingly emphasized staff development. Responsibility for in-service workshops and other staff orientation and training went from an ad hoc committee to an appointed committee to the current standing committee of the college's chief operating academic policy group. The Faculty Resource Center was organized to keep records of curriculum development processes and collect materials faculty can use to improve their courses.

ONGOING CONCERNS AND FUTURE DIRECTIONS

As Alverno identifies and attends to the needs of its students, it does not wish to be linked to a minimum competency movement. When it began pursuing "competence," it had in mind a very high level of achievement. In keeping with that quest, the Office of Evaluation is conducting in-depth interviews of outstanding professionals in several fields to determine what competences distinguish them from their average colleagues.

Recognizing that success rests on more than ability, Alverno plans to investigate personal characteristics—integration, independence, creativity, self-awareness, and commitment—and career competences that help women fulfill their potential and move ahead in their fields and in their whole lives.[21] Alverno realizes its goal when its students have the skills, confidence, and traits to succeed.

University of Minnesota College of Pharmacy

The College of Pharmacy of the University of Minnesota in Minneapolis is a state-operated professional school. A grant from the U.S. Department of Health, Education and Welfare, for developing a competency-based curriculum, resulted in a bold new approach to pharmacy preparation. Dr. Thomas E. Cyrs, Jr., is the former Director of the Curriculum Improvement Office, where instructional strategies and materials were developed and refined. He is now directing the Center for Educational Development and Evaluation at New Mexico State University in Las Cruces to establish a similar program.

WHAT IT IS

Faculty at the University of Minnesota College of Pharmacy have devised a curriculum based upon validated competencies that can be demonstrated. They are committed to training professionals who have mastered technical knowledge and skills and can use good judgment in complex, demanding situations. A pilot program in September 1977 preceded full implementation of the Competency-Determined Curriculum for Pharmacy Education in 1978. One hundred students were involved in the 1977 test.

Competency as defined by the College of Pharmacy involves intellectual processes, professional attitudes, and actual performance of skills built from firsthand analysis of professional performance in a variety of roles and settings where pharmacy is practiced. A competency is usually composed of several terminal performance objectives.

Thirty-four competencies have been designated as "musts" for future pharmacists. Statements of essential competencies were first produced by expert panels drawn from pharmacy practitioners, pharmacy faculty, recent graduates, and a cross section of consumers. These statements were then evaluated by a broad sample of Minnesota pharmacists, all College of Pharmacy faculty, the student body, pharmacists engaged in continuing education, and the original panelists. Trained observers conducted job analyses at 14 sites and validated the relevance of all but two of the 36 competencies being investigated. Each analysis was then reviewed, modified in some cases, and approved by a Professional Review Committee made up of faculty, practitioners, and students. Fourteen other competencies were considered desirable.

The 34 essential competencies fall into eight basic categories; the competent pharmacist (1) evaluates the product, (2) prepares the product, (3) evaluates and monitors therapy, (4) maintains drug information, (5) communicates with patients and health care personnel, (6) complies with standards of practice, (7) manages a system, and (8) maintains basic knowledge.[22] The additional 14 competencies considered desirable involve general public health and civic competencies and expanded clinical roles that are demonstrated by some pharmacists now and are likely to be designated as essentials in the near future.[23]

HOW IT WORKS

Faculty members teach competencies within existing course structures. Each competency is taught in at least one course and many are taught in more than one. Some possible relationships of competencies to courses are shown in figure 4.1.

As professors conduct classes, they draw upon multiple resources to develop student competence—lectures, personalized systems of instruction, computer-aided instruction, programmed instruction, learning contracts, learning packages, independent study, media, laboratory instruction, and simulation exercises.

Each area of competence has been analyzed for all supporting performance outcomes, so that both professors and students know what constitutes mastery. For example, one aspect of communicating with patients and health care personnel is making referrals. The objectives for this competency are shown in chart 4.3.

Mastery of knowledge can be measured by well-constructed paper-and-pencil tests; but ability to perform must be evaluated in lifelike situations. Faculty use the Assessment Center (a method, not a place) to observe students in simulation, role playing, gaming, and situational problem-solving exercises. Evaluative judgments are made by com-

Fig. 4.1 Relationships of Competencies to Courses

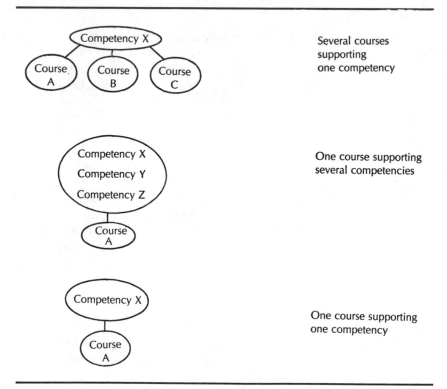

Source: Curriculum Improvement Office, College of Pharmacy, *Progress Report Phase II: An Analysis of Essential Pharmacy Competencies and Identification of Future Competencies* (Minneapolis: University of Minnesota, 1977), p. 13.

Chart 4.3 Supporting Objectives for One Competency in Pharmacy

---

Competency 19: Refers Patients to Other Health Care Professionals and Agencies

---

19.01 Persuades patient to visit other health professional or agency

    19.01.01 00 00   Can select the most appropriate referral health professional or agency for the given condition.

    19.01.02 00 00   Determines the patient's ability to reach the referral health professional or agency.

    19.01.03 00 00   Assists the patient in contacting the referral health professional or agency.

    19.01.04 00 00   Communicates how important it is to seek immediate referral, but communicates without increasing anxiety.

19.02 Suggests alternative action (e.g., first aid, over-the-counter self-medications, no treatment, no referral, etc.)

19.03 Can evaluate information gained and decides the necessity for referral

    19.03.01 00 00   Evaluates seriousness of the problem.

    19.03.02 00 00   Evaluates information in light of knowledge about disease states, their symptomatology, and need for referral.

        19.03.02 01 00   Can state the disease process and side effects of drugs in its treatment.

        19.03.02 02 00   Identifies signs and symptoms of common diseases and chemical side effects.

19.04 Determines the nature of the problem

    19.04.01 00 00   Uses effective communication techniques.

        19.04.01 01 00   Asks probing questions (sequence and branch).

        19.04.01 02 00   Reinforces patient to come to pharmacy.

        19.04.01 03 00   Builds a sense of trust and confidentiality.

    19.04.02 00 00   Listens for pertinent information from the patient.

    19.04.03 00 00   Verifies information obtained.

    19.04.04 00 00   Evaluates information in relation to signs.

Source: Curriculum Improvement Office, College of Pharmacy, University of Minnesota, *Progress Report, Phase II: An Analysis of Essential Pharmacy Competencies and Identification of Future Competencies* (Minneapolis, August 1977), pp. 41–42.

paring individuals' performance with criteria for acceptable performance.

Standards or criteria are still set in individual courses by professors who teach them. However, when total areas of competence are assessed in the future, standards will be drawn from the current state of the art in professional practice.

Maintaining Flexibility.   Modern pharmacy is changing, and the college curriculum must change with it. Consequently, the "should have" competencies that are more and more widely evident in professional practice could become "must have" competencies in the future.

Students benefit from more choice in classroom activities as their professors individualize learning, but they must complete all courses within the quarter system. They can work on units at their own pace, but the number completed bears upon their evaluations.

Management Considerations.   Consultants from the School of Business Administration are helping the College of Pharmacy develop a data-processing system that can be adapted to the needs of the faculty as the new curriculum evolves. The system, which must interface with the University of Minnesota student record systems, will:

- monitor student progress for the Student Affairs Office, students, and faculty advisors, and provide information concerning grades, competencies completed, terminal performance objectives scores, and student demographics
- provide research data on various predictors of student performance, activities completed, and student demographics to assess the effect of particular activities, modules, and courses on student performance
- provide data for administrative decision making, including class lists showing prerequisites completed, course loads, resource allocation, student records, and statistical summaries

Staff Development.   Faculty were involved in the new curriculum development from the beginning by contributing and evaluating competency statements and writing performance objectives. *A Handbook for the Design of Instruction in Pharmacy Education,*[24] prepared at their request, offers information and advice concerning:

- the instructional model
- evolution of the competency-based program
- constructing performance objectives
- designing a learning sequence

- designing learning packages
- preparing classroom tests
- evaluating competency-based programs
- multidimensional assessment procedures
- improving lectures
- designing effective visuals
- personalizing systems of instruction
- developing interpersonal classroom skills
- values education for the health sciences
- copyrighting instructional materials

Faculty development programs have been conducted to meet ongoing needs.

ONGOING CHALLENGES AND FUTURE DIRECTIONS

To date, diverting faculty from general research to involvement in curriculum development has been the foremost problem. Currently, however, with federal funding and state revenue rapidly dwindling, attention has shifted to finding resources to complete the project as originally conceived in the Curriculum Improvement Office.

After investigating many applications of competency-based education, faculty at the University of Minnesota College of Pharmacy conclude that the movement has a future if educators regard it as an assessment model rather than as a curriculum development model. They advocate identifying and validating areas of competency in such a way that the community as well as school officials can make sound value judgments and commitments.

Boy Scout Merit Badge Program

The Boy Scouts of America, with national offices in North Brunswick, New Jersey, focuses on personal development and exploration for youth across the nation in its three divisions (Cub Scouts for boys aged eight through ten; Boy Scouts for boys ten-and-a-half through eighteen; and Explorers for young men and women fourteen through twenty). Michael J. Shyne was Director of Educational Relationships before his recent retirement.

WHAT IT IS

The merit badge program of the Boy Scouts of America[25] has practiced competency-based education since 1911. Through this program Boy Scouts choose specific subjects or skills and work with experts to meet requirements by demonstrating mastery. They are attracted by the opportunity to explore and have hands-on experience, and proudly earn simple cloth merit badges—tangible proof that experts recognize their competence.

At the end of December 1977 there were 1,224,549 boys participating in this self-improvement program devoted to character building, citizenship training, and physical and mental fitness. Merit badge activities help them:

- increase their exposure to career possibilities or leisure activities through broad overviews of available subjects
- gain a wider outlook and understanding of the kinds of work people do for a living
- enjoy life as well-rounded persons
- become capable, confident citizens with useful skills

Competence, in the merit badge program, is "can do"—demonstrated ability recognized by an expert. It is developed by a process involving:

- specific requirements
- clear guidelines to help the Scout meet those requirements
- active participation in the learning situation
- expert guidance as needed
- satisfaction that comes from completing requirements

HOW IT WORKS

Scouts select merit badges from a pool of 118 topics or interest areas. A pamphlet for each describes the competency and its requirements. Each subject is a distinct unit; there is no effort to merge disciplines. Materials are purposely kept simple and understandable. For instance, the merit badge for personal management is written up in a 32-page booklet which offers information on self-management, family budgeting, personal budgeting, buying for a family, putting money to work, planning time, credit rating, looking ahead to a career, and books about personal management. The requirements for this badge are listed in chart 4.4.

The Scout chooses a merit badge—in personal management, or in first aid, camping, computers, or some other area of interest—and notifies his Scoutmaster, who signs a merit badge application and gives him the name of an expert who will be his counselor. The Scout makes an appointment with his counselor and brings the pamphlet describing the competency, the signed badge application, related projects he is working on, and any other signs of preparation.

The counselor discusses requirements with the Scout and finds out what he already knows, so that they can work on remaining items, and then helps the Scout set goals and tentative completion dates. After the Scout understands what he must do, he works at his own pace, with the counselor standing by to help him get information and evaluate his progress. The time involved to complete work on a badge will vary from a week to several months, depending upon the requirements and the boy's time and enthusiasm.

When the Scout feels he has met all requirements for his badge, he has an informal review session with his counselor. The Scout is expected to meet the requirements exactly—no more and no less—so he must pay close attention to terms like "show," "make," "list," "in the field," "collect," "identify," and "label." The standards published in the pamphlets are prepared by volunteer experts chosen by the national office. If these requirements have been met, the local counselor signs approval of the merit badge.

Learning is self-paced, though counselors and leaders work with the boys to encourage progress (part of the monthly advancement report is a list of boys who are not advancing). Scouts may learn in groups—for example, in a course set up in first aid by their rescue squad, or in lifesaving or water safety classes offered by the Red Cross or YMCA. Yet each boy is still evaluated individually.

Scouts accumulate merit badges in accordance with age standards established by the National Boy Scouts of America Executive Board. As they progress through the six-step advancement procedure of Scouting, they are free to develop their own interests but must fulfill certain basic service and merit badge requirements at each level.

Maintaining Flexibility. As society changes, so do merit badges. Suggestions for new badges are common, and national officials make additions and deletions as soon as they can coordinate time, funds,

Chart 4.4   Requirements for a Merit Badge in Personal Management

Personal Management

1. Talk over with parents or guardian how family funds are spent to meet day-to-day and long-term needs. Tell how you can help with the family budget.
2. Make a budget for yourself for 90 days. Keep a record of income and expenses for that period. Review it and report.
3. Help to choose and buy family groceries for one month. Make a report on what you learned.
4. Explain the possible use, advantages and risks in using $100 in each of the following ways. Tell how it might help you and others.
   (a) hide it in a mattress
   (b) put it into a savings account at a bank or savings and loan association (Explain the difference.)
   (c) buy a bicycle
   (d) open a checking account
   (e) buy a US Savings Bond
   (f) buy a power mower or paint sprayer
   (g) invest in a mutual fund
   (h) start a life insurance policy
   (i) buy fishing gear
   (j) buy common stock
5. Talk about things you would like to do within the next 90 days. Tell how you plan to get these done. After 90 days, tell what you did. Tell how you did them.
6. Tell how important credit and installment buying are to our economy and the individual and the family. Visit an officer of a bank or credit department of a store. Find out and tell what you must do to establish a good "credit rating." Tell what it means to you now and in the future.
7. Check out jobs or career opportunities through interviews or reading. Tell what the "next step" would be to prepare yourself for one of these careers.

Source: Boy Scouts of America, *Personal Management,* Pamphlet no. 3270 (North Brunswick, N.J., 1972), p. 3.

staff, and volunteer committees. Recent new additions include American heritage, golf, law, dentistry, consumer buying, and energy. Local councils may devise requirements and develop material for purely local interests, subject to approval of the national office.

Management Considerations.   Record-keeping involves these documents and procedures:

• *Merit badge application:* The Scout prepares an application and the Scoutmaster signs it. After the Scout completes the requirements for the badge, the expert signs the form and the Scout returns it to the Scoutmaster.

• *Advancement report:* The Scoutmaster files monthly progress reports with the local council office.

• *Tabulation sheet:* The local council records the number of merit badges earned in its annual report to national headquarters.

• *Scout progress record book:* The Scout keeps a record of skill awards, merit badges, and advancement from one level to the next.

Staff Development.   Local Scout organizations select experts in merit badge areas and help them assume the role of counselor. At a two-hour orientation session, volunteers can ask questions as they learn about their responsibilities, program purposes, methods, and records. Two pamphlets, *Merit Badge Counseling* and *Merit Badge Counselor Orientation*, describe procedures and provide special suggestions for helping boys acquire the minimum competencies.

ONGOING CONCERNS AND FUTURE DIRECTIONS

Success of the merit badge program rests on well-qualified and respected people volunteering to help boys learn useful skills. Finding capable "solid citizens" who are willing to participate is a steady challenge. The more specialized or professional the badge, the more difficult it is to recruit counselors—especially in rural areas.

The need to keep badges up to date continues, too, as interest in new areas grows. Many new subjects are recommended from time to time; but they can be incorporated only gradually because of national office budget and staff limitations.

Boy Scout leaders like the competency-based approach because it is a practical, down-to-earth technique that works. Individualized learning coupled with experience has done so much for Boy Scouts that leaders of the organization feel similar methods could be adopted by schools. And indeed some classrooms are already using Scouting's merit badge pamphlets to interest underachievers. Some Scouting leaders favor, as a next step, granting some subject or graduation credit for fulfillment of merit badge requirements. They believe students could benefit from contact with a greater range of experts, increased career information, and the opportunity to perform and be recognized. Educators, too, enjoy contact with enthusiastic learners. At the Virginia Polytechnic Institute and State University in Blacksburg, Virginia, for example, some prospective teachers broaden their preparation by becoming Boy Scout counselors.

The Air University

> The Air University, founded in 1946 and headquartered at Maxwell Air Force Base, is a part of the Air Training Command. Dr. John T. Meehan oversees evaluation and research activities for all courses taught within the Air University.

WHAT IT IS

Today's Air Force practices competency-based education to give its officers the skills and knowledge they need to advance in their military careers. The Air University operates four schools to provide professional military education for senior noncommissioned officers (NCOs) and commissioned officers:

- The *Senior Noncommissioned Officer Academy* (SNCOA) trains an average of 240 master sergeants, senior master sergeants, and chief master sergeants each year.
- The *Squadron Officer School* (SOS) trains an average of 700 lieutenants and captains each year.
- The *Air Command and Staff College* (ACSC) trains an average of 425 majors and those selected for promotion to major each year.
- The *Air War College* (AWC) trains an average of 200 lieutenant colonels and colonels each year.

Officers from the active duty Air Force, the Air Force Reserve, and the Air National Guard attend classes at the Air Command and Staff College and the Air War College. In addition, some Army and Navy officers, as well as a varying number of officers from foreign nations, join Air Force personnel in sessions at the Squadron Officer School, the Air Command and Staff College, and the Air War College. Specially convened boards at the Air Force Military Personnel Center select students to attend these residence schools.

The Air University has adopted competency-based procedures to help NCOs and officers master the fundamental skills and knowledge they need to assume positions of increasing authority and responsibility within the military. Competency is recognized as a student's ability to successfully perform a task or demonstrate knowledge according to specific objectives and criteria. The desired competencies are modeled after the behavior exhibited by the more successful Air Force officers and NCOs. The competencies require three types of learning:

- *Common* learning encompasses skills and knowledge needed by all, like staffing procedures and communication skills.
- *Career* learning develops competencies associated with specific skills or functions, as in pilot training, technical skill training programs, or professional graduate education in a functional specialty.
- *Professional* learning prepares officers and NCOs to assume positions of increasing authority and responsibility.

Each school is responsible for specifying what competencies its students must develop. Although exact procedures may vary, since the schools seek to accommodate differences in their target audiences, the schools generally use a systems approach to determine specific objectives and establish performance criteria. After curriculum objectives are organized and arranged in proper sequences, they are reviewed and approved by a board composed of senior officers and civilians within the Air University Headquarters staff. These competencies are taught by expert service personnel who have already demonstrated proficiency in their careers.

General objectives are established for each school; then particular objectives are specified for each course. For instance, the Air Command and Staff College organizes its curriculum to address 11 general objectives:

- know selected command and staff procedures and techniques
- comprehend important aspects of the communication process
- be able to write, speak, and read effectively
- apply selected concepts, principles, and techniques of resource management to command and staff problems
- know how to command, supervise, and manage forces effectively at the intermediate command and staff level
- know the role of the military as an instrument of national policy and the impact of that role on the expertise required of intermediate-level military managers
- apply fundamental aerospace doctrine and concepts in the employment of military forces

- know how military forces and strategies support national security policy
- know national security policies and the factors that affect national security
- comprehend Soviet capabilities, force postures, and doctrine
- comprehend the history of air power and views of aerospace proponents[26]

Four subject areas—staff communications, command and management, military environment, and military employment—are subdivided into phases, each with its own specific objectives and allotted number of hours. For example, phase three of the command and management area devotes 68 hours to staff techniques. Its objectives are:

- comprehend the structures and functions of existing Air Force staffs
- comprehend the role of selected nonquantitative techniques in solving contemporary staff problems
- comprehend the role of selected quantitative techniques in solving management problems
- apply analytical processes in solving resource allocation problems[27]

HOW IT WORKS

The Air University uses a systematic five-step Air Force Instructional Systems Development process that encourages feedback and interaction. Its repetitive cycle forces the user to continually update and validate instruction, and it works equally well whether an instructor wants to teach students to change a tire or to understand the political ideology of the Soviet Union. The five steps:

- *analyze system requirements* to determine needs
- *define education requirements* to help students progress from their present level of learning to a higher one
- *develop objectives and tests* that allow students to demonstrate mastery of a task
- *plan, develop, and validate instruction* to ensure that the lessons allow students to satisfy particular objectives
- *conduct classes and evaluate them* to identify weak areas or additional tasks that may be required[28]

The Air University makes use of Bloom's taxonomy[29] in establishing learning hierarchies. Course objectives tend to follow a uniform format with specific performance criteria. Such standardization facilitates curriculum review and permits a common reference to levels of learning and instructional methods.

Students are informed about objectives in such a way that they understand how they are expected to demonstrate mastery of a given objective. The schools provide samples of behavior (called "samples of evidence") for each objective. Students read assigned materials and attend lectures to get necessary information, then attend seminars in groups of 12 to 15 to consolidate readings and lectures and to probe subject matter. Students are assigned by computer so that the seminars will have experts in different areas who can assist the rest of the group when their specialty is being discussed.

Instructors administer written tests to measure students' academic achievement and to make subjective evaluations to assess how well they synthesize related portions of the curriculum. Before a written examination is administered, formal test review boards judge its relevancy and exercise quality control over the construction of individual items. Afterwards, test results are analyzed statistically to measure the degree of difficulty and the validity of test items. In making subjective evaluations, instructors observe students performing in games and computer simulations.

Maintaining Flexibility. A major decision such as the cancellation of the B-1 bomber or a significant breakthrough in strategic arms limitations requires prompt adjustment of parts of the curriculum—and usually the schools can select new readings and rewrite objectives during an academic year. When new educational philosophy calls for substantial shifts in emphasis in the schools, the changes usually cannot be incorporated until the following academic year.

Ongoing assessment helps the Air University programs remain flexible and responsive to new needs. To keep their offerings current, the schools:

- survey the Air Force to determine the skills and knowledge graduates need
- review and update the curriculum each year
- have the validity of courses measured and confirmed by the Educational Directorate of Headquarters Air University and expert civilian educators
- consider the curricular recommendations of visiting lecturers
- submit new course offerings on a case-by-case basis to the Air Force's functional command or manager if appropriate
- improve curriculum design by examining task analysis data prepared by the Air Force's Occupational Measurement Center

For individuals, some flexibility is achieved through an elective program at three schools—AWC, ACSC, and SNCOA. Otherwise, all students at a given school take the same basic core of instruction. Since they are assigned for specific periods of time, they must complete their work within fixed time limits: ten months for the Air Command and Staff College and the Air War College; eleven weeks for the Squadron Officer School; and nine weeks for the Senior Noncommissioned Officer Academy.

Management Considerations.   Each school establishes its own sets of forms to record student progress. Each step of the subjective and objective evaluation process is documented, and records are kept as a basis for changes in a school's curriculum. Upon graduation students receive a standard Air Force training report that becomes a permanent part of their personnel file.

Staff Development.   Because most Air University instructors have little or no formal training in education, they must attend the Air University's Academic Instructor School (AIS), which emphasizes the use of learning objectives and lesson plans designed to meet them. Persons responsible for developing and implementing curriculum must enroll in a 20-hour elective at the Academic Instructor School to learn the five-step systems approach to instructional development mentioned earlier. A well-balanced mix of theory and practice in the training prepares instructors to assume their instructional roles quickly.

ONGOING PROBLEMS AND FUTURE DIRECTIONS

Students at Air University are adults who have been selected because they have been successful in their careers. With each advance in rank, students have developed their skills through increased experience, making it difficult for teaching staff to identify additional competencies they should acquire. Also, because students have had differing career experiences (e.g., pilots and nonpilots), staff must avoid a curriculum that concentrates on one area so as to favor one group over another.

Because individuals who attend Air University residence schools have gone through a competitive screening process (tough for the Air Command and Staff College, and even more rigorous for the Air War College), the staff must be very careful in dealing with students who do not meet the academic standards in a particular area of study. They consider taking action that could lead to dismissal only if a student fails to meet the standards in several areas, since such action could seriously limit the individual's future in the military service.

Staff feel a continuing need to define their mission and refine their techniques to foster the qualities, knowledge, and skills demanded of a successful military careerist. They must consider what professional military service is and determine what subjects are necessary at what levels. They must survey present and future needs and decide whether they are being met. In the process, they must evaluate their performance to decide why Air University graduates are successful: because of their instruction, or because the selection process provides only individuals who would advance regardless of attendance.

The Air University plans to rely increasingly on some form of competency-based education. Some staff members see value in waiving certain subject matter for students who have demonstrated mastery before coming to an Air University school, because they could then tailor instruction for each student and concentrate on areas of weakness. However, a large number of students per instructor makes individualization difficult.

A competency-based approach does not resolve all of the educational problems within the Air University, but it does guarantee that graduates have mastered skills and subjects intended to maximize their effectiveness in military service.

AT&T Management Training Program

AT&T operates its Large Team Management Training program at the Gouverneur Morris Inn in Morristown, New Jersey. William A. Brantley is director of this corporate training center, which services the entire Bell System.

WHAT IT IS

Each year approximately 1,000 middle managers from across the Bell System attend one-week seminars at AT&T's Large Team Management Training Institute (LTMTI). During the intensive sessions, emphasis is on knowledge and skills necessary for mastery performance as a manager of large team operation systems.

HOW IT WORKS

Instructors use lectures, visual and training aids, open classroom discussion, and individual and group exercises to develop competencies. Because managers must understand their function within the larger system, training involves outside subjects, which are linked back to responsibilities at home. In order to be considered competent, managers must know:

- the physical operation of each company system
- each manager's responsibilities within the system
- the skills each manager needs to execute those responsibilities
- the kinds of interpersonal relationships that managers with different responsibilities should develop
- the behaviors required to meet established, measurable performance criteria

In each course, ranges of competency are based on Bell System average actual performances. On the job, competency is defined through joint target-setting by individual and boss.

The highest level of performance among competing managers is recognized as mastery performance. Deficiencies are identified so that a training program can be devised to bring everyone to mastery level. The program is tested with an expert group of managers, then used with conferees.

Each course has an entrance standard that the manager should meet before attending the Institute. A published synopsis specifies target population, objectives, and entrance requirements, with instructions for meeting them. A course in force management, for instance, trains candidates to provide the right number of operators to meet customer demand at all times of the day and night. It addresses a target population of first- and second-level managers in a Centralized Force Administration Group. These people should have three to six months of on-line experience. The course is also appropriate for staff personnel providing support in large team force management for operating Centralized Force Administration Groups. Upon completion of this course, the manager will be able to:

- force-manage a large team system
- make accurate long- and short-range plans
- develop half-hourly forecasts of operators required
- construct large team schedules
- allocate large team schedules to each operator office
- make good daily adjustments

- coordinate successfully with other large team peer-level managers

These objectives are further broken down into individual class objectives. For instance, instructors use lecture, discussion, an individual exercise, and a group case during a two-hour session centered on long- and short-range planning. At the completion of the lesson, students are able to:

- define a long-range plan
- list the objectives of a long-range plan
- define the responsibility of the force manager in long-range planning
- compute estimated board hours on the long range, using the standard centum-call-seconds/board-hour method[30]
- define a short-range plan
- list the objectives of a short-range plan
- compute estimated board hours on the short range, using either the standard centum-call-seconds/board-hour method or the actual centum-call-seconds/board-hour method

Maintaining Flexibility. Each training course is updated or changed as instructors and training developers identify new needs. Students are asked to fill out critiques at the end of each training session to indicate whether the course met their needs and whether improvements or changes should be made.

Although courses are conducted within fixed time limits, instructors have enough latitude to allow for the differing aptitude and experience levels of each group, which includes a maximum of 18 people. Instructors determine these levels by examining a precourse data sheet on each student and by giving a precourse test. They establish a relaxed atmosphere early, to encourage class participation and increase their awareness of individual and group needs.

Management Considerations. Staff want to offer the best training most economically, so they frequently evaluate the program on the basis of cost records, student profiles, and course performance.

Staff Development. Since the program can be effective only if instructors are very well prepared, those who train must have thorough mastery of:

- subject matter
- course layout
- appropriate use of training aids
- interpersonal skills, including eye contact, rapport, voice control

Staff may acquire necessary competence through private study, assistance from another instructor, or formal course work.

ONGOING CHALLENGES AND FUTURE DIRECTIONS

Explicit program goals and an efficient curriculum plan contribute to a smooth operation for this corporate training area. As staff assess needs, however, they realize that a good professional library would help instructors maintain expertise in their subjects.

AT&T's competency-based approach to training meets the needs of middle managers working in a profit-or-loss system because it ensures that they know what their responsibilities are and how they should be met. In the future, attention will be given to refining the existing concept of mastery and the assessment of deficiencies.

The Large Team Management Training Institute's program is designed to give a specific group of people a specific set of skills; it could not be adopted generally by secondary schools. But its training methods could be applied—especially its procedure for isolating obstacles to mastery performance.

NOTES

1. For more information about Individually Guided Education, consult: Wisconsin Research and Development Center for Individualized Schooling, 1025 West Johnson Street, Madison, WI 53706. 608/263-4200.

2. See Jack Hackett and George McKilligin, "A Study of the Multiunit IGE Elementary Schools" (Paper presented at the request of the Board of Education; Janesville, Wis., August 1972, revised October 1972), p. 5.

3. See Public Schools of the District of Columbia, *The Design and Implementation of the Validation of the Competency-Based Curriculum in Language Arts/English and Science*, pp. 2–3.

4. Ibid., pp. 21–27.

5. Public Schools of the District of Columbia, "Competency-Based Curriculum, Science: Laboratory Science, Grades Nine and Ten," pp. 126–127.

6. Schools using validated Competency-Based Curriculum materials and serving as observation sites.

7. Schools validating (field testing) newly developed Competency-Based Curriculum materials.

8. See Public Schools of the District of Columbia, *Design and Implementation* . . . , pp. 4–6.

9. See Milpitas Unified School District, "Proficiency Standards Curriculum: Language Arts," p. 2.

10. Milpitas Unified School District, "Proficiency Standards: Eighth Grade Reading, Language Arts, Mathematics, Social Science," pp. 10–11.

11. Ibid., pp. 11–12.

12. For information about the Bay Area Writing Project, consult: Dr. James R. Gray, Director, Bay Area Writing Project, School of Education, University of California, Berkeley, CA 94720. 415/642-0963.

13. For a description of guides, see Charles Bowe, "Hood River Valley High School Operational Plan 1977–78," pp. 37–42.

14. For information about V-TECS, consult: Vocational-Technical Education Consortium of States, 795 Peachtree Street N.E., Atlanta, GA 30308

15. For information about Experience-Based Career Education, consult the EBCE Program Director, at one of these locations:

Appalachia Educational Laboratory
P.O. Box 1348
Charleston, WV 25325
304/344-8371

Northwest Regional Educational
  Laboratory
710 S.W. Second Avenue
Portland, OR 97204
503/248–6891

Far West Laboratory for Educational
  Research and Development
1855 Folsom Street
San Francisco, CA 94103
415/565-3127

Research for Better Schools
444 N. Third Street
Philadelphia, PA 19123
215/574-9300

16. For information about the External Diploma Program, consult: Regional Learning Service of Central New York, 405 Oak Street, Syracuse, NY 13203. 315/425-5252 or 315/425-5262.

17. Competency Based Adult High School Diploma Project, *Oregon Competency Based Adult High School Diploma Management Manual 1978*, pp. 10–11.

18. Ibid., pp. 32–59.

19. See Alverno College Faculty, *Liberal Learning at Alverno College.*

20. Ibid., pp. 28–29.

21. See Alverno College Assessment Committee, *Introductory Statement Regarding Characteristics of Advanced Students.*

22. See Curriculum Improvement Office, College of Pharmacy, University of Minnesota, *Progress Report Phase II*, pp. 6–7.

23. Ibid., p. 14.

24. See Thomas E. Cyrs, Jr., *Handbook for the Design of Instruction in Pharmacy Education.*

25. For information about Scouting, consult: Scouting USA, North Brunswick, NJ 08902. 201/249-6000.

26. Air University, *Air University Catalog*, pp. 12, 15.

27. Ibid., p. 16.

28. See Department of the Air Force, *Instructional System Development*, pp. 1.2–1.5.

29. Benjamin S. Bloom, ed., *Taxonomy of Educational Objectives, Handbook I: Cognitive Domain.*

30. "Centum call seconds" is the basic measurement of work on a given call; it is the number of seconds it takes to complete the call, divided by 100.

5

How Can Competencies Be Assessed?

Issues in Role-Based Assessment

H. DEL SCHALOCK

EDITOR'S INTRODUCTION

This chapter concentrates on an important aspect of assessment. We turn from a global examination of the program variations found in chapter 4 to a highly specific concern. The author asks these questions: If a definition of competence based on roles is to be the goal of competency-based education, how can we develop an appropriate system of assessment? If we proceed with this step, what are the implications?

Schalock presents us with a brief review of the literature and identifies key issues that deserve our attention, such as the importance of developing operational definitions of desired outcomes. As the types of outcomes and the standards for performance become more than minimal expectations, assessment becomes much more complex than the simple measurement of basic skills. It is far easier to define outcomes in reading, writing, and computation than in being a parent, learner, or consumer. Yet accurate specifications of such roles are a critical first step. There is little in the literature to guide us, and nothing so concrete as a job description for these objectives.

Using material from Oregon's statewide goals for life role performance, the author supports his observation that such specifications must be defensible and accepted both by those who must teach and by those who are required to demonstrate the outcomes.

Critical issues surrounding the selection of specific functions within roles and the appropriate indicators of performance that could be prescribed as the criteria for judgment are pointed out by the author. He remarks that decisions must also be made about the context of assessment (where it takes place), and the level of performance desired or expected. In addition, selecting appropriate techniques involves choices that pertain to the fairness and the utility of the assessment.

Some conditions that affect the assessment of role performance are also spelled out, including the problem of designing programs for assessment based on roles, when neither the roles themselves nor the conditions within which they are practiced remain constant. These are some sobering realities that must be faced as role-based assessment is considered.

Continuing, the author outlines several conditions needed for effective assessment of role performance. Choosing whether to have real-life or simulated conditions and selecting assessors to evaluate performance are vital considerations. The number of samples of particular behaviors that will be sufficient to verify mastery must be determined, and safeguards against rater bias must be employed to assure reliable and valid judgments.

Evaluating role-based performance is one of the issues in competency assessment generally, and it is a major problem for secondary schools concerned with role-based instruction and certification. However, there are many other assessment problems that demand attention—in programs for adults and for youth out of school. Some of them are less complicated than the one described in this chapter. All of them could benefit from a concerted effort by the measurement community to expand the sophistication of techniques beyond the ubiquitous multiple-choice test.

R.S.N.

WHILE MUCH REMAINS to be understood about competency-based education and the implementation options available appear to be endless, the authors of the previous chapters all agree that the meaning assigned to the concept of competence essentially determines all else. If competence is defined as acquisition of a set of facts or mastery of particular skills, a competency-based education program will be very different from one in which competence is regarded as the ability to function effectively in a job or life role. The potential impact of the program on its participants will also be different, as will the nature of instructional activities pursued and the nature of assessment procedures used.

Without exception, the authors of the previous chapters also recognize that both instruction and assessment are more complex when competence is defined in terms of job or life role performance. In full recognition of this, Chickering and Claxton in chapter 1, and Rubin in chapter 3, argue for such a definition. I have argued for such a definition too,[1] but the complexities involved in assessing role or job performance are so great that they need to be understood fully before commitments are made to implementing a competency-based education program with such a focus.

The authors of the preceding chapters also agree that defensible evidence of the attainment of desired outcomes is essential to any program claiming to be competency based. This is the case whether the assessment of competence is to serve only as a basis for decisions about certification, or whether it influences instruction and the progress of students throughout an educational program.

The purpose of this chapter is to explore the assessment implications of adopting a role-based definition of competency. The chapter opens with a brief overview of the literature that points to the importance of assessment in both competency-based education and minimum competency testing programs. This is followed by a discussion of the assessment problems a role-based definition of competence involves. The remaining sections of the chapter deal with technical and logistical issues. Conditions that complicate assessment and conditions that must be present for it to be carried out effectively are given special attention.

ASSESSMENT IN COMPETENCY PROGRAMS

Whatever else they may be, competency-based education programs are based on goals. The goals pursued within particular programs may vary in kind and level of difficulty and may serve different purposes in guiding curriculum and instruction, but they are always clearly defined. Moreover, because of this orientation, they all carry a clearly recognized obligation to obtain defensible proof of goal attainment. Unless this is carried out, they are not likely to be significantly different from other programs. George Madaus and Peter Airasian point out that:

> Ultimately, the impact of any competency-based graduation program will be dependent upon the evaluation techniques utilized to provide data about student competence and the sanctions associated with failure to demonstrate competence. . . . The fastest way to subvert the meaningfulness of the desired competencies is for a state, district, or other evaluating agency to establish meaningless or watered down evaluation procedures, ones which assure that all pupils are certified as demonstrating mastery of the competencies.[2]

Although competency-based education programs all have this general obligation to specify goals and evidence of goal attainment, they differ greatly in the standards set for performance and the nature of data collected. They also differ greatly in the uses made of the information obtained. The following discussion begins with a technical point, then describes two major patterns of use. These few comments are intended as background to the problems and issues examined in the remainder of the chapter.

Assessment and Operational Meanings.   It is generally recognized in science and philosophy that all things, including ideas, concepts, and educational outcomes, may be defined either abstractly or in terms of the operatior.s used in their measurement.[3] Both approaches are necessary in implementing a competency-based education program. Desired learning outcomes must be described so that they are meaningful to students, teachers, and the community at large. At the same time, since evidence about goal attainment must be obtained, the measures used must be consistent with the abstract goal statements. Ultimately, the real meaning to be assigned to goal statements is no more and no less than the measures used to determine attainment.

This is what is meant by an operational definition of the desired outcomes. This also is why this kind of definition is so important. Care must be taken in designing competency-based education programs to assure a defensible connection between the statements of desired outcomes and the measures used to obtain evidence that they have been attained. Unless there is an obvious connection between the two, and unless the information collected can be accepted as trustworthy, both participants in an educational program and patrons of it will have cause for skepticism.

Assessment in Minimum Competency Testing Programs. As William Spady has indicated, most educational programs claiming to be competency based are actually testing and remediation programs that focus on basic literacy and mathematical skills.[4] These programs are more properly identified as minimum competency or standards programs, since their primary purpose is to certify that students who have completed them are able to demonstrate mastery of a specified set of performance requirements (competencies) established as a prerequisite to high school graduation. There are more than 30 states that have such requirements, as well as some school districts in states that have not yet adopted statewide requirements. Most of these programs have been adopted within the past five years as a response to declining test scores, inadequate vocational preparation, and perceived shortcomings in high school programs generally. The essential thrust of the minimum competency testing movement is to withhold diplomas from students who cannot demonstrate mastery of the prescribed knowledge, skills, or competencies assumed to be needed to function effectively in the world outside the school.

The requirements for assessment in minimum competency certification programs differ considerably from those in programs that are fully competency based, that is, in which outcomes to be attained and evidence of achievement affect curricula and instruction as well as graduation. In minimum competency certification programs, students who have met performance standards and have completed other requirements as well receive a diploma. Those who do not meet the performance requirements engage in remedial activities and take the assessment battery a second or third time.

A host of issues accompanies such an approach. In addition to identifying meaningful outcomes to be demonstrated as a basis for high school graduation, and the attending problem of obtaining defensible measures of these outcomes, there are a number of related questions: When and where in an educational program should such outcomes be demonstrated? What obligation must there be to provide instruction that leads to outcome attainment? What social, political, and legal ramifications are likely to emerge as a consequence of denying high school certification on the basis of a single examination? And what is the evidence that outcomes to be demonstrated as a basis for graduation can in fact be influenced by school programs? Of all issues, however, Madaus and Airasian feel the most prevalent danger of any competency-based certification system is that the process of education may be neglected while attention centers around goals and evaluation methods.[5] The danger is real, and the reader needs to be mindful of it when considering assessment issues related to minimum competency testing at the secondary level.

Assessment in Competency-Based Education Programs.   To Spady, competency-based education, in contrast to minimum competency testing, means a continuous-progress approach to instruction and certification. Instead of taking yearly standardized tests unrelated to their classes, students get regular diagnosis, monitoring, feedback, and correction along with instruction.[6]

Although the role of assessment in educational programs basing instruction on information about the learning strengths and weaknesses of students and their progress toward desired outcomes contrasts markedly with that in programs seeking only the attainment of minimum standards required for high school graduation, some issues are common to both. For example, both need resources and expertise to meet assessment requirements and mechanisms to act upon assessment information, though even here differences are obvious. Other issues, however, take considerably different forms in the two different contexts. The question of how adequately instructional programs can achieve desired outcomes, for example, simply poses different issues for competency-based education and graduation programs. So also does the legal basis for withholding a diploma from students unable to demonstrate competencies required for high school graduation.

BITING THE BULLET: DEFINING COMPETENCE IN TERMS OF ROLE PERFORMANCE

The authors of this volume have adopted a definition of competence that is consistent with the meaning generally conveyed by the term. Competence signifies the ability to do something well. Ordinarily it refers to a job, role, or complex task, like managing a business or a farm, functioning as a scientist or surgeon, or playing tennis or chess. In everyday terms, the concept of competence applies equally well to being a mother, homemaker, student, or citizen. What is important about the general meaning attached to the term is its linkage to a role or position.[7]

From this point of view, a competence to be demonstrated will always be described in general terms and be tied to a particular role or position. Moreover, such a competence will *not* be defined as the set of knowledges, skills, and attitudes that make up the competence or, more accurately, that are needed for competent performance. These should be treated either as enablers of competence or as outcomes desired of education regardless of their relationship to competence.

Adopting a role- or job-based definition of competence has major implications for assessment. Procedures for assessing the acquisition of knowledge or the mastery of skills are well established and widely understood. In programs that choose to go with the majority and define competence in terms of knowledge acquisition or skill mastery, the technology needed for assessment is available. As the definition of competency extends beyond the level of knowledge and skills, however, assessment becomes increasingly complex. In the eyes of many, the assessment of competence in role or job performance requires more than the present technology of assessment has to offer.

This circumstance has been recognized by a number of writers. Spady, for example, notes that:

> Although the choice of CBE outcome goals may impose major constraints and demands on school systems with respect to reconceptualizing, redesigning, and providing adequate curriculum and instruction, the problems are minor compared to those related to the reliable, valid, and timely measurement of applied role performance. The technology surrounding the assessment and measurement of success in life role activities is only in its infancy, even though the rush toward adopting CBE-like programs is upon us. Those systems seriously concerned with the quality of data they will accept as evidence of competency performance will have to pay a steep price in time and personnel resources required for the task.[8]

In much the same vein, though without such clear reference to applied performance testing, Paul Pottinger discusses the assessment tools needed to fully implement competency-based education programs:

> They must be new, not just new names for traditional procedures. Achievement on traditional paper-and-pencil, objective tests correlates highly with performance on all similar types of academic achievement tests; but if the desire is to break out of this closed circuit, there is a need for radically new types of "tests"—tests of learning, critical thinking, problem solving and other newly defined competencies which correlate with competent performance in jobs and other nonacademic situations.[9]

Pottinger goes on to list potentially useful approaches to assessment that have been or are being developed: portfolios; journals; juries; supervisor or peer client ratings; in-basket tests; work sample tests; simulations; contests; and rehearsed performances. Many have been borrowed from techniques and procedures developed by industrial psychologists; but, as Pottinger points out, they are not without their flaws:

> These attempts to break away from the limited traditional measures of verbal ability and scholastic aptitude and achievement have some-times resulted in elaborate, time-consuming, costly and cumbersome techniques and procedures; and most of these assessment techniques are quite subjective. They are not amenable to standardization for comparability among individuals and institutions.[10]

One of the major dilemmas for policy makers contemplating a competency-based approach is whether to proceed without well-established procedures for assessing role or job competence. They have several choices. They can wait until assessment procedures are tested and available, although that means delaying implementation indefinitely. Or they can install a program, either planning to develop the assessment capability needed or to ignore assessment problems and manage with whatever is available. All too frequently the latter choice has been made. It represents one of the most common pitfalls of states and institutions that have attempted to implement minimum competency testing for high school certification.

A related danger, which may be even more serious in the long run, is involved in defining the competencies to be demonstrated in terms of available assessment instruments. Madaus and Airasian speak of this:

> In the rush to implement competency-based programs, the temptation is to focus evaluation efforts upon recall behaviors, since these are the easiest to test and certify. To some extent this tendency is implied by programs' insistence upon classifying social, personal and career development competencies as "skills." Performance objectives involving basic literacy and numeracy skill, and higher level applications, may be ignored in the teaching-learning process if the certifying examination principally focuses on recall.[11]

Given the frequency with which states or institutions have done this or have decided to proceed with minimum competency testing without the assessment tools needed for full program implementation, Pottinger's view of the magnitude of the task ahead is probably accurate:

> The need may be for no less than a new psychology of competence—something on the order of Bloom's and Krathwohl's taxonomies of

cognitive and affective dimensions of learning. But the emphasis must be on *adult* development and learning outcomes with special attention to the interactive nature of psychological variables and how skills and abilities are integrated (as life outside of academia requires). It's a tall order, but a psychology of competence is beginning to emerge.[12]

BASIC CONSIDERATIONS IN THE ASSESSMENT OF ROLE PERFORMANCE

From what has been said thus far it is clear that states, institutions, or classroom instructors wishing to implement programs incorporating role performance in their definition of competence must make their way through essentially uncharted waters with respect to assessment. Many technical problems need to be resolved along the way, some of which are discussed in the next section. A number of basic considerations must guide the overall assessment effort, however, if it is to be successful. These are discussed in the paragraphs that follow.

Beyond Enabling Knowledge and Skills.   To be optimally meaningful, a competency-based education program based on roles or jobs requires assessment of performance in much broader terms than the knowledge or skills assumed to be needed for a particular role or job. Pottinger makes this point when he says that "one cannot *assume* that abilities or skills discretely learned will be integrated in work and life functions and consequently that establishment of minimal levels of performance on isolated skills or 'sub-competencies' have much meaning in themselves."[13] Boyd and Shimberg make the same point, but in a slightly different way:

> Most of us recognize that there is a fundamental difference between *knowing about* a job and being able to *do* the job. "Knowledge of" is really an essential ingredient for doing a complex job correctly, but while it is a *necessary* condition, it is rarely a *sufficient* condition for satisfactory performance.[14]

These authors go on to point out that while people may be able to bluff on a written test, they "can seldom carry off a successful deception when a realistic performance test is required. One of the great virtues of the performance test is its impressive 'face validity' and credibility, because the task one must do so closely resembles the job itself."[15]

Meaningful Role Definitions and Assessment Procedures.   If students, faculty and patrons are to accept an educational program, the proposed outcomes must appear meaningful and important. This is the case whether it takes as its point of departure academic disciplines, life roles, or job preparation. In a program based on roles or jobs, an important first step is establishing the life roles or job definitions that are to guide the program and that will need to be assessed as expected outcomes.

Reducing role definitions to their simplest components is a danger to be guarded against. Desired outcomes need to be stated at a level of generality that has importance as well as meaning for those affected by them, and they must not be so numerous that they are overwhelming. Pottinger focuses on this issue well:

> Competencies cannot be meaningfully defined by seemingly endless reductions of specific skills, tasks and actions which, in the end, fall short of real world requirements for effective performance. . . .
>
> In many competency-based education (CBE) programs, attempts are made to reduce competencies to a series of discrete and hopefully quantifiable action steps. This reductionism follows from the need to clearly communicate as well as to quantify and measure outcomes. However, from the students' point of view, a myriad of overly reductive definitions is awesome, and the definitions, themselves, often lack intuitive meaning; i.e., the "overkill" of subcompetencies lacks the same sense of meaning and relevance to students' lives as the traditional learning agendas from which many have fled. To the student who asks, "What do I have to be able to do to be competent; what do I have to demonstrate in order to be credentialed; and what do these exhibited abilities have to do with the real world?," the current state of the art in defining competence sometimes affords a regrettably inadequate answer.[16]

A related danger is selecting indicators of outcome attainment that do not clearly reflect the focus or intent of the abstractly stated outcomes. When this kind of error is made, there tends to be too much enthusiasm for simplification or too little assurance that the indicators to be used as evidence of outcome attainment are in themselves meaningful. If errors of this kind are to be avoided, the operational definition (measurement) given to an educational outcome must be consistent with its abstract or general definition for either to be trusted. Pottinger speaks pointedly of this interdependence:

> New competency definitions should be readily recognizable as important, and the related assessment techniques or instruments should be easy for faculty and students to understand. There is a need to guard against competency definitions and measures that are so complex, trivial, or esoteric that students and faculty cannot, in the first instance, understand them and, in the second, accept them as meaningful and useful. In other words, educational goals should not be rendered unintelligible; and assessment procedures and instru-

ments should not mystify the process of evaluation of student progress.[17]

More is said about the selection of indicators of effective role or job performance later in the chapter.

Criterion-Referencing. As stated previously, competency-based education is oriented toward goals, which means that criteria or standards must be set for determining when a particular goal has been reached. In this capacity, criteria for goal attainment serve not only as guides for outcome assessment, but also for instruction, student placement in an instructional program, and student progress through a program, including graduation.

A great deal of confusion has entered the assessment literature with respect to criterion-referenced testing. Technically speaking, neither "criterion-referenced" nor "norm-referenced" should be used to describe a test, since both terms refer to *interpretations* made from test data. Tests that have been developed and standardized against the distribution of scores attained by a population of learners (typically referred to as norm-referenced tests) can be used for making criterion-referenced decisions. The problem with using them in this way is that they lack clear reference to desired learning outcomes. More typically, criterion-referenced instructional decisions are made from tests that have established performance levels against specified educational goals.

Producing Trustworthy and Useful Information. Irrespective of an assessment system's focus or form, it must produce trustworthy and usable information. Concern for the extent to which collected data can be believed is reflected in traditional measurement terms such as reliability and validity. Since these are well known and procedures are well established for dealing with them, little more needs to be said about them here. It is important to understand, however, that traditionally both have been treated from the perspective of norm-based assessment and that they take somewhat different form from the perspective of goal-based assessment. Spady and Mitchell explain:

> . . . in CBE programs teachers will have to "teach to the test" to the same extent that it is necessary to "teach to the goals" which students are trying to reach. Since CBE requires that both performance indicators and instructional experiences reflect explicit and known outcome goals, and since the purpose of evaluation is to diagnose and determine student progress toward those goals, neither the content nor the occurrence of evaluation experiences should be a "surprise" to students. Another clear implication of the foregoing is that both "pencil-paper" and typical "standardized" tests will have limited utility in

measuring life-role competencies. Consequently, the "test" toward which teachers will be directing the instructional program will most often be locally determined and program-relevant. Since "standardized" assessment instruments are not and cannot be explicitly program-relevant, they are not likely to become a central focus of CBE programs, as many educators currently fear.[18]

Other dimensions of the validity question, face validity and predictive validity, for example, are as appropriate to assessment systems based on goals as to those based on norms.

Feasibility of Implementation.   Apart from all other considerations, assessment methods used in competency-based education programs must be feasible to implement. They cannot be overly time-consuming for teachers to administer and score or for students to take; they cannot require extensive new resources; and they must be acceptable to all. More than this, the benefit derived from them must be considered worthy of the effort and cost involved. Competency-based education is vulnerable on many counts, but its Achilles' heel is clearly the quality of data on competency attainment and the political and economic feasibility of collecting those data.

TECHNICAL CONSIDERATIONS IN THE ASSESSMENT OF ROLE PERFORMANCE[19]

Beyond these basic considerations are a host of conceptual and technical matters: identifying the roles or positions for which competence is to be demonstrated; specifying the functions (competencies) to be performed within each role or position selected; specifying the indicators of effective performance; developing trustworthy and defensible measures of performance; and establishing defensible standards. The nature of these various tasks and the issues that are central to them are discussed briefly in the following paragraphs.

Specifying Roles or Positions.   If a competency-based education program is designed to prepare a person to function effectively within a particular job or class of jobs, a number of decisions have to be made. In the preparation of teachers, for example, a first-level decision involves a choice between preschool, elementary, middle school, and secondary school. A second decision involves the nature and degree of specialization. At the elementary level, for example, it must be decided whether reading specialists, counselors, music specialists, or generalists are to be prepared, while at the middle and secondary levels decisions have to be made about content specialities as well.

Beyond these choices, which most teacher education programs

make at present, there are decisions about the forms that schooling should take at the different age levels. Programs may decide to prepare teachers to function within traditional schools, open schools, schools without walls, individualized learning contexts, or team-teaching contexts, among others. These are more difficult decisions, for they involve projections about the future and commitments to points of view that may not be commonly accepted at the time.

With little more that can be given as guidance, program developers must arbitrarily arrive at a list of life roles to be performed and defend their selection as well as they can. Steps need to be taken to be sure that participants and patrons find the proposed list meaningful and agree to it before a great deal of energy is invested in program development. Beyond this cautionary step, however, and the basic consideration of meaningfulness, there are few guidelines that can be provided on role selection.

Specifying Functions to Be Performed. Job analysis procedures typically define a function as the largest or most inclusive subdivision of work within a particular job or position.[20] Applying this definition to a job, such as teaching, any position is made up of a number of functions, such as setting objectives for instruction, selecting instructional materials and procedures, facilitating interaction between pupils and materials, and assessing outcomes. These are of course arbitrary subdivisions, and the designers of teacher education programs may choose to make functions more or less inclusive. Taking care to specify the functions to be performed within a given job description is critical in the design of a competency-based teacher education program for two reasons. The description of functions to be performed is what defines the parameters of a job, and it is in relation to the performance of functions that the competence of a teacher is to be judged.[21] Given this frame of reference, *the functions to be performed within a teaching position become the basic units of analysis in preparing curricula within a teacher education program. They also become the basic units of analysis in assessing the competence of those going through the program, for the outcomes expected from teaching are linked to functions.* Because of this, performance standards and the indicators that they have been met are both tied to functions. An overall judgment about the competence of a teacher or prospective teacher is linked to performance across functions.

Since functions are arbitrary subdivisions of work, they not only vary in focus and size across programs, but also may vary within a given program over time. This could be due to changes in job definitions, reassignment of work responsibilities, or a simple redefinition of meaningful units of work. It is also the case that a given function may serve more than one job description. For example, setting instructional objectives is a function performed in both elementary and secondary teaching positions. In spite of the arbitrariness of function definitions, however, the ability to identify large units of work within a job is possible. It is also *necessary* if a definition of teaching competency is to be linked to job performance.

Following much the same logic, performing life roles such as citizen or consumer involves a number of related functions. These are comparable to functions in training programs related to jobs. Identifying the functions related to life role performance may be more arbitrary than identifying functions necessary for a particular job, but the process and the type of product are much the same. Examples of role-related functions that have been developed by the Dayton School District in Oregon are presented in chart 5.1. The functions to be carried out within a role or job definition become the competencies to be demonstrated.

Specifying Indicators of Competence. An equally important activity, and one that is often taken too lightly, is identifying what kinds of evidence will be accepted as indicators of competence. In Oregon these specifications are referred to as "performance indicators." Functionally they point to categories of evidence to be collected and used as a basis for judging competency attainment. As used in Oregon, performance indicators are not the actual measures to be used in assessing competence.

In most competency-based education programs, the specified indicators of outcome attainment will only be examples of those that are acceptable. The range of expected outcomes is so great and the indicators are so varied that it is impossible to identify an exhaustive set for all possibilities. Nevertheless it is necessary to provide examples so that students, staff, and certifying officials will know what kind of achievement is expected and what the basis for judgments will be.

Developing Trustworthy Performance Measures. Once proper links between roles, functions, and performance indicators have been established, developing measures to assess a student's ability to perform the functions (competencies) within a particular role or job is reasonably straightforward. "Test item equivalents" that reflect the intent of each performance indicator are established, and from these the actual measure for each competence is created. Following are examples of test item equivalents that might be used to obtain "evidence that a student

Chart 5.1   Role-Related Competencies Being Considered by the Dayton (Oregon) Public Schools as Graduation Requirements

---

THE ROLE OF INDIVIDUAL

1. Able to communicate (read, write, speak, listen) at a level of proficiency that enables one to function effectively as an ADULT learner, producer, citizen, consumer, and family member
2. Able to apply basic computation skills at a level of proficiency that enables one to function effectively as an ADULT learner, producer, citizen, consumer, and family member
3. Able to establish and maintain a healthy body

THE ROLE OF LEARNER

1. Able to identify one's own interests and abilities in relation to 11 life roles
2. Able to learn independently
3. Able to apply logical processes to the solving of problems

THE ROLE OF CITIZEN

1. Able to describe one's own values in relation to the values that are dominant in one's community of residence
2. Able to identify the major needs of one's community of residence, and able to determine how best to contribute toward meeting those needs
3. Able to function as a responsible citizen on streets and highways

THE ROLE OF CONSUMER

1. Able to manage one's personal property and resources
2. Able to function as a wise and responsible consumer
3. Able to analyze the costs and benefits of alternative solutions to environmental problems

THE ROLE OF PRODUCER

1. Able to describe at least three occupations of interest, the short and long term benefits that go with them, and their requirements for entry and success
2. Able to assess with a reasonable degree of accuracy personal characteristics and abilities that relate to occupational success
3. Able to find and obtain work

THE ROLE OF FAMILY MEMBER

1. Able to cope with everyday stresses and problems
2. Able to function effectively as a member of a social group
3. Able to apply knowledge of the demands of marriage and family living to personal plans for career and marriage

---

Source: H. Del Schalock, *Alternative Models of Competency Based Education,* 2d ed. (Monograph prepared under National Institute of Education contract no. 400-76-0028 by the Oregon Competency Based Education Program, Salem, October 1976), p. 32; Bethesda, Md.: ERIC Document Reproduction Service, ED 147 951.

162

is able to use published resources, knowledgeable others, and consumer assistance agencies when doing comparative shopping":

- School-based measure: a report prepared by a student which identifies publications, persons in the community, and consumer assistance agencies that can be approached when making price and quality comparisons, and a discussion of how these various resources can best be used for this purpose
- Community-based measure: a report describing the actual use of such resources in making price and quality comparisons for goods and services[22]

One of the decisions program developers must make with respect to the assessment of competence is whether it will occur in real-life or simulated settings. Ideally, evidence should be obtained in real-life settings, for example, homemaker roles performed in a home, carpenter roles on a construction project, teacher roles in ongoing school settings, and citizenship roles in the community. However, since access to such real-life settings is often difficult to arrange, and evidence of performance is costly to obtain, something less than the ideal may have to do.

One alternative is to demonstrate the ability to perform role functions under simulated conditions. These may occur within such well-established laboratories as the woodworking and automotive shops or the homemaking facilities maintained by most schools, through simulation games that call for the application of knowledge and skill in social situations, or through other applied performance demonstrations that are in use or could be developed by a creative teacher.

Barring evidence of the ability to apply knowledge and skill in real-life or simulated settings, a school may accept the mastery of knowledge and skills *assumed to be needed* to perform role-related tasks competently. This of course is less persuasive as proof of competence, but may be the best that a school is able to manage.

While decisions a school makes about the definition and assessment of competence will always represent a trade between what is desired and what is possible, the value gained from strong definition and assessment should not be underestimated. The general assumption is that the stronger the evidence of competence, the better one can predict success in job or life roles following graduation, an assumption that becomes important for classroom instruction and for certification of what a student should be able to do after school. The relationship between the kind of evidence used to judge competence and the ability to predict success outside school settings is illustrated in figure 5.1.

Generally speaking, the rule to be followed in developing assessment systems for competency-based education programs is to measure desired performance under the most realistic conditions and in the most direct way possible. When the number of individuals to be tested is large, however, direct measurements are often too costly and time-consuming to manage.

Although the technology for assessing role or job performance is still relatively primitive, persons interested in implementing a role- or job-referenced competency-based education program will find assistance from two sources. The first is David McClelland's landmark article on testing for competence rather than intelligence.[23] In the last half of that article McClelland offers a series of far-reaching and sound suggestions as guides to the assessment of competence. The second is

Fig. 5.1   Alternative Measures as Predictors of Competence Outside the School

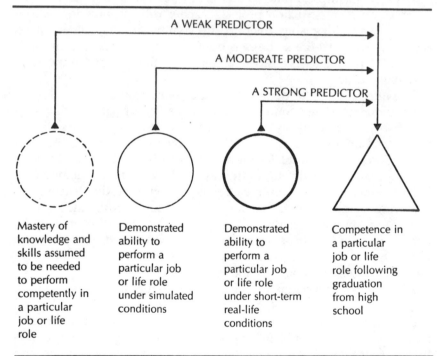

Source: H. Del Schalock, *Alternative Models of Competency Based Education* (Monograph prepared under National Institute of Education contract no. 400-76-0028 by the Oregon Competency Based Education Program, Salem, October 1976), p. 57; Bethesda, Md.: ERIC Document Reproduction Service, ED 147 951.

the Clearinghouse for Applied Performance Testing that has been established by the National Institute of Education at the Northwest Regional Educational Laboratory in Portland, Oregon. The Clearinghouse has been in operation for several years now, and has collected descriptive information about the nature of essentially all applied performance testing programs in the nation. As used by the Clearinghouse, applied performance tests are "designed to measure performance in an actual or simulated setting. In education, performance tests focus on the measurement of performance on tasks significant to a student's life outside the school or to adult life."[24]

Establishing Defensible Standards.   Having established measures that permit the meaningful assessment of role or job performance, there remains the task of setting standards against which performance is to be judged. Put in other terms, the level of proficiency to be required before a particular job or role performance is considered adequate must be decided. To complicate the matter, the question of standards must be addressed with respect both to the demonstration of individual competencies (the various functions to be performed within a life role or job description), and to performance of the role or job as a whole. Embedded in the issue of standards are such questions as these: Should the standards be treated as a minimally acceptable level of performance, or a higher level? How does one proceed to establish desired standards? How does one determine whether they are appropriate or sufficient?

As experience is gained with competency-based education programs, the issue of performance standards is gradually being recognized as one of the most complex for designers of competency. Pottinger states the issue well:

> The determination of criteria or standards of competence is one of the most difficult problems to be addressed. In every case, whether standards of competence of new or more traditional outcomes are determined, appropriate *levels* should be established by empirical evidence sufficient to ensure that they will not be viewed as arbitrary. Many educators have been satisfied with *a priori* judgments of what skills and levels of performance are adequate. It is startling to realize how much we accept the face validity of credentials and how little we really know about the correspondence between ability and levels of performance these credentials represent and what in fact is needed for adequate performance in life's tasks. We have no sound bench marks for evaluating the standards and offerings of postsecondary institutions.[25]

It is also being recognized that setting standards for demonstrating competencies is one of the least understood aspects of competency-based education. In an excellent review of the practices and issues involved, Larry Conaway concludes:

> Although increased attention has been given to the issue in the past few years, it is apparent that practitioners cannot obtain validated standard-setting procedures, either off-the-shelf or out of the literature. Instead, they must devise their own standard-setting procedures, relying upon their own experiences and philosophies in competency-based measurement and upon any guidance they can get from available literature and fellow practitioners.[26]

Conaway goes on to say that practitioners can obtain some information relevant to their standard-setting problems from the literature, but that

> they should not expect to find ready-to-use procedures that have been validated or undergone extensive use. Millman and Meskauskas each acknowledged that most passing scores have been set arbitrarily in the past, based upon such things as tradition and the intuition that the chosen score represents mastery but does not demand perfection. Kosecoff and Fink also found that most of the commercial criterion-referenced tests they reviewed either left the passing score decision to the test user or reported "mastery" and "non-mastery" scores based upon correctly answering an arbitrarily selected number of items per objective. At the present time there is no indication that the literature has had a great impact on practitioners, and conversely there is no indication that the practitioners have made major contributions to the literature.[27]

In setting standards, the initial focus is the level of proficiency required for each competency or function related to roles or jobs to be demonstrated, for this is the level at which performance indicators take their meaning. The complicating feature of this task is that learners can show they are competent to perform job or role functions only by demonstrating mastery of specified outcomes. In competency-based teacher education, for example, a teaching competency could be described as the demonstrated ability to bring about the *outcomes* expected from the *successful* performance of a teaching function. Those training prospective teachers would need to specify the outcomes expected of each teaching function.

Specifying the outcomes expected from the successful performance of a teaching or life role function is not a simple task! In part this is because educators are used to thinking in terms of process rather than outcomes. In part it is simply hard work. Moreover, it is a task that will not and need not yield similar results across programs. The designers or a teacher education program, for example, are free to identify the outcomes they expect from a particular teaching function, so outcome statements are likely to vary across programs even when they are dealing with the same function for the same general job description.

The definition of a competency in terms of the outcomes expected for the successful performance of a role or job function represents a major departure in thinking about education, *for it moves the criteria for competency to output rather than process.*

One of the nagging realities of assessing competencies within role or job preparation is that the ability to carry out one required function is one thing; the ability to carry out all functions and integrate them into successful role performance over time is quite another. To be judged competent as a teacher, for example, one would have to demonstrate the ability to carry out the various functions called for in a particular teaching position, and *also* demonstrate the ability to integrate them to meet the overall requirements of the position. The same would be true for high school students required to demonstrate their ability to function in life roles outside the school.

Unfortunately, there are no better guidelines for setting standards with respect to the performance of a role or job as a whole than there are for individual competencies. In a competency-based teacher education program, for example, such standards might require successful performance of *all* teaching functions within a particular position, or they might allow for uneven performance across functions. It also is possible to set them so that success is required only in a majority of functions, or in an essential set of functions, with uneven performance permitted in others.

Still another approach might require the successful performance of each function within a teaching position at least once, but permit any number of failures in the process of demonstrating the one successful performance.

It is evident from this discussion that there probably is no one preferred set of standards that could be applied to the performance of a particular role or job function, or performance in a role or job as a whole. In judging the competence of a teacher in a particular teaching position, the standards used may vary with the position that is being considered, the commitments of supervisors, or the standards of the institution or school district. The same would hold for the performance of persons in life roles generally. The critical point is that standards need to be established for performance in a job or life role as a whole, as well as for the performance of the individual functions. The two are related, but are not the same.

Whether life roles as a whole or separate functions are being considered, the issue of level of performance or proficiency must be addressed. Spady warns that in setting standards there will always be tension between required minimums and desirable maximums, especially when graduation depends upon the demonstration of competence according to whatever standards are set.[28] The assumptions underlying competency-based education are open on this issue, though most programs tend to have required minimums as performance standards.

Conaway points out that content and standards are two aspects of the problem of proficiency definition:

> In terms of content, if students are not required to be exposed to some areas (e.g., social studies, science, the arts) to graduate or if these areas receive much less instructional and evaluative emphasis, there is no way to assure reasonable attainment . . . if proficiency levels are set at low levels and if exit with full legal rights is provided for those who meet these standards, it is possible that many students will choose this route; and it may be found at a later date that this has adversely affected the individual or society. Either of these aspects may occur in a competency-based program, or both of them may be present.[29]

Conaway goes on to say that it is too soon to determine the effects of setting minimum performance standards for competency-based education programs, but there is clear cause for concern. A recent report of an interim committee established by the Oregon legislature to investigate the nature and effects of Oregon's competency requirements highlights the nature of the concern and why it is justified.[30]

CONDITIONS THAT COMPLICATE ASSESSMENT

If what has been said thus far is at all accurate, it is clear that fully functioning competency-based education programs would be very different in focus and operation from most elementary and secondary education programs that exist today. Implementation of competency-based education would simply require a new way of thinking about education and about the preparation of teachers. It would require a major restructuring of curriculum, instruction, and assessment procedures. Although individual programs would vary in emphasis and procedural detail, they would undoubtedly be much different from most educational programs as we now know them.

As complex as the assessment function appears to be within fully operational competency-based education programs, at least as that function has been outlined in the present chapter, the full measure of its complexity extends beyond what has been signaled in these pages. The purpose of this section is to describe two conditions that add immeasurably to the complexity of assessment within a role- or job-referenced competency-based education program.

Evolving Role or Job Definitions.   As indicated previously, the definition of a role- or job-referenced competency must be linked to a particular role or job function. Competence cannot be demonstrated abstractly. It must be demonstrated for a particular role or job that is played out in a particular context at a particular time. Since this is the case, competency-based education programs must assume that the functional demands of a role or position are reasonably constant across settings and time. Neither institutions nor students can afford to spend time and energy preparing for a role or position that is here today and gone tomorrow. For educational programs to be economically and functionally viable, there must be some assurance that the life roles or job positions serving as guides to program operation have a reasonable degree of stability.

The obvious problem is that this may not be the case! Role and job descriptions are constantly changing, which poses a dilemma for those who are responsible for designing competency-based education programs. If they adopt roles or positions that will no longer exist when students complete their programs or that do not emerge as anticipated, students are put at a great disadvantage and a great deal of energy stands to be wasted by individuals and institutions.

No simple solution to this dilemma exists, though program developers are engaged in futurist and manpower projections with a degree of seriousness not felt by most educational planners thus far. A serious commitment to role or job performance as a basis for the design of education programs requires dealing with issues that simply do not arise when the purpose of education is to help students develop basic skills or learn various bodies of subject matter. Given the reality of having to implement a role- or job-referenced competency-based education program, it should come as no surprise that only a handful of institutions or states have even attempted to do so.

Different Performance Styles and Conditions.   People, and the contexts in which they work and play, differ. Another truism is that some roles and job definitions are reasonably stable. Stable roles or job definitions, however, do not imply that individuals within those roles or jobs will perform them in the same manner. The designers of role- or job-referenced competency-based education programs must recognize that the *manner* in which a role or job is performed is not the primary focus of a competency assessment system. The style with which a thing gets done is important, but it is not as important as *how well* it gets done. The critical focus of a role- or job-referenced competency assessment system must be on the *outcomes achieved* with respect to a role or job held.

Competency assessment systems must accommodate not only individual differences in style, but also various conditions under which role or job performance is carried out. For instance, the ability to function effectively as a parent or spouse under tranquil conditions is one thing; to do so under adverse conditions is quite another. The same applies to performance in school, on the job, as a neighbor, or as a friend. The assessment of competence in the performance of a role or job must always take circumstances into account. There are no established guidelines for doing this, but experience has shown that competency assessment systems failing to take contextual factors into account are viewed by all concerned with a great deal of suspicion. Research on the effectiveness of workers in industry and of teachers in elementary schools points consistently to the impact of settings.[31]

CONDITIONS NECESSARY FOR ASSESSING ROLE PERFORMANCE

In order to implement a fully operational system for assessing role or job performance, a number of conditions must exist. The availability of appropriate measures and standards are only two of them. The following pages outline additional conditions that must be present if role or job performance is to be assessed effectively within the context of a competency-based educational program.

Contexts for Assessment. One of the major logistical requirements of a role- or a job-referenced competency-based education program is to establish contexts in which competency can be demonstrated and assessed. To demonstrate competence as a teacher, for example, one must have access to classrooms. To demonstrate competence as a consumer of goods and services, one must have opportunities to act as a consumer. Ideally, students should demonstrate their abilities under real-life conditions, but because of political, economic, or logistical considerations, simulation may have to be used instead.[32]

Another major logistical requirement, and one that has political as well as economic implications, is the necessity of having trained persons present as competence is demonstrated to determine whether performance adequately meets pre-established standards of performance. There are no rules or guidelines that govern who this should be, how many persons should be involved, or how they should go about making judgments. In fact, nothing requires that conclusions about competence be drawn at the time of performance. Electronic or written records can be kept so that quality can be assessed at a later time. Under either set of conditions, however, the introduction of observers raises a host of methodological issues. And if assessment occurs in real-life settings, these issues are often accompanied by political considerations.

As a means of overcoming the various problems associated with the assessment of role or job performance, program designers are beginning to look to the concept of assessment centers. These have been developed within the business community for purposes of identifying future managers, but they appear to hold considerable promise for competency-based education programs. William Byham describes a typical operation:

> In a typical center aimed at identifying the potential of first-level managers for middle-level management positions, 12 participants are nominated by their immediate supervisors as having potential based on their current job performance. For two days, participants take part in exercises developed to expose behaviors deemed important in the particular organization. A participant may play a business game, complete an in-basket exercise, participate in two group discussions and in an individual exercise, and be interviewed. Six assessors observe the participants' behavior and take notes on special observation forms. After the two days of exercises, participants go back to their jobs and the assessors spend two more days comparing their observations and making a final evaluation of each participant. A summary report is developed on each participant, outlining his or her potential and defining development action appropriate for both the organization and the individual.[33]

While the specific procedures used by the business community to select candidates for middle management positions may not be appropriate to the assessment of role or job performance in competency-based education programs, the concept has had sufficiently wide acceptance within business and industry that its potential should be explored.

Sampling Guidelines.   Under the best circumstances the assessment of competence in role or job performance will always be based on a sample of behavior observed in one or two contexts. Because of this, program designers must always decide how many contexts and how much behavior to sample. Does observing a teacher in one subject matter area with one set of children for an hour provide a sufficient sample of contexts and behaviors on which to judge competence? Would three observations in one subject area be better than three distributed across subject areas? Would three hours of observation distributed across three subject areas and repeated for two or three groups of children be better still? Obviously, the larger the sample of contexts and behaviors, the greater the confidence one can place in judgments about competence.

The issue must be resolved through compromise. There are practical limits to how many contexts and observations can be justified as an operational requirement for all students progressing through a competency-based education program. Somehow a balance must be struck between the practical and the ideal. As with so many issues discussed in this chapter, there are no commonly accepted guidelines for such matters; it must be left for the designers of particular programs to resolve. It can be anticipated that evidence will ultimately be available on the predictive validity of competency measures using various contexts and time samples; but until the evidence is in, each program must make the best compromise it can between what is desired and what can be obtained.

Measures Accommodating Differences.   Measures that accommodate different performance styles and settings must be available in a fully fuctioning program. The essentially unending variability in role or job definitions and functions and the impact of contexts and stylistic preferences demand that such measures be developed. The dilemma is that assessment measures must be flexible enough to accommodate variability and standard enough to give commonly accepted judgments about competence. Whatever form assessment procedures must take to achieve these ends, it is clear that they will not resemble the procedures reflected in standardized achievement and intelligence tests.

Standards Accommodating Differences.   The sources of variability in role or job performance must be accommodated without penalty. Operationally, this requires setting general standards for the demonstration of a particular role or job competence, then adapting them to meet the demands of specific situations by providing samples of the indicators of successful role or job performance in a particular situation.

Practically, this means that *program level* standards established for a given role or job must be free of content and context. Standards at this level can function only as guides to what must be demonstrated. The substance and context enter the picture as *specific indicators* of the successful performance of a *specific role or job*. Two practical consequences result from this. First, only *sample* indicators of satisfactory role or job performance are provided at the program level. Second, a great deal of trust must be placed in persons making on-site judgments about the adequacy of role or job performance. Since no absolute standards of competence in role or job performance exist, and only sample indicators can be provided, on-site professional judgment becomes a critical ingredient in the process of assessing competence.

Realistic Time Lines.   States or institutions attempting to implement a competency-based program of the kind described in the present volume need to be realistic about the time lines involved. This is particularly important with respect to a fully functioning assessment system. Identifying the outcomes to be achieved through a competency-based education program is a time-consuming task in itself. Establishing instructional programs that facilitate the development of these outcomes and assessment systems to determine outcome attainment are still more time-consuming. Pilot efforts will have to be carried out on both instruction and assessment systems, and refinements will be needed for many years. Experience in the arena of competency-based teacher education has shown that at least five years are needed for such programs to become fully operational. Oregon's experience in attempting to convert elementary and secondary programs to a competency-based mode of operation suggests that five years may be a conservative estimate.

The point is that shifting to a competency-based mode of operation at any level of education is an unusually complex process; and unless the time and energy required are perceived realistically, there is danger that programs will be judged as failures before they have received a reasonable test.

NOTES

1. See H. Del Schalock, *Alternative Models of Competency Based Education*.

2. George F. Madaus and Peter W. Airasian, "Issues in Evaluating Student Outcomes in Competency-Based Graduation Programs," p. 83. All quotations by permission.

3. See Abraham Kaplan, *The Conduct of Inquiry: Methodology for Behavioral Science*.

4. See William G. Spady, "The Concept and Implications of Competency-Based Education," pp. 16–22.

5. See Madaus and Airasian, p. 81.

6. See Spady, p. 21.

7. Larrie E. Gale and Gaston Pol, "Competence: A Definition and Conceptual Scheme," p. 20. Used by permission.

8. William G. Spady, "Competency-Based Education: A Bandwagon in Search of a Definition," p. 11. Copyright 1977, American Educational Research Assn., Washington, D.C. All quotations by permission.

9. Paul S. Pottinger, *Comments and Guidelines for Research in Competency Identification, Definition and Measurement,* p. 12. All quotations by permission.

10. Ibid., p. 13.

11. Madaus and Airasian, p. 86.

12. Pottinger, p. 23.

13. Ibid., p. 22.

14. Joseph L. Boyd, Jr., and Benjamin Shimberg, *Developing Performance Tests for Classroom Evaluation,* p. 3.

15. Ibid.

16. Pottinger, pp. 7–8.

17. Ibid., p. 10.

18. William G. Spady and Douglas E. Mitchell, "Competency-Based Education: Organizational Issues and Implications," p. 13. Copyright 1977, American Educational Research Assn., Washington, D.C. Used by permission.

19. The content of this section has been adapted in large part from H. Del Schalock, "Defining and Assessing Teacher Competence" (unpublished paper).

20. The treatment of work descriptions is always arbitrary. Job definitions and functions to be performed, for example, may be extremely broad or narrow. In describing work, five levels of differentiation are commonly employed: jobs; functions (the largest units of work within a job); activities (the largest units of work within a function); tasks (the largest units of work within an activity); and actions (the largest units of work within a task). While no hard-and-fast boundaries surround any of these levels of differentiation, they are intended to indicate the level of detail at which a particular analysis of work is focusing.

21. A competent teacher is one who performs satisfactorily all or the majority of the functions included within a particular position; a teacher demonstrates a competency by demonstrating the ability to perform successfully a given function.

22. Adapted from Schalock, *Alternative Models,* p. 34.

23. See David C. McClelland, "Testing for Competence Rather Than for Intelligence."

24. Clearinghouse for Applied Performance Testing, *Applied Performance Testing: What Is It? Why Use It?* p. 4.

25. See Pottinger, p. 18.

26. Larry E. Conaway, "Setting Standards in Competency-Based Education: Some Current Practices and Concerns," p. 1.

27. Ibid., pp. 7–8.

28. See Spady, "Competency-Based Education: A Bandwagon."

29. Conaway, p. 14.

30. See Joint Interim Task Force on Minimum Competencies/Graduation Requirements, *Report*.

31. See Edwin E. Ghiselli and Clarence W. Brown, *Personnel and Industrial Psychology;* and Walter Doyle, "Paradigm for Research on Teacher Effectiveness."

32. For references to simulations used in various fields, see Clearinghouse for Applied Performance Testing, *Annotated Bibliography;* and H. Del Schalock, "Situational Response Testing," pp. 163–83.

33. William Byham, "The Assessment Center as an Aid in Management Development," p. 10. Reproduced by special permission from the December 1971 *Training and Development Journal*. Copyright 1971 by the American Society for Training and Development, Inc.

6

Competency-Based Education and Secondary Schools:
Current Practice and Some Implications

SCOTT THOMSON

EDITOR'S INTRODUCTION

This chapter makes one point very clear: Practice in secondary schools at this time is overwhelmingly focused on minimum competency testing rather than on the broader concepts characterizing more sophisticated programs. Why? Because secondary education is using minimum competency testing as a quality control device in response to public pressure. The public generally wants confirmation that the schools can teach, and does not consider restructuring a means to this end.

At the heart of Thomson's thesis is the view, shared by many administrators and practitioners, that minimum competency testing *is* a *part* of competency-based education, even if it is a modest effort. Consequently, schools have made very few of the structural changes that characterize many programs in postsecondary education and outside the schools. Minimum competency testing verifies student achievement in certain basic subject matter areas, and schools have embraced it. But few have seriously undertaken basic restructuring.

"Few secondary schools, indeed, have used the competency-based concept to rethink their goals, to reorganize their curriculum, to re-study their credit requirements, and to realign their evaluation systems on a performance-based model." With these words the author prefaces a review of the "many faces of competency-based education" in secondary schools and of some of the implications and some of the promise that wearing of the masks involves. And, as a prelude to discussion of current activities, worthy of examination because they represent what *is*, Thomson tempts us with a sketch of what *might be*: a new learning system based on the broad application of a competency-based education philosophy.

This new approach would clarify learning objectives and their relation to real-life adult roles, take advantage of opportunities to use new learning environments, give students credit for performing rather than merely spending time in classes, support continuous progress toward documented outcomes, and test students' ability to apply knowledge to life situations rather than their ability simply to memorize and recall facts.

Acknowledging that such an effort will not be easy, the author explains why this is so. Several social and cultural issues are contributing to a focus on "accountability"—a direct result of public disenchantment with schooling. These issues include doubts about schools' effectiveness, expectations for documentation of results, and the swiftly changing nature of the even more widely ranging young people who are or ought to be in schools.

In a second section, the author reviews the stated goals for secondary education over the past fifty years. As he remarks, they have remained very stable. What does vary to some degree, is the instructional content designed to achieve them, as well as some of the processes employed.

Next, the activities of specific schools are described. Strikingly different perceptions of competency are reflected by examples of the objectives of their assessment practices. The content range of the tests covers basic skills and some life skills, but the predominent method for evaluation, for obvious reasons, is still the paper-and-pencil test. Fortunately, there are a few examples of programs that require demonstrations of competence in appropriate settings. Advantages and disadvantages of these approaches are discussed, and some results of the effects of minimum competency testing on student performance are reported.

Then, stepping beyond the current scene, the author gives us a vision of the future. He lists some administrative and structural changes that will be necessary to implement a comprehensive program that goes beyond the goals of minimum competency testing. We envision community learning stations established and maintained by citizens; expanded guidance services to improve diagnostics and to broker learning experiences; professional review committees to verify competence; and computerized record systems to track students' continuous progress.

Such changes are exciting to imagine. They are also significant. Before they can become a reality, many questions must be asked and difficult decisions must be made. Certainly such a serious undertaking requires important research and development efforts. What are the implications of moving in this direction? Can we afford not to?

R.S.N.

O NE GOOD illustration of the adage that a profession is defined not by its literature but by its practice is provided by an analysis of competency-based learning and its relationship to secondary education today. This is not to argue that empirical definitions necessarily are more valid than conceptual definitions. It does, however, point out that conceptual definitions tend to go considerably beyond empirical practice. It is inordinately easier to conceive a system, or even to establish it, than to make that system perform as desired on location!

The tendency for people and established institutions to modify the most elegant of constructs is especially common in the field of education. Social realities cause accommodations to be made; and the forces playing upon secondary schools are especially powerful. To begin with, the students are in transition toward adulthood—physically, emotionally, economically, legally, and socially. Public debate about the purpose of schooling is relentless. Public priorities themselves shift year by year. Little agreement exists concerning the most effective pedagogies, and serious questions arise as to the impact of schooling upon youth in any event. The list of uncertainties extends straight to the foundation disciplines of education. It ranges from the physiology of thought processes to the psychology of learning, from contending philosophies to conflicting values.

A concept called "competency-based education" enters this unsettled scene. Little wonder that definitions tend to range widely. Small agreement exists, even among the more ardent advocates, as to its constituent elements and their derivation. The objectives of competency-based education are in dispute, as are its processes and their applications.

One point is clear, however. Competency-based education as it developed in schools during the decade of the 1970s tended to be limited to minimum competency testing. With few exceptions, the focus of competency testing fell upon the basic cognitive skills of reading, writing, and computation. To most of the public, and to the profession, competency-based education meant competency testing to determine student achievement in certain subject fields, not a broad application of the concept of competency. Consequently the structure of schools has remained virtually unchanged even in states where competencies of various sorts were required for the diploma.

Few secondary schools, indeed, have used the competency-based concept to rethink their goals, to reorganize their curriculum, to re-study their credit requirements, and to realign their evaluation systems on a performance-based model. Rather, the schools have applied minimum competency testing as a kind of quality control device in response to public demands for accountability. It became a vehicle to provide specific answers to some hard questions about student achievement in the traditional subject areas and in certain life skills. The school campus continued to be the location for learning, and classes continued to be held 180 days a year for all students regardless of individual performance. Competency-based education has come to mean minimum competency testing to most of the nation.

This rather cautious approach to competency-based education, as an empirical fact, should come as no surprise, given the conditions at hand. The public of the late 1970s was not in an experimental mood about schools, given the questionable outcomes of many innovations of the late 1960s and early 1970s. Concern about rising crime rates and lower test scores in schools reinforced notions that schools were becoming inadequately controlled, and too costly, and led by teachers of marginal effectiveness. Add to this the contending definitions of competency-based education and the dearth of visible models actually operating in comprehensive high schools: the circumstances clearly point to a circumspect, rather than a bold, approach to the concept. Most practitioners would at this time urge theorists to define, clarify, and agree upon the constituent elements of competency-based education for adolescents attending a comprehensive high school. An appropriate administrative framework is also necessary. Principals do not feel comfortable "working out the details" of these matters, on-site, for legal minors and their cautious, critical parents.

THE MANY FACES OF COMPETENCY-BASED EDUCATION

Considering purposes alone, it is possible to identify at least five content objectives and five social objectives for competency-based education. These objectives may be relatively modest (e.g. teaching cognitive skills to remedial students) or they may be very ambitious (e.g. preparing students fully for the many contingencies of adulthood).

Other definitions of purpose for competency-based education are less singular. They may include three or four objectives concurrently, such as the application of basic skills to qualify for the diploma as well as for purposes of grade promotion. The full potential of objectives advanced for competency-based education is illustrated by the matrix in figure 6.1.

Fig. 6.1   Potential Objectives for Competency-Based Education

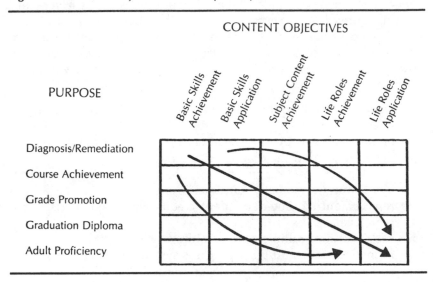

These 25 objectives need not be mutually exclusive, but their individual expression is represented by the various definitions of competency-based education found in the literature and operating in schools. Commonality in this respect does not exist either among theorists or among practitioners; and it is from this reality that the application of the concept of competency-based education to secondary education must be viewed.

Some observers define competency-based education as essentially an evaluation system based on outcomes and not a philosophy of education.[1] Others describe it as a comprehensive learning system involving objectives, processes, and evaluation systems, with the potential for a powerful impact upon secondary education.[2] Still others describe definitional points along a continuum spanning simple assessment through revolutionary change. Some persons even see competencies as learning objectives rather than as models of education or evaluation.

The definitions of competency-based education are so fluid, in fact, that they tend more to reflect the philosophical biases of the writers than to represent coherent, independent constructs. Many enthusiasts see the competency-based approach as a vehicle to steer education in a direction of their own choosing. Consequently, it is inaccurate to label it as progressive or conservative, as child-centered or curriculum-centered. It is any or all of these, depending upon the advocate.

Despite these definitional problems—or perhaps in part because of them—ideas about competency-based education suggest a very interesting potential for secondary education. Looking beyond the schools' current involvement with minimum competency testing, a broad application of the competencies philosophy could result in a flexible and responsive learning system for students. These would be among its advantages:

- clarification of learning objectives and their relationship to adult roles
- opportunities to pursue learning in a variety of environments depending upon the objectives at hand
- development of a diagnostic and program-planning service to identify and remediate deficiencies
- replacement of time-dependent credits with credits based on performance
- provision for multiple opportunities to document outcomes
- formation of a continuous-progress system of student advancement
- development of testing environments that reflect life situations

The implications of such a system, fully implemented, are enormous. A significant restructuring of secondary schools would result. Delivery systems would become extremely flexible, joining and rejoining subject fields, depending upon the performance objectives at hand. Students could pursue learning in a variety of school and community contexts. Graduation might come in three years for some students, five years for others. Teachers would diagnose and propose alternative learning situations as well as instruct students. Various forms of contracts for learning would define expectations and mutual obligations. The focus in all this would be verified performance based upon predetermined criteria approved by the school and its teachers.

Such changes would come like a revolution to most of the nation's secondary schools. While many ideal elements are contained in competency-based education, the transition from current practice would extend into uncharted waters. For example, the schools' difficulties with independent study for students have given rise to new caveats about the questionable ability of the majority of adolescents to study unless supervised by persons as well as by structure. Provision for continuous progress in learning, recognized as ideal from the standpoint of student motivation, can create a nightmare of logistical problems for teachers, registrars, and administrators.

Concerns about the practical applicability of competency-based education to a large comprehensive high school, together with the lack of definitional concurrence among theorists, might suggest that little movement can be expected toward competency-based schools. Why, then, is enthusiasm so widespread today for minimum competency testing which is one form—perhaps an initial form—of competency-based education? Why do the advocates of education for competencies represent such a broad spectrum of educational and social philosophies? (And why do their critics, in fact, represent a similar range?) What do teachers, parents, board members, administrators, and the general citizenry expect to gain by shifting secondary education to a competency base? What are the visions? Where are the energies and the rewards?

COMMON INTERESTS, DIVERSE PERSPECTIVES

While the forces supporting competency-based education are manifold, basically they intersect at six points:

- dissatisfaction with the anomie infecting secondary education
- expectations for documenting the outcomes of schooling
- growth of consumerism in society
- new consensus about priorities for schools
- transitional needs of today's youth
- evolution of a pedagogical emphasis upon individualization and experiential learning

Anomie and Secondary Education.   Significant sectors of the public appear to be disenchanted with the schools.[3] Their attitude may be expressed by a negative tax vote or by other acts. Frequently they have a feeling of disengagement, of discomfort about the perceived drift in secondary education. The old confidence in schools has waned. As schools have assumed more social responsibilities, their instructional responsibilities have become blurred.[4] Citizens have begun to view schools less clearly and have developed doubts about their effectiveness. To the public eye, secondary education seems weakened by a certain formlessness.

Competency-based education promises to sharpen the definitions. Some tangible outlines could be restored to secondary education, proponents argue, with a competencies approach. Thus Barbara Lasser and Allan Olson describe competency-based education as a management process that aims at bringing greater precision to objectives and methodology through evaluation.[5] William Spady concurs, asserting that

> CBE takes the surprises out of the instructional-certification process by encouraging collaborative decision making regarding goals, by placing these goals "up front" as guides for both teachers and learners, and by attaching those goals to explicit and reasonably concrete behavioral referents.[6]

Such descriptions offer hope to critics of various hue, who have felt schools are flabby with humanism, insufficiently articulated to motivate students, too badly designed to accommodate individualities, or merely aimless. For those who desire precise definitions, competency-based education has a pragmatic appeal. It offers a container to shape the soft outline.

Documenting Outcomes. The public displays an increasingly strong inclination to hold institutions accountable for results. Private sector personnel have historically been expected to produce tangible outcomes; now this yardstick is being applied to the public sector as well:

> No social program gets governmental approval these days without an accountability clause—some requirement to evaluate the people who administer the program (social workers, counselors, teachers, politicians). These "helping agents" must account for their success or failure either to those who request the service (supervisors, the government, the taxpaying public) or to those who receive it (the poor, the sick, the unskilled). The rationale for these evaluative measures is that people who are responsible for their efforts will work harder and more efficiently in order to gain praise from their bosses or clients and to keep their jobs; accountable agents should thus be more attentive to their clients' needs.[7]

The accountability mood of today's public probably is not a simple fancy. Its roots lie in a strong behavioral base. The most modern personnel evaluation practices, both in the private sector and in government, include job targets or other approaches to articulated objectives for professionals in service occupations as well as in the industrial world. The establishment and attainment of performance objectives for much of middle-class America has modified thinking about the outcomes of schooling. Many people are saying, "If we can do it in our organization, then why can't the schools? I want some tangible objectives for schooling in return for paying my tax bill."

This hardening of purposes is one part of the "back to basics" movement. The current interest in cognitive skills relates to new accountability systems for the teaching of basic skills, and it derives primarily not from political conservatism but from a new sophistication in connection with evaluating the performance of individuals and institutions. Citizens want from schools what their jobs require of them. They expect a report on the outcomes, and one opportunity for realizing these expectations is to tie learning outcomes to graduation requirements or grade promotions.

Consumerism in Education. Citizens also want a voice in determining the shape and quality of outcomes. The consumerism movement has hit education with noticeable force. The quality of the schools' product has become a national issue.[8]

The consuming public demands that schools be responsible for more than reflecting citizen interests in the curriculum, lowering energy costs, or accommodating new social goals. It also demands a product free of defects. It wants high school graduates to be personally and vocationally proficient. Functional illiterates—the drones of education—are no longer acceptable. Consumer advocacy has come to secondary schools.

Some school districts have responded directly to these demands. For instance, the Salt Lake City schools now practice a policy of open disclosure, which informs parents, students, and community citizens of the objectives of each course and the skills to be learned in each course. Student progress reporting is conducted within this framework.[9] Thus consumers may decide whether or not they are receiving the quality of goods they have been asked to pay for.

Public Consensus. For secondary schools, the "basics"—if this means the important things—are defined in countless ways, depending upon the philosophical orientation of the writer. Certainly the three Rs are included in most statements, either explicitly or implicitly. But the "basics" for public schools turn out to be more complicated than the neatly written statements. They tend to reflect the priorities of the times, and these shift with public policy.[10] If schools fail to respond to these priorities, then school board members are replaced and administrators are dismissed.

The "basics" for schools in the late 1950s included improved math and science instruction. During most of the 1960s they encompassed racial desegregation, First Amendment rights for students, "relevant" curricula, and less structure. By the middle 1970s the public understanding of "basics" had taken a new turn. People wanted to reverse the decline in test scores and to assure that students could read, write, and compute. The question at school board meetings ceased to be "What is your dropout rate?" It became "What are your reading scores?"[11]

Today consensus about the priorities for schools is focused upon the basic cognitive skills.[12] The public apparently wants schools to pull reading, writing, and arithmetic out of the pack of competing concerns and place them up front. If schools do nothing else, the common argument goes, then at least they should teach the basic skills. This new consensus forms a relatively straightforward priority for schools, in contrast to the cacophony of the competing and imprecise demands of the past decade. It is a small step from establishing this priority to expecting specific documentation of its attainment through competency testing either by the application of those skills or by more traditional means.

Transitional Youth.   During the late 1960s and early 1970s student activism shook loose some old perceptions about the political and social outlook of youth. Many adults attempted to respond constructively to various student demands, but a strong unease remained. The new patterns seemed contradictory and unclear. Events may have troubled youth, but the causes and effects of hyperactivism distressed adults even more. Somehow the force of the movement seemed more pervasive than could rationally be explained by the Vietnam conflict or by experimentation with strong drugs.

Two reports, *Youth: Transition to Adulthood*[13] and the report of the National Panel on High Schools and Adolescent Education,[14] did much to clear the air. These reports asserted that the youth subculture with its attendant behaviors was a product of the larger social environment rather than of one or two separate sources. The social circumstances of youth were summarized as follows:

> Youth are segregated from adults by the economic and educational institutions created by adults, they are deprived of psychic support from persons of other ages, a psychic support that once came from the family, they are subordinate and powerless in relation to adults, and outsiders to the dominant social institutions. Yet they have money, they have access to a wide range of communications media, and control of some; and they are relatively large in number.[15]

Educators began to realize that schools play a part in this segregation. The trend in secondary education over the past hundred years has been to keep students in school to a later age. Meanwhile, opportunities in the adult working world have become limited. As youth have grown more and more segregated from adult society, the transition to that society has become more difficult. Youth have found themselves fenced off by abstract, passive, synthetic experiences. The formal and informal links of earlier years between adults and youth have been broken.

The most immediate response to these and other reform reports was to reestablish links through community-based work and service experiences. This led, in turn, to a focus upon marketable skills, adult proficiencies, job training, and other performance indicators common to the business and professional world. Secondary education began to pay more attention to performance on the job and to the evaluation of specific performance objectives. As schools became comfortable with performance evaluation systems for students in the community, it was a small step to applying this technique to sharpen evaluation practices within the school. Easing the transition of youth to adult settings in turn caused school programs to accept competency-based procedures.

Individualizing Student Achievement.   The sixth major force moving schools toward competency-based education has been the evolution of the pedagogical ideal of individualized education. An individualized approach to learning advanced beyond rhetoric as schools established behavioral course objectives, experimented with computer-assisted instruction, flirted with programmed learning, launched independent study projects using learning packages, and organized continuous-progress curricula. The sum of these efforts has forced schools to articulate objectives more clearly and to document their attainment more carefully. As secondary education had begun to group students less by age and time, schools have begun to pay more attention to performance measures.

By emphasizing goals over traditional student roles, and by expanding learning opportunities for students, the new approaches to individualization have moved schools toward competency-based education. According to Lorin Miller, competency-based education encourages new outcomes, individualization, and community learning, thus providing stimulation for development of the very program it was established to evaluate.[16]

While it may be argued that all education that encounters formal evaluation is competency based, individualized approaches to learning require that the evaluation systems be tightened and made more specific. Outcomes must be defined precisely. Competency-based evaluation systems meet those specifications.

The relationship of cognitive achievement to individualization of instruction is sufficiently close that the Wisconsin Research and Development Center for Cognitive Learning, the large federally funded effort to improve learning in secondary schools, has been renamed the Wisconsin R&D Center for Individualized Schooling.[17] Competency-based evaluation systems are used by such affiliates of the center as Hood River Valley High School in Oregon.

The pedagogical roots of competency-based education extend beyond the new efforts at individualization, to be sure. They can be found in technical and vocational education, in cooperative education programs, in the military service schools, and even in the course examination "practicals" of the land grant colleges where students two generations ago were required to provide actual demonstrations of concepts and techniques taught in class.

These six forces fueling the movement toward a competency-based accountability for the outcomes of schooling must contend with another reality of American society: the continuing central goals of secondary education. These goals act as a framework around which all contemporary pressures and forces must flow.

GOALS FOR SECONDARY EDUCATION

Despite the constant changes in American society, the central goals for secondary education have remained extraordinarily stable for many years. When commissions meet to develop broad goals for secondary schools, their formal statements convey a common emphasis. From the *Cardinal Principles of Secondary Education*, published in 1918 by the Commission on the Reorganization of Secondary Education, to *The Reform of Secondary Education*, published in 1973 by the National Commission on the Reform of Secondary Education, the similarities are striking. Chart 6.1 illustrates the comparability of these two landmark documents.

The two lists are closely related except that the 1973 version includes two distinctly new goals: "critical thinking" and "environmental understanding." The central purposes of secondary education, then, have tended, even as new routes to learning have been charted and recharted, to remain essentially fixed.

General acceptance of these purposes has been confirmed by annual Gallup polls on education. When asked what requirements, if any, they would set for graduation from high school for those students who do not plan to go on to college, the American people in 1978 indicated the priorities shown in chart 6.2. These opinions support the first four of the seven *Cardinal Principles* and eight of the thirteen goals for the *Reform of Secondary Education*.

Basic skills, good health, career preparation, and civic competence— these are the areas of secondary schooling that the public takes most seriously. When these goals are combined with social forces, the significance of their relationship becomes apparent. Competency test-

Chart 6.1   Comparison of Educational Goals in 1918 and 1973

Cardinal Principles of Secondary Education (1918)*	Goals for Reform of Secondary Education (1973)**
I. Health	Ability to adjust to change
II. Fundamental processes	Achievement of communication skills Achievement of computation skills
III. Vocation	Acquisition of occupational competence
IV. Civic education	Acceptance of responsibility for citizenship Respect for law and authority Appreciation of others Economic understanding
V. Home membership	Knowledge of self
VI. Use of leisure	Clarification of values
VII. Ethical character	Appreciation of the achievements of man Attainment of proficiency in critical and objective thinking Clear perception of nature and environment

*Source: Commission on the Reorganization of Secondary Education, *Cardinal Principles of Secondary Education,* Bulletin no. 25 (Washington, D.C.: U.S. Government Printing Office, 1918), pp. 11–16.
**Source: National Commission on the Reform of Secondary Education, *The Reform of Secondary Education,* ed. B. Frank Brown (New York: McGraw-Hill Book Co., 1973), pp. 32–34.

ing, as it has developed, is not a peripheral movement. Rather, it weds the most important purposes of secondary education with powerful historical pressures.

There should be no surprise, then, about the rapid growth of competency testing. The movement is advanced more by public perception of the public weal than by intellectual forces attempting to establish a useful conceptual model. If the movement appears to have loose ends and contradicting definitions, this is caused not merely by varying perspectives on "minimums" but also by its formation amidst the heat and dust swirling around hundreds of schools as they thrash in desperate response to public pressures.

This review of the goals of secondary education also helps explain why school boards and practicing educators have embraced life role versions of minimum competency testing less enthusiastically than the

Chart 6.2 Responses to 1978 Gallup Poll on Graduation Requirements

	Very Important %	Fairly Important %	Not Important %	Don't Know or No Answer %
How important is it that these students . . .				
. . . be able to write a letter of application using correct grammar and correct spelling?	90	9	*	1
. . . be able to read well enough to follow an instruction manual for home appliances?	86	12	1	1
. . . know enough arithmetic to be able to figure out such a problem as the total square feet in a room?	84	14	1	1
. . . know the health hazards of smoking, use of alcohol, marijuana, and other drugs?	83	14	2	1
. . . have a salable skill, such as typing, auto mechanics, nurse's aide, business machines?	79	17	3	1
. . . know something about the U.S. government, the political parties, voting procedures?	66	30	3	1
. . . know something about the history of the U.S., such as the Constitution, Bill of Rights, and the like?	61	31	7	1
. . . know something about the major nations of the world today, their kind of government, and their way of life?	42	46	10	2
. . . know something about the history of mankind, the great leaders in art, literature?	30	48	21	1
. . . know a foreign language?	16	32	50	2

Source: George H. Gallup, "The 10th Annual Gallup Poll of the Public's Attitudes Toward the Public Schools," *Phi Delta Kappan* 60 (September 1978): 40.
*Less than 1%

teaching or application of basic skills. Of the five content objectives named in figure 6.1, "life roles" application and achievement take a back seat to "basic skills" and "subject content." Life roles simply are not a central target for schools as conceived by the public, which currently lacks the patience or the dollars to focus upon peripheral purposes. Moreover, strong suspicions are aroused when the state proposes social role standards and instructional treatment thereof. Many citizens do not want governing bodies shaping life role behavior except in extremely broad terms. Some people object because they see potential value conflict; others view the prescription of social role outcomes as a totalitarian device inimical to individual self-determination. As Leonard Waks points out:

> . . . when the compulsory school, an instrument of state power, frames up minimal conceptions of acceptable parenting behavior, and even minimally correct uses of leisure time, and sets in motion compulsory treatments effective in establishing these minimum competencies and tests to ascertain success, the question "by what right?" arises immediately. The state will find no justification for such practices in existing democratic theory.[18]

Although arguments could be made that the "general welfare" clause of the Constitution would permit schools to engage in some life role curricula, the elections of the late 1970s indicated that the public would favor limiting the programs and powers of government. Citizens apparently want fewer, not more, initiatives and prescriptions from government. They prefer that students *first* be taught traditional cognitive skills and that these *then* be applied to practical activities. People want schools to develop tools for students, not blueprints. The commission members who developed the seven *Cardinal Principles*, more than 60 years ago, may continue to rest in comfort.

COMPETENCY TESTING IN PRACTICE

With many philosophical schisms evident among the advocates of competency-based education, it was to be expected that the movement—insofar as it was *a* movement—would soon be all but exhausted by internecine conflict. The traditionalists have wanted strong instruction in basic skills, the moderates have sought more affective objectives, and the progressives have proposed that schools should plan individual student programs in rather broad social terms and hold records (if in fact schools are required at all to provide an education oriented toward specified outcomes).

Yet the minimum competency testing movement has grown vigorously over the past decade; by 1978 it had become a force in secondary education in all 50 states.[19] Why is this so? What factors constitute the common appeal? Most citizens are not much interested in the fine points of educational methodology. Theoretical models, however elegant, are viewed with little interest and much suspicion. But people appreciate that minimum competency testing does focus upon expected outcomes. The public wants results in the form of adequate cognitive and occupational skills; and minimum competency testing is clearly oriented towards results.

The public also appreciates that minimum competency testing provides a vehicle for gaining agreement on common priorities for schools at the operational level. Traditionally, most goal statements have been far up on the ladder of abstraction and accordingly difficult to track through to outcomes.

The emergence of competency testing from a developmental-empirical base, as distinguished from a conceptual base, is illustrated by the variety of competency-oriented programs advanced by the 50 states. While theorists propose various refined models, even more various forms of minimum competency testing are taking shape, piece by piece, throughout the land.

Some theorists argue that a full and legitimate competency-based curriculum must cut across different subject areas, provide opportunity for individualized learning, span a sequence of grade levels, and incorporate real-world experience. Spady, for instance, defines it as

> a data-based, adaptive, performance-oriented set of integrated processes that facilitate, measure, record, and certify within the context of flexible time parameters the demonstration of known, explicitly stated, and agreed upon learning outcomes that reflect successful functioning in life roles.[20]

Actualization of this definition would of course constitute a revolution in secondary education. It implies redirected goals, revised methodology, modified structures, and comprehensive evaluation systems. Neither the public nor practicing professionals have embraced this or other such ambitious definitions, however. The tendency has been to focus upon more limited objectives, such as teaching students to read and compute. The possibilities for competency-based education as described by theorists do not appear to intrigue the public. Rather, people prefer to focus upon improved confirmation systems for current objectives and practice. Their concern is to improve reading and math scores, not to restructure schooling.

Actions by state legislatures or boards of education have emphasized the basic skills and their application. Programs that began more ambitiously, such as Oregon's, which was devised in answer to a mandate to teach to certain life roles, have been modified or else moved toward postponed implementation. It is infinitely easier to conceptualize a learning system than it is to make that system perform as desired.

STATE-MANDATED COMPETENCY PROGRAMS

A survey of activity by states[21] shows five different approaches to competency-based education at the secondary school level. These approaches can be briefly characterized in these terms:

- basic skills
- life roles
- equivalency tests
- external programs
- external examinations

By June 1978, some 24 states had mandated competency testing programs, and 15 more had authorized the development and use of competency tests by local districts. Without exception, reading competencies were part of the mandate for each of these states. Mathematics was included in all but three states, and writing in all but four. Only ten states required competency in citizenship or government, and only seven required competency in consumerism, which represents a precipitous drop in consensus. Clearly, the states are focusing upon basic skills rather than on the other possibilities for competency-based education as outlined in the matrix of objectives in figure 6.1.

Basic Skills. The application of basic skills in terms of functional literacy is the most common mandate, with Arizona's eighth-grade reading requirement being a prominent exception. The purposes for which basic skills mastery is sought, however, range from simple diagnosis and remediation to grade promotion, graduation, and limited adult proficiency. Some states, such as New York, require the use of tests developed by the state, whereas others, including California and Idaho, allow districts the option of using tests selected locally or at the state level.

Life Roles. Oregon, the first state to initiate competency testing programs tied to the diploma, has been the leading advocate of life role competencies. In addition to using the basic skills, graduates of Oregon high schools are expected to be competent in maintaining health, acting as informed citizens, being informed consumers, using scientific processes, and functioning in an occupation or advanced educational setting. These life role requirements have now been postponed until 1981.

With the development of Project Basic, Maryland is the second state to work toward life role competencies. This competency-based plan supplements basic skills with four other areas:

- *survival skills*, to include consumer competencies, parenting skills, mechanical skills, and interpersonal proficiencies
- *world of work*, to include skills and attitudes for success in the job world
- *world of leisure*, to include constructive use of leisure by proficiencies in lifetime sports and the arts
- *citizenship*, to include understanding and participating in the political and legal systems[22]

Both Maryland and Oregon are tying these life competencies to the high school diploma. In neither case, however, is a full competency-based educational program under development. Rather, the thrust is toward assuring competencies at the threshold level only. Traditional courses such as English and U.S. history still are required. Student achievement in these courses typically is evaluated by norm-referenced measures.

A full competency-based curriculum tied to life roles would need to recognize specific occupational requirements as well as general occupational requirements. For example, a person aspiring to be a research chemist or an engineering salesman would need certain specific mathematical competencies as well as general attitudes related to successful employment. In a school of a thousand or more students, the sum of these requirements, added to specific and general citizenship, leisure, consumer, and family skill requirements, would cause a highly complex instructional and reporting system. Conceivably there could be literally thousands of sets of combinations to meet the various life role expectations of a thousand students. Schools have hesitated to move toward a full competency-based curriculum resting upon life roles because of the severe logistical and administrative problems involved. Most schools in Oregon, for example, have moved to a computer tracking system just to monitor the 20 minimum competency areas required for a diploma in that state. Twenty-one subjects are required, as well, that include competency test criteria.

The difficulty of defining life role competencies beyond minimum levels creates another problem for schools aspiring to a life role approach. Clearly, significant theoretical work is also needed prior to the application of a comprehensive life role curriculum.

Equivalency Tests. Florida and California provide that equivalency tests for the diploma may be taken by students aged sixteen or older. The Florida program has been overshadowed by that state's new minimum competency testing program for the regular high school diploma. The California program is administered through the Department of Education. Candidates who pass both an essay test and a multiple-choice test measuring reasoning skills are awarded a certificate of proficiency, which is recognized as an equivalent to the high school diploma. Other states have not passed equivalency diploma legislation for youth below the age of majority. Rather, they have supported use of the General Educational Development (GED) tests for youth aged eighteen or older.

External Examinations. The GED tests are accepted for high school graduation in nine states.[23] Requirements and limitations differ from state to state, the most common being that students must exceed the age of compulsory schooling before the tests may apply to graduation. The GED examinations and the California Equivalency Tests are both batteries of criterion-referenced achievement tests. They evaluate student learning in traditional subject fields. Most adult evening schools offer preparation programs for the GED examinations.

External Programs. Correspondence courses and extension programs leading to the high school diploma are available in most states. Some of these programs are managed by state university systems, others by proprietary schools. Students gain credit by examinations tied to textbooks, course study guides, or course enrollment. Course content includes the required and elective courses typically found in the high school diploma program.

A new direction for this road to graduation is provided by the New York State External High School Diploma Program. Inaugurated in 1975, this approach involves a competency-based, applied performance assessment system. Students aged eighteen and over may demonstrate competencies for a diploma through simulated adult life experiences.[24]

While the system was created primarily to assess competencies, it includes a diagnostic and guidance function to help students attain the required competencies. It directs student learning efforts while also assessing the outcomes of prior experiences:

> The new diploma recognizes performance in basic skills areas (math, reading) as well as in life skills (consumer, scientific, citizenship and

health awareness, and occupational preparedness); it rewards advanced occupational/vocational, academic, and specialized skills . . .

To complete the first portion of the diploma program, one must
pass five tests designed to elicit the performance of the 64 designated
"life-skill" competencies. An open testing technique is used; it is
characterized by flexibility in time and location (there are three take-
home tests), use of several communication modes (two oral interviews), explicit understanding of and open discussion of competencies to be demonstrated, and continuous feedback on progress.[25]

Clearly, of the five approaches used by states to initiate competency-
based diplomas, the New York external diploma program most closely
meets the definitions for competency-based education advanced by
Spady and other theorists. The program involves life roles (individualized competencies) as well as the application of basic skills (generalized
competencies). Not only is it based on outcomes, as are all the other
state approaches described here; it also includes variable locations for
learning and individualized approaches to needs assessment and
learning activities. The program is highly flexible and adaptable to a
variety of settings.

However, the interests of the vast majority of states in competency-
based education are more limited, being expressed in less ambitious
programs to advance and guarantee basic skills. Course requirements
are not being replaced by competency tests; rather, competency tests
are being viewed by state boards of education and state legislatures as
an additional guarantee that graduates are functionally literate. Oregon, for instance, has increased the number of courses while also
initiating competencies for graduation requirements.

Secondary education operates within certain economic and political
constraints. These include most centrally the attitudes of the public as
expressed through elected or appointed state officials. Currently the
focus appears to be preemptive: limited intercession of competency
testing to shore up weaker high school students. The citizens' objective
is not to reform the educational system at this point, but rather to
reform the exit system for secondary education. The public wants a
guaranteed product. Its central interests are expressed in figure 6.2,
which fills in the matrix of objectives presented earlier in the abstract.

COMPETENCY TESTS AND LOCAL SCHOOL DISTRICTS

The assertion that competency-based education is a hollow paradigm that can be packed according to the wishes of the community is
borne out by activities of school districts nationwide. The Denver
(Colorado) schools, first to tie competency testing to the diploma, use a
basic skills achievement test battery. The application of basic skills, a

more popular approach nationally, is employed by the Gary (Indiana) school system, among others. Achievement in subject content is the objective of continuous-progress institutions such as Mariner High School in Everett (Washington). Competency in life roles describes programs in Hood River (Oregon) and Jefferson County (Colorado). And comprehensive adult proficiency is the goal for students attending the St. Paul (Minnesota) Open School. All of these approaches are identified in figure 6.2. It should be noted that the Mariner and St. Paul approaches involve competency-based education, not minimum competency testing. The continuous-progress approach, for example, requires students to pass a series of criterion-referenced tests within each subject or project area. Optional units are provided to accommodate student interests. Time requirements do not exist, as students proceed according to their own rate. The St. Paul approach includes the demonstration by students of adult proficiencies in appropriate settings. The vast majority of secondary schools, however, are confining their current activities to minimum competencies verified by paper-and-pencil tests.

While few of the hundreds of high schools using competency testing in one of its forms tie competencies to grade promotion, almost all require the demonstration of competencies for the diploma.[26] Local school districts have tended more than states have to connect com-

Fig. 6.2 Typical Public Objectives for Competency-Based Education

CONTENT OBJECTIVES

PURPOSE	Basic Skills Achievement	Basic Skills Application	Subject Content Achievement	Life Roles Achievement	Life Roles Application
Diagnosis/Remediation	✓	✓	✓		
Course Achievement	✓	✓	✓		
Grade Promotion	✓	✓			
Graduation Diploma	✓	✓			
Adult Proficiency	✓	✓			

petency testing to graduation requirements. All of the early schools—
Denver; Westside (Omaha, Nebraska); Gary; Kern County (Bakersfield, California); Duvall County (Jacksonville, Florida); and the St.
Paul Open School—require demonstrations of specified competencies
for the diploma.

Any discussion of minimum competency testing must acknowledge
its populist roots. The hundreds of secondary schools now employing
minimum competency testing in its various forms were responding,
with very few exceptions, to local public opinion rather than to state
rulings. The Westside schools in suburban Omaha, for instance, began
in 1975 a program of testing competencies in seven areas (reading,
writing, arithmetic, consumerism, democratic concepts, oral expression, and health) upon the conclusion of a broad review of educational
purposes and priorities by the school district. No precipitous act was
involved. No state or federal mandate was imminent.

Involvement of the community appears to be important to the success of minimum competency testing at the local level. The Kern
County schools in California collaborated with over 300 frontline job
supervisors to develop their competency program. A pool of test items
was formed that reflected the reading and computational requirements
of entry-level jobs in the Bakersfield area, so students would be
economically self-sufficient upon graduation.[27]

Alternative high schools at the local level often use competency
measures other than paper-and-pencil tests. For instance, at North
Central High School in suburban Indianapolis, the alternative program
provides for students to demonstrate competencies as described in
Walkabout, a series of newsletters published by Phi Delta Kappa. The
"walkabout" is a series of summit experiences marking the transition
from adolescence and schooling to adulthood and community life. It
requires the student to select, plan, and perform challenging activities
that reflect adult skills and responsibilities. It requires demonstrated
competence in seven areas: creativity, logical inquiry, volunteer service, practical skills, adventure, cognitive development, and world of
work. The students perform the "walkabout" challenges in addition to
meeting certain course requirements.

The tests typically used by secondary schools to measure minimum
competency skills come from a wide range of developers: local educators, state personnel, proprietary firms meeting local specifications,
and corporations with national distribution. In some school districts
both commercial and local tests are employed.

The many local competency testing efforts are interesting not only
for the diversity they represent but also for the value of on-site experi-

ence they promise. As Goldhammer and Weitzel have noted (in chapter 2 of this book), since theory about competency-based education is currently based upon mixed notions and convictions, both systematic trial and error and empirical evidence are needed before assurances about its relative effectiveness with students may be given. And as Rubin reports (in chapter 3), practitioners see matters that way; they recommend beginning small and then later broadening the scope of competency-based education programs.

The work of individual schools often goes unrecognized. While state legislation, planning activities, and conference proceedings tend to dominate the professional media, reports of implementation by local schools tend to go unnoticed. This situation is ironic indeed, when one considers that in the final analysis concepts must be implemented by teachers, site by site, if they are to affect students. Attempts at reform must include practice or they remain plans, not programs. The successful practice of a concept in school settings ultimately determines its growth or demise in the profession.

SCHOOL SITE POSITIVE FACTORS

Setting aside the larger forces and conditions affecting secondary education and its relationship to competency-based education, which of its specific features are attractive to a school and its community? Why would individual secondary schools and local school systems initiate competency-based evaluation programs? Why would they take the risk of experimentation and possible failure?

Keefe and Georgiades explain that competency-based education can change a school setting in any of these ways:

- forcing a community-needs assessment
- offering functional validity to the diploma
- encouraging early diagnosis of student learning needs
- suggesting remedial programs tailored to specific targets
- providing a firmer accountability base for the school and community[28]

These are changes sought not only by citizens at large but also by many educators. For instance, a community-needs assessment provides school personnel with documents that aid goal planning and management of resources. Remedial programs can be specifically focused and their support broadened when they are directed toward clearly stated graduation requirements. And confusion over grade-reporting systems is reduced when the criteria for student evaluation are defined.

Setting specific expectations provides security for participants at parent-student conferences in local schools as well as for members of boards of education at large public meetings.

New research on the high school indicates that organizational structures tend to be undifferentiated, perhaps adding to uncertainties about which persons are presently responsible for which objectives, including instructional objectives.

> Organizationally, high schools are less differentiated, more participatory, and more loosely structured that some people claim. . . . Principals participate in decision-making arenas on a wide range of issues, but so do others—teachers, specialists, other administrators, counselors, and parents—particularly in their spheres of responsibility. Rules exist to govern what students do. Some rules exist for teachers, but *not in instructional matters* [italics mine]. The internal parts of high schools are not related to each other in ways that conventional organization theory predicts, and many of these "nonrelationships" violate the expectations of logic and reason. . . . For instance, one might have reasonably expected that, in a school with numerous courses and nonclassroom arrangements, meetings would occur more frequently, in the interest of control. However, they do not.[29]

Whether this disconnectedness is a cause of the many undifferentiated goals that became attached to secondary education during the decade 1965–1974, or, more likely, is the result of these forces, the end effect is weak administrative control. Therefore, the redefinition of objectives and the setting of priorities that ordinarily accompany competency-based education could have a salutary effect on school management. It should tighten the internal organization, since administrators would likely be expected to look after the attainment and measurement of competencies. It could help a school's leaders define job roles, relationships, and responsibilities.

Other positive outcomes tend to emerge when secondary schools attempt to implement the various components of competency-based education:

- good relationships between teachers and students as they work together to meet external test requirements
- attention by teachers to the objectives and content of approved curricula
- understanding by students of job requirements and the relationship of those requirements to schooling
- certification of competencies required in the broader world rather than those used within the educational system

- reporting of student progress based upon clearly formulated criteria
- the audit and treatment of eleventh- and twelfth-grade students with deficient skills
- development of instruction according to the learning styles of individual students
- immediacy of goals and rewards
- development of effective remedial loops by focusing attention upon the diagnosis and correction of skill deficiencies
- motivation for older students to review and improve cognitive skills in basic fields.[30]

Other benefits claimed by schools with competency-based education programs, as variously expressed, include these:

- growth in spontaneous or self-motivated learning
- development of problem-solving skills
- growth in initiative and responsibility
- ability to cope with the social milieu
- growth in social awareness

The measurement of progress toward such goals is difficult, at best, since they tend to be aspirations and assertions rather than descriptions of behaviors that can be verified.

Aims such as these for schooling are not new. Most programs advocated since the advent of John Dewey have included this dimension of education. Advocates of competency-based education have as much claim as anyone else to potential success with the elusive treasures of affective education. Since affective traits form slowly and tend to be wrapped in the family umbilical cord, however, educators should be cautious about quick claims to success. As Rubin points out (in chapter 3), it is important to distinguish between Utopia and reality.

The "positives" reported by schools reflect back upon the aspirations of those institutions. Schools with limited definitions of competency-based education may report ease of implementation and evaluation. Ordinarily it is not difficult to tie basic reading skills to diploma requirements. It is quite another matter to develop a life role curriculum that applies to effective adulthood. Some secondary schools, notably the St. Paul Open School, have taken the larger step. But comprehensive high schools are not alternative high schools, either in mission or in composition. Since they lack a volunteer student body and the flexibility provided by small enrollment, they face a different set of conditions.

SCHOOL SITE NEGATIVE FACTORS

A paper prepared for the Education Commission of the States points out that competency testing can have negative or positive effects, depending upon its application. Of the "negatives" possible with a minimum competency program, the commission says:

> They could send schools backwards to the days when students dropped out if they could not meet the minimum standards. Or they could discredit the schools for what society is doing. Or narrow the curriculum to what is testable. Or drive out creative teaching in favor of routine drill and practice. Or force teachers to concentrate on the bottom of the class at the expense of the top. Or increase the amount of testing time and decrease the amount of teaching time. Or label the disadvantaged as incompetent. Or isolate them in remedial classes.[31]

These fears, however, reflect more the dark clouds than the falling rain. Commentary about the difference between original conceptions of competency-based education and its common application ignores the survival instincts of school personnel, who do not intend to be rained upon—not by these dark clouds or by other more ambitious ones looming or forming on the horizon.

Many objections to competency-based education have been raised in the professional literature. Edgar Kelley, writing in *Catalyst*, the journal of the Nebraska Council of School Administrators, comments on the minimum competency testing versions of competency-based education:

> Life's demands are subject to expectations which others have as well as expectations which we, as individuals, place upon ourselves. For each individual, these demands are likely to be different from the demands which others face. And, for the same individual, these demands may change with changes in role and setting.[32]

His warning is echoed by Gene Glass,[33] among others, and by numerous practitioners. For instance, Leonard Hanson, principal of South High School in Omaha, warns that competency testing will lead to external controls and outside interference. And in his opinion, "Each [student] is entitled to a diploma. If the student makes an honest effort, this has to be given consideration."[34]

Practitioners experienced with minimum competency testing, however, do not view it so dourly. In fact, the many practitioners with such testing on line are positive about the benefits to date.[35] Moreover, some practitioners invoking broader applications of competency-based education—for instance, Wayne Jennings, principal of St.

Paul Open School—also argue for the value to students of minimum competency testing.

Even the most enthusiastic school administrators, however, acknowledge that certain problems may arise from the application of a minimum competency version of competency-based education to school settings. The following points have been made repeatedly:

• *It can cause a major burden in record keeping and general paper work*, even when computerized. If additional clerical personnel are employed, the teachers and counselors still face a heavy load of paper processing.

• *It may raise the costs of schooling*. Remedial programs to assist students to acquire the required competencies must be organized and staffed. The alternative is to reduce elective courses and assign those teachers to remedial centers. Teacher workshops to organize and implement the new curricula require funding, as well.

• *It may be opposed by many teachers*. The National Education Association is cool toward the concept, and some local teacher groups are strongly opposed, fearing that their performance evaluations will be based upon student test scores or rates of student progress.

• *It may focus upon the trivial*, causing learning to be fragmented. Students should learn by approaches that are more holistic, integrating the affective and cognitive through thought processes.

• *It cannot be applied to evaluate life role proficiency*. Paper-and-pencil tests are inadequate for this. Simulations and on-site performance tests are awkward, time-consuming, and highly subjective.

• *It can focus too much attention on a limited number of cognitive skills*, to the detriment of other educational goals. Care is needed to maintain balance in the curriculum.

• *It may make certification procedures more difficult.*

• *It requires the careful in-service education* of professional staff and *increased communication* with students, parents, and citizens prior to and during implementation.

• *It faces court challenges* before its legal status is assured.

Warnings by Merle McClung and action by the NAACP legal fund in Florida attest to the force of the issue of court challenges.[36] Keefe and Georgiades comment on the legal dimensions as they apply to a school's instructional program:

> Many competency programs are targeted for students well along in their secondary education experience, with little prior notice. Traditional application of due process requires adequate notice of any law that can jeopardize a person's educational or job prospects.

Then there is the problem of test validity. Most people would agree that a test would be unfair if it measured what a school did not teach. At question here is not only how well test items represent competency domains (content validity) or whether they reflect the objectives of the curriculum (curricular validity), but whether or not these competencies and objectives are actually taught in the classroom ("instructional" validity). A school or district that is not sure of the comprehensive validity of its proficiency tests should not use them to deny promotion or the diploma.

And, of course, there is the matter of potential racial or ethnic discrimination. Some evidence exists that competency tests may disqualify disproportionate numbers of black and Hispanic students. The point here is not that minorities should be excused from minimum standards but that great care must be taken to avoid creating a new form of discrimination. McClung suggests careful articulation of instructional and test development to reflect all aspects of our pluralistic society, and a lengthy phase-in period with ample opportunity to utilize diversified learning, remediation, and evaluation strategies.[37]

This list of school site negatives is formidable but not fatal. Implementation of new educational programs always requires schools to muster high levels of initiative and pragmatism. Flexibility is a key factor in the success of new programs, whose theoretical models must be adjusted to accommodate local attitudes and resources. Purists may be horrified, but the alternative is protracted conflict and rejection. Those who adopt new processes expect the freedom to revise them.

Most secondary schools operating minimum competency testing programs have overcome the major hurdles. Budgets have been established, staff workshops held, community meetings conducted, and countless questions answered. Paper work has been streamlined and curriculum balance maintained. In Oregon, with schools committed to life role or survival competencies as well as to the application of basic skills, the greatest number of problems occurred in actually writing and defining competencies. According to Earl Anderson, school personnel were not sufficiently trained in these areas, and not enough models existed to be of assistance. In many instances school districts found it helpful to form consortia to develop programs in conformity with state requirements.[38]

ANALYZING THE RESULTS

To date, most schools and their communities have expressed satisfaction with the results of minimum competency testing. Very few students have been denied diplomas because of competency test requirements, indicating that fears of mass failure were premature. The public has found it reassuring that students and teachers can get serious about school if necessary.

The student pass rate for secondary schools with minimum competency tests has been impressive. In 1977, Denver reported that only 1.5 percent of its seniors had failed to graduate because of inability to pass the minimum competency tests. The Gary school system held back only 10 seniors from the class of 1978, although 400 had failed either the reading or the math requirement on the first test. In 1977, in Phoenix, none of the seniors in the district's high schools failed to graduate because of low test scores. In 1978, Omaha's Westside School District denied the diploma to 8 students, but 4 of these lacked course requirements. In Kern County, only 8 of 3,000 seniors in the class of 1977 were held back.[39]

Success has been more difficult to achieve in Oregon, where schools struggling with the life skills graduation requirements were authorized to postpone them for two years. A serious challenge to the entire Oregon program, mounted in the state legislature, was accommodated by this compromise.

Generally, however, the public—from Greenville County, South Carolina, to Anchorage, Alaska—has seemed satisfied with the initial results of requiring competency testing as a condition for granting the high school diploma. More comprehensive forms of competency-based education, such as those represented by the careers theme of Hood River Valley High School in Oregon or the life role focus of St. Paul Open School in Minnesota, appear to be solidly in place.

Teacher resistance to basic skills minimum competency testing programs appears to diminish with experience. For example, James Fillbrandt, reporting on the Kern County program, gives this view:

> . . . in the experience of the author, teachers are most receptive to minimum competency where the approach to test correction is more global than detailed, more novel than conventional. For these reasons, it seems that English teachers have more quickly embraced minimum competency in writing than reading or mathematics teachers have accepted minimum competency in their disciplines.[40]

Changes in responsibilities for some teachers were less than anticipated, as well. Geraldine Houser, a reading teacher at Roosevelt High School in Gary, reports, "I'm doing basically the same things as I did before but now the objectives are more clearly defined."[41] Although some in-service education is required to acquaint teachers with the purposes and procedures related to competency testing, the methods—including individualized remedial instruction—have been promoted by schools of education for a decade or more.

Rather than focusing upon minimum competencies tied to high school graduation, Maryland in 1975 launched a comprehensive program in elementary and secondary schools to diagnose and overcome reading deficiencies. The Iowa Tests of Basic Skills and the Maryland Basic Skills Reading Mastery Test are used to assess student achievement in the five reading goals established by the State Board of Education:

- utilize a variety of reading materials
- use a word recognition system
- comprehend various reading materials
- meet the reading demands for functioning in society
- select reading as a personal activity

All reading diagnosis, instruction, and testing in Maryland is based on these categories. The central purpose of the program is to assess the strengths and weaknesses of individual students in the five basic functional reading areas and to plan individualized instructional programs to accommodate the identified deficiencies.

Improvement in reading scores was made in 1976 and again in 1977 at the two secondary school levels assessed, grades 7 and 11.[42] Success with the reading program encouraged Maryland to launch Project Basic, a competencies program encompassing five broad areas of human activity and scheduled for implementation in 1982.

Accountability for schools involves two dimensions important to parents and other taxpayers. At one level citizens want to know if teachers are providing programs of real importance. For instance, are schools attending to the priorities identified by the community and the state? At a second level citizens want to know the results of instruction. Are test scores improving or dropping or remaining stable? Is student behavior acceptable? Only if test scores improve and student social habits are tolerable will the public maintain its current interest in competency-based education.

The secondary schools' flirtation with modular scheduling ended because students had difficulties using independent study time constructively, not because they scored poorly on achievement tests. People are primarily interested in the products of competency-based education, not in the processes employed or the philosophical framework. If the product does not meet the promise, then pragmatic citizens will become disenchanted and look elsewhere for ways to

improve outcomes. They become doctrinaire about secondary education only when they perceive that their own current priorities are being
ignored.

Questions about the *results* of teaching must raise the question of
what is *teachable*. What skills and concepts can the school seriously and
realistically expect to transmit to students? Most educators agree that
basic cognitive skills and processes are teachable behaviors. As
Madaus and Airasian point out, however, there appears to be less
certainty that such higher level skills as analysis, synthesis, and evaluation can be taught successfully to many pupils:

> Certainly the relationship of general intelligence to mastery of these
> higher level behaviors belies the notion that they are readily available
> to all students. . . . Moreover, and perhaps most crucially for a
> competency-based certification approach, it is not at all clear how
> pupils acquire these behaviors or what types of instructional mate-
> rials are most appropriate for developing them. The key issue here is
> not that these behaviors cannot be taught, but rather that teaching
> them, given the present state of knowledge, is as much an art as it is a
> science. Techniques useful with some pupils are not useful with
> others; strategies adopted by one teacher are not readily exportable to
> other teachers. Certainly, teaching higher level cognitive behaviors
> involves a degree of complexity far removed from the simple "di-
> agnose and prescribe" language contained in most competency-
> based programs.
>
> Moreover, the domains of personal, social and career develop-
> ment, if these domains are seen as involving more than cognitive and
> psychomotor competencies, pose particularly difficult areas in which
> to match appropriate instructional techniques to the development of
> pupil competence. Even when the issues regarding whether the
> school *should* teach patriotism, self concept, work ethic, or job pre-
> paredness are put aside, there is a serious question about whether
> schools *can* teach such competencies.[43]

Whether complex thought processes and affective behaviors can be
taught (and this is clearly debatable), it is likely that student cognitive
skills can be improved through competency *testing* programs. The
most efficient method of altering the instructional emphasis in a school
is to alter the content or form of important school examinations. The
European external examination system operates upon this premise,
primarily because of the importance attached to these examinations.[44]
Similarly, a competency testing program in the United States that
requires basic cognitive skills for course credit or the diploma will find
schools giving more attention to the teaching of those skills. And since
those skills at least *are* (presumably) teachable, achievement should

improve in most circumstances, despite the initial findings in Kern County.

When teachers have a choice between emphasizing tested or non-tested objectives, they generally favor the tested objectives. Madaus and Airasian explain:

> Faced with a choice between one set of objectives which are explicit in the course outline and a different set which are explicit in the certifying examinations, students and teachers generally choose to focus upon the latter. This finding holds true over different countries and over many decades. . . . Most studies have found that the proportion of instructional time spent on various objectives was seldom higher than the predicted likelihood of their occurrence on the external examination.[45]

The question, then, is not whether schools should expect to improve student achievement in the skills to be examined. Rather, the question is whether some learnings are being displaced and what the relative value of those learnings is.

Will testing for cognitive skill competencies, for example, displace learning of questionable worth or will it replace learning of the highest value? Schools will need to review these questions carefully; for part of evaluating any new program honestly is determining what is lost as well as what is gained. Competency-based education may claim a beneficial impact on secondary education only if schools keep all goals in mind and evaluate the total expectations.

EXAMINING THE POTENTIAL

The meaning of competency-based education for secondary education may be as broad as the field itself or as narrow as the teaching of one cognitive skill. Although the changes found in most schools are not terribly dramatic because of the focus upon minimum competency testing, a few reflect substantial conversions of goals and processes. The competency concept undergirds a broad continuum of practice. Beyond the pragmatic changes implemented step by step lies the power of the concept itself. As Chickering and Claxton point out in chapter 1, competency is an eternally contemporary notion.

The implications of current activity in secondary education suggest a Hegelian synthesis. The forces generating support for competency-based education are vital and broad. The forces of resistance are based on a skepticism buttressed by tradition. Given the conservative nature of educational institutions, as well as the public's current cynicism about innovation in schools, all signs point to a modest but undramatic shift toward competency-based systems. This shift can already be observed as states and local districts scurry to establish minimum competency tests. It is less readily observable in other important aspects, such as continuous-progress evaluation systems. Proudly but still less visible at the head of the line are a very few programs thoroughly oriented toward life roles, using time-free learning and a variety of performance measures.

Competency-based education is an attractive concept in most of its manifestations. Its focus on outcomes, alternative learning arrangements and time flexibility makes it appealing to many educators. And it is supported by trends in the broader society and by developments within education toward individualized instruction. Although the multiple definitions of competency-based education complicate its full implementation, none of secondary education's traditional goals are in conflict with its objectives.

Throughout this century, secondary education has concentrated upon four categories of learning:

- cognitive (basic) skills
- citizenship
- health
- career or job preparation

Of the many possible categories of learning, these four are valued most by commissions of educators and by people responding to public opinion polls. They constitute the modern *quadrivium* of the curriculum. Whether competency-based education is viewed as an objective, an evaluation system, an implementation plan, or a new construct for education, its definitions all lean toward supporting these priorities.

Schools that use competency approaches to teach basic skills are simply applying a new technology to the first responsibility of secondary education. They may use this technology as an evaluation or accountability instrument only, or they may employ the entire individualized system of diagnosis and prescription proposed in the competency-based education literature. They may maintain essentially a traditional orientation toward school organization, or they may revise substantially their structures and teaching roles. Whatever specific strategy is used, implementation of the concept of competency-based education appears to be in harmony with the long-standing central purposes of education.

The acquisition of citizenship skills can also be sharpened by a competency-based education program that identifies objectives and certifies their attainment. Whether documentation is by paper-and-pencil tests or by more sophisticated techniques, it is important that the concepts not be neglected.

Career or job preparation goes hand in hand with a performance evaluation system. The growth, over the past decade, of *community*-based education, or action learning, may be traced to certain facts, ideals, and needs also identified with *competency*-based education:

- competency evaluation plans used by business and the professions
- identification and evaluation of specific job skills
- desire to make learning relevant and practical
- need to increase contacts among various age groups
- desire of youth for adult responsibilities
- views of secondary education as being more comprehensive than classroom schooling

In addition, the difficulties that college-educated generalists encounter in obtaining good employment, together with a new interest in artisanship, have also caused a strengthening of competency-based approaches to the evaluation of job and career skills in secondary education.

The fourth priority for secondary education, physical and mental health, also finds useful applications through competency-based education. Competency measures have been used for first-aid tests and various safety examinations such as swimming tests. They can easily be expanded to include drug identification, nutrition, and physical fitness. The relationship of verified competencies to mental health opens the door that is labeled "values," however; and this door for secondary education has people pushing both ways.

This discussion of the relationship between competency-based education and the central concerns of education illustrates the reasons competency-based education has been applied to secondary schooling conservatively rather than comprehensively. Each area, as articulated, is primarily aligned with content that can be taught within the traditional subject matter framework. Basic skills can be taught and examined in mathematics and English classes. Job preparation can be taught in business or industrial arts classes and applied in related work experience programs. Citizenship education is still U. S. history, American government, and city council meetings to most of the public. Health and physical education tend to be personal matters, and community interest is addressed toward interscholastic teams as much as toward drug education or nutrition.

Competency-based education has been applied by schools to stimulate and verify achievement of these traditional goals rather than to redefine them or to reformulate the desired outcomes. It has been used to reinforce a weary structure rather than to replace that structure with another. This explains why the application of competency-based education contrasts so markedly with theory about it. Theory often argues for a broader reform of curriculum, instruction, and evaluation than can typically be accommodated by schools. Spady states that the curricula developed to facilitate competencies must begin with an assessment of the demands and contingencies associated with major life roles and not with the content fields. This reflects an interesting view of competency-based education but does not represent the actual practice of secondary schools with competency-based programs.

The question is not whether the broader view can be implemented under any circumstance, because Nickse and her associates in New York State have proved that for adults a life role curriculum can be organized and competencies measured. Neither is it a question of whether the broader approach can be implemented with adolescents, because some alternative high schools operate within this framework. Rather, the question is: Given the learning objectives and the social expectations operating for the comprehensive high school, can an interdisciplinary, individualized life role program make a broad impact upon secondary education?

Three possible scenarios are suggested to address this question. One entails the evolution of current programs. A second involves a rounding-out of the status quo. The third considers actions by countering forces and the swing of the pendulum to new interests.

Scenario I. A fusion occurs as various versions of competency-based education come together. Schools now testing for basic skills begin to teach students to apply those skills to life situations and then to career roles. Other schools with competency-based, continuous-progress plans begin to identify and teach for extraschool goals as well as intraschool goals. The public maintains its demand for accountability of learning. Student performance improves and an appreciative public provides additional remedial and developmental monies. Schools begin to look toward broader goals than testing for graduation requirements. Alternative schools using life role criteria adapt these through experience to the requirements of comprehensive high schools. Traditional time and age expectations are modified. Evaluation systems become more sophisticated and certification questions are resolved. Not all schools move to a comprehensive life role program, but much of secondary education is clearly competency based and is shifting from school-related content to community-oriented content. The movement evolves from minimum competency testing to the full application of competency-based education as shown earlier in figure 6.1.

Scenario II.   The current programs stabilize rather than evolve toward a life role orientation. Almost all states continue to require some form of minimum competency testing, with half of the states tying basic skills competencies to the diploma. Remedial programs are widely required for students failing the tests. A few schools remain committed to a competency-based, subject-oriented, continuous-progress curriculum. Still fewer, mainly small alternative schools, establish competency programs involving walkabout challenges or some other form of integrated, broad performance criteria. Some school districts table life role competencies after encountering difficulties in defining and evaluating them. The public, satisfied that high school graduates can read and compute, and not really attracted to progressive or experimental systems of education, turns its attention to other matters.

Scenario III.   Under this scenario, a series of circumstances pushes the competency testing movement back to an earlier position. Critics of the basic skills competency programs contend it is costly and wasteful to test all students to identify the few who require remediation. Litigation is directed successfully against states and school districts that do not provide sufficient lead time or who underfund remedial programs. Schools utilizing competency testing for course credit decide that maintaining the computer evaluation system is too costly and complicated. Voter groups challenge the value and the democracy of requiring competency measures for graduation. The states committed to life role competencies, Oregon and Maryland, are unable to define and measure family competencies, career competencies, and group or social competencies to the satisfaction of consumers, and fall back to a basic skills program. In other states a reduction in tax revenues causes schools to cut personnel, increase class size, and dismiss all expenses related to remedial instruction and accounting for competencies. Economic problems also result in the elimination of most alternative schools, including those with a competency base.

Good arguments can be mounted for the first scenario. A competency-based system can implement educational priorities as articulated by the public. It also offers a clear delineation of objectives, citizen involvement, and flexible routes toward the objectives. Priorities can be defined and school programs focused toward their attainment.

Also, individualization of instruction is encouraged by competency-based education, building upon current trends. Research on reading achievement shows the type of diagnosis and prescription suggested by competency-based education is a practical and effective approach to individualization. The advent of PL 94–142 requires individualized educational plans for handicapped students. Will not interest grow in developing these plans for all students? New information about student learning conditions suggests that a teaching methodology, to be effective, must reflect a variety of student learning styles.[46]

In addition, the public seeks accountability, and competency-based education affords that service. The public is in a practical mood, as well, wanting students to learn marketable skills. It seeks to involve students educationally in the broader society. Youth, in any event, are moving in that direction legally and socially. Some, about 7 percent, are graduating early from high school, and more than 60 percent hold jobs at age seventeen while attending school.[47]

Competency-based education can improve curriculum organization, since its development requires a school to reorganize its curriculum according to explicit goals. Classes can respond more directly to learning objectives. In short, by making outcomes and achievement explicit, ambiguity in the instructional process is reduced. A life role focus should respond to the interests of older students.

A few high schools are on the threshold of a comprehensive competency-based program of education. The Fairfield-Suisun high schools in California, for instance, are implementing a full competency-based curriculum that includes a group of 37 skills together with competency majors grouped by career fields (e.g., public service, communications, and agriculture). The schools also maintain a more traditional university preparatory major.[48]

Any school moving toward a full competency-based curriculum must recognize the considerable structural changes required to implement the concept. Traditional administrative arrangements must be revised in a number of areas, to include the following:

• Learning stations will need to be identified with community assistance and managed with the cooperation of citizens offering to help students learn.
• Guidance centers will need to be expanded to accommodate new functions, to include diagnosis of learning needs and the brokering of learning opportunities in the community.
• Systems of student supervision must be established to provide acceptable behavior without visual control. Legal protection must be afforded to all concerned.

• Data-processing equipment and procedures will be needed to accommodate an expanded records system based on outcomes.

• Subject area departments will need to be restructured to provide support for student objectives that may be interdisciplinary and oriented toward adult roles.

• Professional review committees will be needed to verify the quality of student outcomes for a multitude of completed projects.

• Criterion-referenced measures will need to be developed for courses and life role activities.

• Decisions must be made about graduation requirements. Will certain group activities, such as science laboratory work, be required? What about writing and computing skill levels? Are common learnings expected? Will a "critical path" route be expected of all students?

• How will group activities, such as band or team sports, be accommodated in the total school schedule?

• What new procedures and instruments will be required for evaluation of professional staff in a system that diminishes the importance of classroom instruction?

• What will constitute the basic organizational structure of the school in the absence of a class schedule? Will it be a clock schedule, learning contracts with specific reporting times, a daily homeroom period, an office or base for each student, a guidance class, or some other mode?

• Will progress reports be sent to parents each month, each semester, at the completion of each unit, or at other times?

All of these structural changes are significant and must be considered fully by a school before implementation of competency-based education in its more comprehensive form.

PROJECTING THE IMPLICATIONS

Despite the many arguments that may be advanced for the unfolding of Scenario I, other conditions militate against rapid movement of schools toward a full competency base. Casting economic questions aside, even though levels of tax support and inflation may well be major determinants, at least three factors possess strong implications for the implementation of competency-based education in the secondary schools of America.

First, the view of competency-based education as a life role curriculum strays from the two main aspirations of students and their parents. Simply stated, graduates of secondary schools want either to enter college or to get a job. They want the competence they need to be undergraduates or employees. The expression of this interest was substantiated as recently as 1977 in a national study.[49] Parents concur with these aspirations.

For students entering higher education, approximately 45 percent of the twelfth-grade class, the central concern is still school learning, not adult circumstances. They lack a clear perception of themselves as adults because they are still in the process of deciding about many matters, including their major field of study. Their immediate goal is to be successful in college. Other more distant roles, however important, take a back seat. They ask, "What do I need to get into college?" not, "Will I be a successful parent or community member?"

Job-bound high school graduates are somewhat oriented to their life in the community because they have in mind an immediate job. School is valued, however, in direct proportion to its capability for preparing students for employment. It is not valued for the more abstract purposes suggested by a full life role competency-based education program. Students are seeking occupational competency and placement; and this has been attainable through traditional schooling, especially since the advent of the Vocational Educational Acts of 1963 and 1968.

A second consideration in projecting the impact of competency-based education on secondary schools involves the expectations of the public for schools to provide custodial care as well as the corollary desire of students to be with their peers. The tendency for students passing the California proficiency test to remain in school has been mentioned. The teaching of college subjects in high schools is growing as students increasingly select this option over early college entrance.[50] Recommendations to lower the compulsory attendance age have been stonily ignored by state legislatures.

Schools in the United States are expected to socialize students as well as to conduct instruction. Parents want students to mature socially as well as intellectually. They expect supervised athletics, dances, clubs, field trips, lunches, elections, and even bathrooms. The public is not likely to drop this expectation overnight, especially with the advent of unsupervised homes. The public wants not only demonstrated competence, but also demonstrated nurturing of youth.

A third major factor involves the identification and evaluation of life roles as a major component of competency-based education. Several problems occur. First, the criteria for delineating life role performances are not adequate. These definitions must precede the identification of life role competency requirements. Second, as Waks points out, in the development of life role competence, nonpedagogical cultural instrumentalities and self-determined learning are dominant. How can the schools, then, develop effective life role treatments for students? Third, rapid technological change compounds the problem. Preparation for a career role may be less defendable in today's constantly· changing world than it was a generation ago. And fourth, the lack of value consensus in society complicates the search for ready definitions to guide schools.

Considering these constraints, schools are not likely to forge ahead with a curriculum based on roles. They are more likely to shy away from the uncertainties involved and to fall back upon areas of consensus, such as the teaching of basic skills.

A major research and development effort must precede the serious incorporation of life roles in the secondary school curriculum. This analysis must be mounted from at least two perspectives: what tasks are performed by students after graduation, and how well does the current curriculum prepare students for these tasks? The serious implementation of life role competency-based education at the secondary school level must await a further formulation of life role proposals. These models are not as yet prepared for field trial. Too much of what is educationally valuable to consumers cannot at this point be translated into measurable objectives. Also, how does a school articulate life roles with admissions requirements in selective colleges?

The implications of competency-based education for secondary schools are clear. Some of the elements can be implemented successfully: for instance, the use of criterion-referenced, performance-based tests in the application of cognitive skills or the employment of an individualized mastery learning pedagogy. The call for accountability and the public's interest in clarifying goals remain strong, as well.

The opportunity for students to participate more fully in setting the objectives and circumstances of their learning provides a strong motivational element to competency-based education. Older students, especially, respond positively to being involved in planning their learning. The dilemma is to balance aspirations and inclinations with certain social expectations such as informed citizenship.

Additional leverage for the implementation .of competency-based programs is provided by broadening the options for student learning and basing credit on performance criteria rather than traditional factors.

These are not superficial elements, and their impact is being felt in secondary schools. Curricula are being defined more precisely, graduation requirements are being recast, school organization is being sharpened, instruction is becoming more individualized, guidance services are being refocused, reporting is becoming more precise, community opinion is gaining impact, and the evaluation of program outcomes is being published with increasing candor.

But these changes will not modify interest in traditional subject content for most people, or their expectations for schools as socializing institutions. Citizens will continue to hold schools primarily responsible for reading, computation, and citizenship. This emphasis, together with the better capabilities afforded by competency-based education for applying these skills and improving occupational proficiency, should provide a useful meld of competency-based and traditional education.

Human competency is an amalgam of skills, knowledge, attitudes, expectations, motivations, intuitions, emotions, and values. Competency-based education can contribute to the strength of this amalgam. This is the implication of competency-based education for secondary schools.

NOTES

1. See J. Michael Palardy and James E. Eisele, "Competency Based Education," p. 545.

2. See Robert B. Howsam, "Performance-Based Instruction: Some Basic Concepts," p. 333.

3. See George H. Gallup, "The 10th Annual Gallup Poll of the Public's Attitudes Toward the Public Schools," p. 35.

4. See National Commission on the Reform of Secondary Education, *The Reform of Secondary Education*, pp. 8–12.

5. See Barbara R. Lasser and Allan L. Olson, *Strategies for Implementation of Competency Based Education Programs*.

6. William G. Spady, "Competency Based Education: A Bandwagon in Search of a Definition," p. 10. Copyright 1977, American Educational Research Assn., Washington, D.C. All quotations by permission.

7. News and Comment, "The Consequences of Accountability," p. 12. From *Human Nature*, September 1978. Copyright © 1978 by Human Nature, Inc. Reprinted by permission of the publisher.

8. See National Assn. of Secondary School Principals, *Competency Tests and Graduation Requirements*, pp. 3–5.

9. See Salt Lake City School District, *Basic Skills in Reading and Language Arts: Second Grade*, p. 10.

10. See Task Force on Secondary Schools in a Changing Society, *Secondary Schools in a Changing Society*, pp. 1–3.

11. See George Weber, "How You Can Make Sure the Students in Your Schools Are Learning the Basic Skills."

12. See Gallup, pp. 35–41.

13. See James S. Coleman et al., *Youth: Transition to Adulthood.* Copyright © 1974 by the University of Chicago. All quotations by permission.

14. See National Panel on High School and Adolescent Education, *The Education of Adolescents: Final Report and Recommendations.*

15. Coleman et al., p. 125.

16. See Lorin L. Miller, "The New State Graduation Requirements," p. 30.

17. See *Wisconsin R&D Center News,* Fall 1978, p. 8.

18. Leonard J. Waks, *Education for Life-Role Competence,* p. 17. Used by permission.

19. See Chris Pipho, "Minimum Competency Testing in 1978: A Look at State Standards."

20. Spady, p. 10.

21. See Scott D. Thomson and Nancy De Leonibus, "Minimum Competency Testing . . . An Update," pp. 9–11.

22. See Project Basic Office, *The Comprehensive Plan for Maryland Competency-Based Prerequisites for Graduation.*

23. See Thomson and De Leonibus, pp. 9–12.

24. See Ruth S. Nickse, "The Central New York External High School Diploma Program," p. 123.

25. Ibid. Quoted by permission.

26. See Pipho, pp. 586–87.

27. See Thomson and De Leonibus, p. 3.

28. See James W. Keefe and Constance J. Georgiades, "Competency-Based Education and the High School Diploma," p. 101. All quotations by permission.

29. Susan Abramowitz, Ellen Tenenbaum, et al., *High School '77: A Survey of Public Secondary School Principals,* pp. 58–59.

30. See Thomson and De Leonibus, pp. 3–5.

31. Henry M. Brickell, *Let's Talk About Minimum Competency Testing,* pp. 6–7. Copyright © 1978. Used by permission.

32. Edgar A. Kelley, "Minimum Competencies: A Cause for Concern," p. 55.

33. See Gene V. Glass, "Minimum Competence and Incompetence in Florida," *Phi Delta Kappan* 59 (May 1978): p. 602.

34. Leonard E. Hanson, quoted in Edgar A. Kelley, "Commentary: Minimum Competencies for High School Graduation," p. 6.

35. See Chris Pipho, guest ed., "Minimum Competency Testing," special issue *Phi Delta Kappan* 59 (May 1978).

36. See Merle S. McClung, "Competency Testing: Potential for Discrimination."

37. Keefe and Georgiades, pp. 102–03.

38. See Earl N. Anderson, "Coping with Oregon's New Competency-Based Graduation Requirements."

39. See Wayne Reilly, *Competency Based Education: Some Educational, Political and Historical Perspectives.* See also Thomson and De Leonibus, pp. 2–4.

40. James Fillbrandt, ed., "An Approach to Minimum Competency Programs in Mathematics, Reading, and Writing," p. 47.

41. See Reilly, p. 18.

42. See Maryland Accountability Program, *Functional Reading for Test Results.*

43. George F. Madaus and Peter W. Airasian, "Issues in Evaluating Student Outcomes in Competency-Based Graduation Programs," pp. 81–82. All quotations by permission.

44. Ibid., pp. 83–84.

45. Ibid., p. 85.

46. See Rita S. Dunn and Kenneth J. Dunn, *Teaching Students Through Their Individual Learning Styles.*

47. See National Commission on Resources for Youth, *New Roles for Youth in the School and the Community.*

48. See Sydney Thompson, *Competency-Based Education: Theory and Practice,* pp. 21–23.

49. See Richard A. Gorton and Kenneth E. McIntyre, *The Effective Principal.*

50. See Franklin P. Wilbur and David W. Chapman, *College Courses in the High School.*

Conclusion

RUTH NICKSE

COMPETENCY-BASED EDUCATION is here. Regardless of the versions, whether as narrow and cautious as the minimum competency testing programs practiced widely in elementary and secondary education, or as broad and comprehensive as the External High School Diploma Program in New York, the program at Alverno College, or many efforts outside the schools, its presence cannot be ignored.

Like Pandora's box, it has burst upon us, scattering possibilities for good use and misuse in every direction. The very real longing of some besieged educators to figuratively stuff it back in the box and forget it can be understood, but the time is past. The task at hand, which will preoccupy us for some time, is how to make the most of the opportunities it presents and how to minimize the inevitable disappointments and unattractive side effects.

Many opportunities for improved learning and teaching are present in this movement toward educating for competence. Support comes from at least two different quarters: changing attitudes and behaviors related to effective learning, and new technologies to assist in it. Examples of changing attitudes include interest in such concepts as lifelong learning and recurrent education.

These phrases are simple descriptors that are based in part on changing conceptions about the nature of education, work, and leisure. Formerly we viewed our life activities as consecutive, with education, work, and leisure or retirement following one another sequentially through orderly cycles. A period of preparation (education) was followed by a period of application (work), followed in turn by a period of leisure to review both (retirement).

220

The changing nature of society and the demands upon us to accommodate change, increased life spans, and the measure of affluence enjoyed by many have enabled a more flexible ordering. No longer do we have to pack our educational knapsack with enough skills and knowledge at age eighteen (or twenty-two) to last a lifetime. We all have a second, third, or fourth chance. We can refresh our skills at any point in our lives. And our behavior offers concrete evidence that we are taking the opportunity seriously.

Community colleges and universities are full of middle-aged and elderly individuals who have overcome their personal fears that old dogs can't learn new tricks. These new learners bring a wealth of experience to the classroom, and many of them want and deserve credit for prior learning. They are benefiting from exciting learning opportunities formerly considered inappropriate or off limits to all but the young. Evidence about our propensity to learn throughout life is accumulating. Alan Tough's research indicates the 90 percent of us engage in five or more in-depth, self-designed learning projects each year. The learning society, in fact, has arrived.

Secondly, there are technologies that can be used to deliver education, both within classrooms and also, ever increasingly, in the community and in our homes. Consider the possibilities: radio; television; video discs; and now QUBE tube, interactive television, which is transforming communication in Columbus, Ohio. In addition to the media, there are many electronic devices for instruction and record-keeping. Hand-held calculators, electronic games, home computers, and sophisticated data-processing equipment are available to assist and keep track of learning progress. That they exist is not news. One of the problems with these wonders is that they emerge faster than we humans are capable of making intelligent use of them. Too often their full potential is limited by our mistrust and ignorance.

But how do these observations and facts link or converge with competency-based education? The authors of this book correctly agree that there is no one way to teach for competence. A variety of instructional strategies to teach and reinforce learning is a necessity. The rate at which knowledge, skills, attitudes, and values are learned varies within as well as across individuals, and there are various instructional strategies and technologies to accommodate the differences. The argument over which one is "best" should be laid to rest forever, since they are all good ways for most of us to learn at some time or another, depending on the nature of the desired outcome and our personal characteristics and abilities.

Not only is there no one best way to learn to be competent, there is no one best site. Learning is valuable and legitimate whether it is in the classroom, on the job, in the community, at home, or at Scout head-quarters. Some places are better than others at a particular time, depending again on the types of outcomes desired, the facilities necessary for learning, and the type of instruction (such as guided or independent), that will enhance the attainment of a particular objective. The trick is knowing how to use this apparent chaos of opportunity and to give it form and structure. A competency-based approach to learning can do this. It is a system well suited to the management of instruction and assessment because of essential structural elements that can be used to plan and manage both individualized and group learning activities. These include the use of known outcomes with explicit criteria for judgment; written, mutually derived learning contracts that outline instructional activities; and the identification of assessment techniques or appropriate documentation for verifying performance. The beauty of the competency-based approach is its ability to manage diversity.

Admittedly, much needs to be done to pull together available technologies, instructional strategies, and sites to achieve a comprehensive system for a learning society. It is not an easy task, so it cannot be expected to happen overnight. But the success of programs, both those identified in this book and the many others that they represent, encourages us to think that it can be done.

There are dual concerns—inflation and energy—that will increasingly affect the delivery of education as we know it. Building enormous energy-consuming complexes set aside to house a community of learners may fast become a luxury that society will be unable to afford. New structures for the delivery and management of education will become a necessity. Fortunately, both the climate for change and the necessary technology are on hand.

Assuming that these forces will encourage us to respond boldly, where will we first direct our efforts? Certainly there is no need to despair, for there are practices and models to follow. We need to study what we have, use it in new ways, and borrow and adopt from others.

Some administrative changes suggested by Scott Thomson in chapter 6 are directed at secondary education, but they have implications for colleges and universities as well. In addition, some currently underused activities will need to be expanded to develop a sophisticated management system. For example:

• Regional guidance and educational brokering services can provide counseling for learners of all ages and abilities. They can also diagnose progress and provide information about both formal and informal learning and teaching opportunities within communities, as well as assist in planning. Telephone counseling will become common-place.

• Regional assessment centers can assess competence, on request. These can provide opportunities for learners to check their progress and offer them a choice of techniques to document and evaluate their learning.

• Regional credit banks can record and store information on learner progress throughout a lifetime, if the learner wishes. These can make full use of data-processing techniques and can be reached by telephone.

• Learning exchanges can provide learners with information and opportunities.

Finally, in order to make full use of competency-based education as a management system, there will be a need for research. The list of possible topics is very long, as always seems to be the case. However, two areas stand out, at least for me personally.

One is that we need to know more about the cognitive aspects of instruction—how teaching styles influence learners' attention, under-standing, and motivation, which in turn influence learning behavior. A cognitive model emphasizes the active, constructive role of learners and views them as responsible and accountable for their own learning. This will be important because competency-based education depends upon learner activity, motivation, and responsibility.

A second is that we need to know more about independent learning. Learners seem to need help with their planning and confirmation that they are making progress toward their goals, so studies of how to enhance self-directed learning would be of value. This is important because competency-based education in its more comprehensive form relies on this approach both within and outside school settings.

The chapters in this book are a snapshot in time of the current status of competency-based education. They give us the flavor of the variety of activities in progress which are perhaps more closely related through the power of the concept, that of education for competence, than they are in practice. At this juncture in the history of the move-ment, this is as it should be, for it is only through the support and study of many different approaches that we will begin to sort out those that are most useful. Whatever versions ultimately predominate, and it seems certain that there will continue to be several, the competency-based approach to instruction will serve as a powerful management tool for formal and informal education both within and outside tradi-tional institutions.

Bibliography: References Cited

ABRAMOWITZ, SUSAN; TENENBAUM, ELLEN; ET AL. *High School '77: A Survey of Public Secondary School Principals*. Washington, D.C.: U.S. Department of Health, Education, and Welfare, National Institute of Education, 1978.

ADKINS, WINTHROP R. "Life Skills Education for Adult Learners." *Adult Leadership* 22 (June 1973): 55–58, 82–84.

ADULT HIGH SCHOOL COMPLETION TASK FORCE. "Annual Report 1977–78." Mimeographed. Salem, Oreg.: Chemeketa Community College, 14 June 1978.

ADULT HIGH SCHOOL DIPLOMA PROGRAM. "Student Information Booklet." Mimeographed. Salem, Oreg.: Chemeketa Community College, April 1978.

AINSWORTH, DAVID. "Examining the Basis for Competency-Based Education." *Journal of Higher Education* 48 (May/June 1977): 321–32.

AIR UNIVERSITY. *Air University Catalog*. Maxwell Air Force Base, Ala., September 1976.

ALVERNO COLLEGE ASSESSMENT COMMITTEE. *Introductory Statement Regarding Characteristics of Advanced Students*. Mimeographed. Milwaukee, Wis.: Alverno College Productions, 1978.

ALVERNO COLLEGE FACULTY. *Liberal Learning at Alverno College*. Milwaukee, Wis.: Alverno College Productions, 1976.

ALVERNO EDUCATORS. *Faculty Handbook on Learning and Assessment*. Milwaukee, Wis.: Alverno College Productions, 1977.

ANDERSON, EARL N. "Coping with Oregon's New Competency-Based Graduation Requirements—View from a Practitioner." Paper presented at the annual meeting of the American Educational Research Assn. Washington, D.C., April 1975; Bethesda, Md.: ERIC Document Reproduction Service, ED 105 594.

BERLINER, DAVID C., and Gage, N. L. "The Psychology of Teaching Methods."
    In *The Psychology of Teaching Methods*, Seventy-fifth Yearbook of the
    National Society for the Study of Education, edited by N. L. Gage. Chica-
    go: University of Chicago Press, 1976.
BLOCK, JAMES H. "The 'C' in CBE." *Educational Researcher* 7 (May 1978): 13–16.
———. "Learning for Competence." *VIER Bulletin* 40 (1978): 27–43.
BLOOM, BENJAMIN S., ed. *Taxonomy of Educational Objectives.* Handbook I:
    Cognitive Domain. New York: David McKay Co., 1956.
BOWE, CHARLES. "Hood River Valley High School Operational Plan." Mimeo-
    graphed. Hood River, Oreg., n.d.
BOY SCOUTS OF AMERICA. *Merit Badge Counseling.* Pamphlet no. 6517. North
    Brunswick, N.J., 1972.
———. *Merit Badge Counselor Orientation.* Adult Leader Development pam-
    phlet no. 6540. North Brunswick, N.J., n.d.
———. *1978 Guide to Scouting Literature for Librarians and Teachers.* Pamphlet no.
    12–116. North Brunswick, N.J., 1978.
———. *Personal Management.* Pamphlet no. 3270. North Brunswick, N.J., 1972.
BOYD, JOSEPH L., JR., and SHIMBERG, BENJAMIN. *Developing Performance Tests for
    Classroom Evaluation.* TM Reports, no. 4. Princeton, N.J.: ERIC Clearing-
    house on Tests, Measurement and Evaluation at Educational Testing
    Service, June 1971.
BRICKELL, HENRY M. *Let's Talk About Minimum Competency Testing.* Education
    Commission of the States, May 1978.
BROUDY, H. S. "CBE—A Dissenting View." *Educare Journal.* Publication of the
    College of Education, University of Wisconsin-Oshkosh. 5 (Spring 1978):
    3–6.
BRUNER, JEROME S. *The Process of Education.* Cambridge, Mass.: Harvard Uni-
    versity Press, 1960.
BRUNER, JEROME S.; OLIVER, ROSE R.; GREENFIELD, PATRICIA M.; ET AL. *Studies in
    Cognitive Growth; A Collaboration at the Center for Cognitive Studies.* New
    York: Wiley, 1966.
BYHAM, WILLIAM C. "The Assessment Center as an Aid in Management De-
    velopment." *Training and Development Journal* 25 (December 1971): 10–22.
CAWELTI, GORDON. "Requiring Competencies for Graduation—Some Curricu-
    lar Issues." *Educational Leadership* 35 (November 1977): 86–91.
CHEMEKETA COMMUNITY COLLEGE. "Graduation Requirements: Adult High
    School Diploma." Mimeographed. Salem, Oreg., 8 December 1977.
CLEARINGHOUSE FOR APPLIED PERFORMANCE TESTING. *Annotated Bibliography.*
    Portland, Oreg.: Northwest Regional Educational Laboratory, n.d.
———. *Applied Performance Testing: What Is It? Why Use It?* Portland, Oreg.:
    Northwest Regional Educational Laboratory, n.d.
COLE, MICHAEL, ET. AL. *The Cultural Context of Learning and Thinking.* New York:
    Basic Books, 1971.
COLEMAN, JAMES S. ET AL. *Youth: Transition to Adulthood. Report on Youth of the
    President's Science Advisory Committee.* Chicago: University of Chicago
    Press, 1974.

COMPETENCY BASED ADULT HIGH SCHOOL DIPLOMA PROJECT. *Oregon Competency Based Adult High School Diploma Management Manual 1978.* Salem, Oreg.: Department of Education; Roseburg, Oreg.: Umpqua Community College, 1977.

CONAWAY, LARRY E. "Setting Standards in Competency Based Education: Some Current Practices and Concerns." Paper delivered at Symposium on Test Development Issues in Competency-Based Measurement, National Council on Measurement in Education, New York, April 1977.

CORCORAN, THOMAS B. "Prospects and Problems of Competency-Based Education." In *Renewing Higher Education: The Competency-Based Approach,* edited by Vance T. Peterson. Toledo, Ohio: Center for the Study of Higher Education, University of Toledo, 1976.

CROSS, K. PATRICIA. *Accent on Learning: Improving Instruction and Reshaping the Curriculum.* San Francisco: Jossey-Bass, 1977.

CURRICULUM IMPROVEMENT OFFICE, COLLEGE OF PHARMACY, UNIVERSITY OF MINNESOTA. *A Competency-Based Pharmacy Curriculum: What Is It?* Working paper no. 1. Minneapolis, 1976.

————. *Progress Report, Phase I: Competency Identification—Including Evaluation and Validation.* Minneapolis, June 1976.

————. *Progress Report, Phase II: An Analysis of Essential Pharmacy Competencies and Identification of Future Competencies.* Minneapolis, August 1977.

CYRS, THOMAS E., JR. *Handbook for the Design of Instruction in Pharmacy Education.* Minneapolis: College of Pharmacy, University of Minnesota, 1977.

DEPARTMENT OF THE AIR FORCE. *Instructional System Development.* Air Force Manual no. 50–2. Washington, D.C.: Air Training Command, 31 July 1975.

DOYLE, WALTER. "Paradigm for Research on Teacher Effectiveness." In *Review of Research in Education,* Vol. 5, edited by Lee Schulman. Itasca, Ill.: Peacock Press, 1978.

DUNN, RITA S., and DUNN, KENNETH J. *Teaching Students Through Their Individual Learning Styles: A Practical Approach.* Reston, Va.: Reston Publishing Div. of Prentice-Hall, 1978.

EBEL, ROBERT L. "The Case for Minimum Competency Testing." *Phi Delta Kappan* 59 (April 1978): 546–49.

ERIKSON, ERIK H. *Childhood and Society.* 2d ed., rev. New York: W. W. Norton, 1964.

EWENS, THOMAS. *Think Piece on CBE and Liberal Education.* CUE Project Occasional Paper Series, no. 1. Bowling Green, Ohio: Bowling Green State University, May 1977.

FILLBRANDT, JAMES, ED. "An Approach to Minimum Competency Programs in Mathematics, Reading, and Writing." Mimeographed. Bakersfield, Calif.: Kern High School District, 1978.

FLAVELL, J. *The Developmental Psychology of Jean Piaget.* Princeton, N.J.: Van Nostrand, 1963.

FREIRE, PAULO. *Pedagogy of the Oppressed.* Translated by Myra B. Ramos. New York: Seabury Press, 1970.

GALE, LARRIE E., and POL, GASTON. "Competence: A Definition and Conceptual Scheme." *Educational Technology* 15 (June 1975): 19–25.

GALLUP, GEORGE H. "The 10th Annual Gallup Poll of the Public's Attitudes Toward the Public Schools." *Phi Delta Kappan* 60 (September 1978): 33–45.

GHISELLI, EDWIN E., and BROWN, CLARENCE W. *Personnel and Industrial Psychology.* 2d ed. New York: McGraw-Hill, 1955.

GLASS, GENE V. "Minimum Competence and Incompetence in Florida." *Phi Delta Kappan* 59 (May 1978): 602–05.

GORTON, RICHARD A., and McINTYRE, KENNETH E. *The Effective Principal.* The Senior High School Principalship, vol. 2. Reston, Va.: National Assn. of Secondary School Principals, 1978.

HACKETT, JACK, and McKILLIGIN, GEORGE. "A Study of the Multiunit-IGE Elementary Schools." Paper prepared at the request of the Board of Education. Janesville, Wis., August 1972, revised October 1972.

HANSON, LEONARD E. Quoted in Kelley, Edgar A. "Commentary: Minimum Competencies for High School Graduation: A State of the Scene Report for Nebraska." *Catalyst* 1 (September 1977): 3–8.

HARVEY, O.J.; HUNT, DAVID E.; and SCHRODER, HAROLD M. *Conceptual Systems and Personality Organization.* New York: Wiley, 1961.

HATHAWAY, WALTER. "Competency Based Education: Definitional Issues and Implications for Cooperation Across Educational Institutions and Levels." Paper prepared for Competency Based Education Workshop of the Council of Chief State School Officers Study Commission, 13–16 July 1976, Salem, Oreg. Mimeographed.

HOWSAM, ROBERT B., and NEA Association of Classroom Teachers. "Performance-Based Instruction." *Today's Education* 61 (April 1972): 33–40.

HUFF, SHEILA. *Problems in Implementing Competency-Based Programs.* Mimeographed. Syracuse, N.Y.: Educational Policy Research Center, Syracuse University Research Corp., 30 June 1975.

INKELES, ALEX. "Social Structure and the Socialization of Competence." *Harvard Educational Review* 36 (Summer 1966): 265–83.

JOINT INTERIM TASK FORCE ON MINIMUM COMPETENCIES/GRADUATION REQUIREMENTS. *Report.* Oregon Sixtieth Legislative Assembly. Salem, December 1977.

KAGAN, JEROME, and KOGAN, NATHAN. "Individual Variation in Cognitive Processes." In *Carmichael's Manual of Child Psychology,* 3d ed., Vol. 1, edited by Paul H. Mussen. New York: Wiley, 1970.

KAGAN, JEROME, ET AL. "Information Processing in the Child: Significance of Analytic and Reflective Attitudes." *Psychological Monographs: General and Applied* 78, no. 1 (1964).

KAPLAN, ABRAHAM. *The Conduct of Inquiry.* New York: Harper & Row, 1964.

KEEFE, JAMES W., and GEORGIADES, CONSTANCE J. "Competency-Based Education and the High School Diploma." *NASSP Bulletin.* Publication of the National Assn. of Secondary School Principals, Reston, Va. 62 (April 1978): 94–108.

KEETON, MORRIS T. "Credentials for the Learning Society." In *Experiential Learning*, edited by Morris T. Keeton and Associates. San Francisco: Jossey-Bass, 1976.

KELLEY, EDGAR A. "Minimum Competencies: A Cause for Concern." *Catalyst*. Journal of the Nebraska Council of School Administrators. 1(September 1977): 55–56.

KNOTT, BOB. "Competency Based Education: State-of-the-Art Position Paper." Paper prepared for Oregon Department of Education, Salem Oreg., 1976. Mimeographed.

———. "What Is a Competence-Based Curriculum in the Liberal Arts?" *Journal of Higher Education* 46 (January/February 1975): 25–39.

KOLB, DAVID A. "Student Learning Styles and Disciplinary Learning Environments: Diverse Pathways for Growth." In *The Future American College*, edited by Arthur W. Chickering. San Francisco: Jossey-Bass, in press.

KRIS, ERNST. *Psychoanalytic Explorations in Art*. New York: International Universities Press, 1952.

LASSER, BARBARA R., and OLSON, ALLAN L. *Strategies for Implementation of Competency Based Education Programs*. Salem, Oreg.: Oregon Competency Based Education Program, Northwest Regional Educational Laboratory, April 1977; Bethesda, Md.: ERIC Document Reproduction Service, ED 147 950.

LESSER, GERALD S. "Cultural Differences in Learning and Thinking Styles." In *Individuality in Learning: Implications of Cognitive Styles and Creativity for Human Development*, edited by Samuel Messick. San Francisco: Jossey-Bass, 1976.

LESSINGER, LEON M. "Implications of Competency-Based Education for Urban Children." *Educational Technology* 12 (November 1972): 58–61.

LOEVINGER, JANE. *Ego Development: Conceptions and Theories*. San Francisco: Jossey-Bass, 1976.

MADAUS, GEORGE F., and AIRASIAN, PETER W. "Issues in Evaluating Student Outcomes in Competency-Based Graduation Programs." *Journal of Research and Development in Education* 10 (Spring 1977): 79–91.

MAEROFF, GENE I. "Education Now: Brouhaha over Competency Testing." *Saturday Review*, 8 July 1978, p. 43.

MARLOWE, JOHN. "Testing, Testing . . . Can You Hear Me?" *Phi Delta Kappan* 58 (November 1978): 256–57.

MARYLAND ACCOUNTABILITY PROGRAM. *Functional Reading for Test Results: Maryland Assessment of State Goals in Reading*. Year III. Baltimore: Maryland State Department of Education, 1 May 1976.

McCLELLAND, DAVID C. *Pedagogy and Competency-Based Education*. Paper developed under National Institute of Education contract no. 400–75–0036 for Educational Policy Research Center, Syracuse University Research Corp., Syracuse, N.Y., n.d. Mimeographed.

———. "Testing for Competence Rather Than for 'Intelligence.'" *American Psychologist* 28 (January 1973): 1–14.

————. "Toward a Theory of Motive Acquisition." *American Psychologist* 20 (May 1965): 321–33.

McClung, Merle S. "Are Competency Testing Programs Fair? Legal?" *Phi Delta Kappan* 59 (February 1978): 397–400.

————. "Competency Testing: Potential for Discrimination." *Clearinghouse Review* 11 (September 1977): 439–48.

McDonald, Frederick J. "Assessing Competence and Competency-Based Curricula." In *Renewing Higher Education: The Competency-Based Approach*, edited by Vance T. Peterson. Toledo, Ohio: Center for the Study of Higher Education, University of Toledo, 1976.

Miller, Lorin L. "The New State Graduation Requirements: An Overview and Discussion." *OSSC Bulletin* (Publication of the Oregon School Study Council, Eugene, Oreg.) 20, no. 7 (March 1977).

Milpitas Unified School District. "Proficiency Standards Curriculum: Reading, Mathematics, Language Arts, Social Sciences." Mimeographed. Milpitas, Calif., n.d.

————. "Proficiency Standards: Eighth Grade Reading, Language Arts, Mathematics, Social Science." Mimeographed. Milpitas, Calif., 1978.

Murphy, Gardner. *Human Potentialities*. New York: Basic Books, 1958.

National Academy of Education Committee on Testing and Basic Skills. *Improving Educational Achievement: Report of the National Academy of Education Committee on Testing and Basic Skills to the Assistant Secretary for Education*. Stephen K. Bailey, Chairman. N.d.

National Assn. of Secondary School Principals. *Competency Tests and Graduation Requirements*. Reston, Va.: The Assn., 1976.

National Commission on Resources for Youth, Inc. *New Roles of Youth in the School and the Community*. New York: Scholastic Book Services, Scholastic Magazines, 1974; Bethesda, Md.: ERIC Document Reproduction Service, ED 106 182.

National Commission on the Reform of Secondary Education. *The Reform of Secondary Education*. Edited by B. Frank Brown. New York: McGraw-Hill, 1973.

National Panel on High School and Adolescent Education. *The Education of Adolescents: Final Report and Recommendations*. HEW publication no. (OE) 76-00004. Washington, D.C., 31 August 1976.

News and Comment. "The Consequences of Accountability." *Human Nature* 1 (September 1978): 12.

Nickse, Ruth S. "The Central New York External High School Diploma Program." *Phi Delta Kappan* 57 (October 1975): 123.

Northcutt, Norvell. "Functional Literacy for Adults: A Status Report of the Adult Performance Level Study." Mimeographed. Austin: University of Texas at Austin, n.d.

O'Malley, J. Michael. "Perspectives on Competence: Research on Definitions of Social Competence." Paper presented at symposium, Definitions of Social Competence, at the annual meeting of the American Educational Research Assn., Washington, D.C., April 1975.

PALARDY, J. MICHAEL, and EISELE, JAMES E. "Competency Based Education."
    Clearing House 46 (May 1972): 545–48.
PARSONS, MICHAEL J. "The Notion of Competence and Competency as Educa-
    tional Objectives." *CCBC Notebook* 6 (February 1977): 2–6; Bethesda, Md.:
    ERIC Document Reproduction Service, ED 133 900.
PIAGET, JEAN. *The Place of the Sciences of Man in the System of Sciences.* New York:
    Harper & Row, 1974.
PIPHO, CHRIS. "Minimal Competency Standards." *Today's Education* 67 (Febru-
    ary/March 1978): 34–37.
————. "Minimum Competency Testing in 1978: A Look at State Standards."
    Phi Delta Kappan 59 (May 1978): 585–87.
POTTINGER, PAUL S. *Comments and Guidelines for Research in Competency Identifica-
    tion, Definition and Measurement.* Paper developed under National Institute
    of Education contract no. 400–75–0036 for Educational Policy Research
    Center, Syracuse University Research Corp., Syracuse, N.Y., 19 June
    1975.
PROJECT BASIC OFFICE. *The Comprehensive Plan for Maryland Competency-Based
    Prerequisites for Graduation.* Baltimore: Maryland State Department of
    Education, 1978.
PUBLIC SCHOOLS OF THE DISTRICT OF COLUMBIA. *Competency-Based Curriculum
    Guide.* Washington, D.C., 1978.
————. "Competency-Based Curriculum, Science: Laboratory Science, Grades
    Nine and Ten." Preliminary draft. Washington, D.C., 1978.
————. *The Design and Implementation of the Validation of the Competency-Based
    Curriculum in Language Arts/English and Science.* Washington, D.C., June
    1978.
RAVEN, JOHN. "On the Components of Competence and Their Development in
    Education." *Teachers College Record* 78 (May 1977): 457–75.
REBELL, MICHAEL A. *Legal and Legislative Implications of Competency- Based Educa-
    tion.* Paper prepared for Educational Policy Research Center, Syracuse
    University Research Corp., Syracuse, N.Y., 30 June 1975. Mimeographed.
REILLY, WAYNE. *Competency Based Education: Some Educational, Political and His-
    torical Perspectives.* Ford Fellows in Educational Journalism Report.
    Washington, D.C.: George Washington University, Institute for Educa-
    tional Leadership, 1 September 1977.
ROTH, EDITH. "APL: A Ferment in Education." *American Education* 12 (May
    1976): 6–9.
SALT LAKE CITY SCHOOL DISTRICT. *Basic Skills in Reading and Language Arts:
    Second Grade.* Mimeographed. Salt Lake City, Utah, n.d.
SCHALOCK, H. DEL. *Alternative Models of Competency Based Education.* 2d ed.
    Monograph prepared under National Institute of Education contract no.
    400–76–0028 by the Oregon Competency Based Education Program,
    Salem, October 1976. Bethesda, Md.: ERIC Document Reproduction Ser-
    vice, ED 147 951.
————. "Defining and Assessing Competence." Interpretive paper no. 1.
    Implications of the Oregon Board of Education's Proposed Process Stan-

dards for the Design and Operation of Teacher Education Programs. Monmouth, Oreg., 1973.

––––––. "Situational Response Testing: An Application of Simulation Principles to Measurement." In *Instructional Simulation: A Research, Development and Dissemination Activity,* edited by Paul A. Twelker. Monmouth, Oreg.: Teaching Research Division, Oregon State System of Higher Education, 1969.

SCHLESINGER, MARK A. *Reconstructing General Education: An Examination of Assumptions, Practices, and Prospects.* CUE Project Occasional Paper Series, no. 2. Bowling Green, Ohio: Bowling Green State Univ., May 1977.

SIGNALL, KAREN A. "Cognitive Complexity in Person Perception and Nation Perception: A Developmental Approach." *Journal of Personality* 34 (December 1966): 517–37.

SPADY, WILLIAM G. "Competency Based Education: A Bandwagon in Search of a Definition." *Educational Researcher* 6 (January 1977): 9–14.

––––––. "The Concept and Implications of Competency-Based Education." *Educational Leadership* 36, no. 1 (October 1978): 16–22.

SPADY, WILLIAM G., and MITCHELL, DOUGLAS E. "Competency Based Education: Organizational Issues and Implications." *Educational Researcher* 6 (February 1977): 9–15.

STABEL, C. "The Impact of a Conversational Computer System on Human Problem Solving Behavior." Working paper of the Massachusetts Institute of Technology Sloan School of Management, Cambridge, Mass., 1973.

STRIKE, KENNETH A. "What Is a 'Competent' High School Graduate?" *Educational Leadership* 35, no. 2 (November 1977): 93–97.

TASK FORCE ON SECONDARY SCHOOLS IN A CHANGING SOCIETY. *Secondary Schools in a Changing Society: This We Believe.* Scott D. Thomson, Chairman. Reston, Va.: National Assn. of Secondary School Principals, 1975.

THOMPSON, SYDNEY. *Competency-Based Education: Theory and Practice.* School Management Digest, no. 9. Prepared by ERIC Clearinghouse on Educational Management. Burlingame, Calif.: Assn. of California School Administrators, 1977.

THOMSON, SCOTT D. and DE LEONIBUS, NANCY. "Minimum Competency Testing . . . An Update." *Practitioner.* Newsletter of the National Assn. of Secondary School Principals, Reston, Va. 4 (June 1978).

VENN, GRANT. "Accountable for What? Measuring Up to the World of Work." In *The Courage to Change,* edited by Roman C. Pucinski and Sharlene P. Hirsch. Englewood Cliffs, N.J.: Prentice-Hall, 1971.

VOCATIONAL-TECHNICAL EDUCATION CONSORTIUM OF STATES. *Fifth Annual Report of V-TECS.* Atlanta, Ga.: Commission on Occupational Education Institutions, Southern Assn. of Colleges and Schools, 1978.

WAKS, LEONARD J. *Education for Life-Role Competence.* Paper prepared for Life-Role Project, National Institute of Education, Washington, D.C., June 1977, with minor revisions August 1977. Mimeographed.

WEATHERSBY, RITA. "Ego Development and Adult Learning." In *The Future American College*, edited by Arthur W. Chickering. San Francisco: Jossey-Bass, in press.

WEBER, GEORGE. "How You Can Make Sure the Students in Your Schools Are Learning Basic Skills." *American School Board Journal* 165 (June 1978): 31–33.

WHITE, ROBERT W. "Motivation Reconsidered: The Concept of Competence." *Psychological Review* 66 (September 1959): 297–333.

———. "Sense of Interpersonal Competence." In *The Study of Lives*, pp. 72–93. Edited by Robert W. White. New York: Atherton Press, 1963.

WILBUR, FRANKLIN P., and CHAPMAN, DAVID W. *College Courses in the High School.* Reston, Va.: National Assn. of Secondary School Principals, 1978.

WILLINGHAM, WARREN W. "Critical Issues and Basic Requirements for Assessment." In *Experiential Learning*, edited by Morris T. Keeton and Associates. San Francisco: Jossey-Bass, 1976.

WISCONSIN RESEARCH AND DEVELOPMENT CENTER FOR COGNITIVE LEARNING. *The Whole IGE Catalog.* Madison: University of Wisconsin, n.d.

———. *Wisconsin R&D Center News.* Madison: University of Wisconsin, Fall 1978.

WISE, ARTHUR E. "Minimum Competency Testing: Another Case of Hyper-Rationalization." *Phi Delta Kappan* 59 (May 1978): 596–98.

WITKIN, HERMAN A. "A Cognitive Style Approach to Cross-Cultural Research." *International Journal of Psychology* 2, no. 4 (1967): 233–50.

WODITSCH, GARY A. *Developing Generic Skills: A Model for Competency-Based General Education.* CUE Project Occasional Paper Series, no. 3. Bowling Green, Ohio: Bowling Green State University, May 1977.

———. "Jonathan Livingston Student: Competence for What?" In *Renewing Higher Edsucation: The Competency-Based Approach*, edited by Vance T. Peterson. Toledo, Ohio: Center for the Study of Higher Education, University of Toledo, 1976.

Index